PENGUIN BOOKS

RUTH
CRACKNELL

Ruth Cracknell lived in Maitland in early childhood, before her family moved to Sydney. She was educated at North Sydney Girls' High School and began a professional career in radio at the age of twenty. She travelled to England, where she worked for the BBC in radio, returning to Sydney in 1954. In theatre she was known for her interpretations of both classical and contemporary drama as well as for her particular flair for comedy. She also worked extensively in film, television, radio and animation, and won numerous industry awards. She is, perhaps, best-known for her role as Maggie Beare in the ABC series *Mother and Son*.

Ruth, a Member of the Order of Australia, was awarded honorary doctorates from Sydney University and the Queensland University of Technology.

RUTH
CRACKNELL

A BIASED MEMOIR

PENGUIN BOOKS

Penguin Books

Published by the Penguin Group
Penguin Books Australia Ltd
250 Camberwell Road
Camberwell, Victoria 3124, Australia
Penguin Books Ltd
80 Strand, London WC2R 0RL, England
Penguin Putnam Inc.
375 Hudson Street, New York, New York 10014, USA
Penguin Books, a division of Pearson Canada
10 Alcorn Avenue, Toronto, Ontario, Canada M4V 3B2
Penguin Books (NZ) Ltd
Cnr Rosedale and Airborne Roads, Albany, Auckland, New Zealand
Penguin Books (South Africa) (Pty) Ltd
24 Sturdee Avenue, Rosebank, Johannesburg 2196, South Africa
Penguin Books India (P) Ltd
11, Community Centre, Panchsheel Park, New Delhi 110 017, India

First published by Penguin Books Australia Ltd 1997
This edition published by Penguin Books Australia Ltd 1999

13 15 17 16 14

Cover design by Deborah Billson, Penguin Design Studio
Text design by Ellie Exarchos, Penguin Design Studio
Typeset in 11.5/18 pt Centaur MT by Post Pre-press Group, Brisbane, Queensland
Printed and bound in Australia by McPherson's Printing Group, Maryborough, Victoria

National Library of Australia
Cataloguing-in-Publication data:

Cracknell, Ruth.
Ruth Cracknell : a biased memoir.

Includes index.
ISBN 0 14 027588 6.

1. Cracknell, Ruth. 2. Actors – Australia – Biography. I. Title.

792.028092

www.penguin.com.au

for Eric Phillips

Contents

Acknowledgements

I am indebted to many friends and colleagues who assisted in clearing up doubtful points, and others who read certain pages with keen eyes. In particular, I would like to thank Kirrily Nolan, who read an early set of proof pages. I am also grateful to Ron Haddrick, Gillian James, Ron Blair, Peter Woodley from Information Services at the Maitland Library, Peggy Leinas, John McKellar, Diana Davidson, staff at the Sydney Theatre Company and the Melbourne Theatre Company, Monica Maughan, Rodney Fisher, Jurgen Zielinski, Graham Wills, Kathleen Wall, Maureen Fitzpatrick, Kerry Walker, Ann Churchill-Brown, Richard Wherrett, Chris Willcox and Pamela Rabe. Pamela Rabe surprisingly owned sheet music for that old ballad 'Marchéta' which I have referred to. I have also referred at times to the Currency Press publication *Companion to Theatre in Australia*.

Thanks, too, to Bryony Cosgrove for her sensitive approach to editing, along with the laughs; and to Barbara Mobbs for wise counsel at all times.

Finally, heartfelt gratitude to my husband, Eric, who in a week that presented a publishing deadline on the one hand and the preview week of the play *Vita and Virginia* on the other, performed the final proofreading of the following pages on my behalf.

'A Tribute to Ruth'
(with apologies to Dr Seuss)

The truth about Ruth is that nobody knows,
Why her presence commands from her head to her toes,
But it does, so let's praise the forces that forced her
To start on her path to the courses that sourced her,
In the magical world of the footlights and spot,
The flies and the wings and the greasepaint and grot.

You've given us pleasure we cannot repay,
And that's why we're here to grovel today.
So down on your bellies and down on your knees,
And say to her 'Ruth' you *must* hear our pleas,
Keep going, keep going, your seventy years,
Are but a mere trifle, a changing of gears.

Why only last year you were like a gazelle,

Bounding up stairs in a play that was — well —

A little bit risqué for one of your stature,

With flashing male bottoms, and sensual rapture,

I know, I was there, the force in the rear,

And I swear you can wing it another ten year.

Remember the days of The Love of Four Colonels,

The Tempest, The Father, and those old eternals,

A Delicate Balance, Chalk Garden, Trelawney,

Forget me not Lane, the Revues fast and corny,

Remember The Seagull, and Mother and Son,

The Importance of Earnest, — we've barely begun.

I'm sure there are moments you'd like to forget,

And plays whose point you fail to see yet,

I'm sure some directors have earned your invective,

And critics — well let's not malign the defective.

I'm sure there are actors who've driven you spare,

We'd never name names, — there's Henri down there.

But surely it's true that your forge will keep forging,

Your boiler keep boiling, your gorge will keep gorging,

Your engine keep revving, your kettle keep steaming,

Your bollards keep firm and your gun barrels gleaming,
Your rockets igniting, your circuits plugged in,
Your toaster ejecting, your Zeitgeist in trim.

So there's no need to urge you to stick to your last,
We'll simply salute now your glorious past,
And cheer for the pleasure you've given us all,
The Empress of Sydney, the Westerly Squall,
The Southerly Buster, the Patron's Delight,
The standing ovation on opening night.

The timing precision that shames a Swiss clock,
The subtle subtexting that rescues sheer schlock,
The withering presences, the lightness of being,
The humour so funny that infants start weeing,
You've given it all, you're a gem of showbiz,
So let's hear it now for Theatre's first Ms.

*This delectable hyperbole was written by David Williamson
and read by Garry McDonald at The Wharf Theatre during the
afternoon tea party given by the Sydney Theatre Company
on the occasion of my 70th birthday.*

SANCTUARY

I look out through the diamond-paned windows and my garden is ablaze. We are in the midst of a brilliant autumn, and
the spread of the liquid amber fills the bay of the window.
The Japanese maple in the back garden is a flick of fire.
Lovely, when I stand at the sink. My house is surrounded by
trees – two liquid ambers, one huge fir, one immense oak,
palms, ferns, two China pears . . . and a partridge . . .

In the ever reducing circumstances of my girlhood/
young womanhood, whatever space we dwelt in was graced if
the outlook incorporated a tree, trees. When I at last became
a professional actress we were living in Chatswood at the top
of an old house at the corner of Brown Street and Railway
Street, where the Hotel Charles now stands. Our part-
enclosed side verandah sat in the treetops. I slept in this room;
my sister, Gwenyth, and her husband, Bill, just returned from

the war, had the second bedroom. This is what happened in post-war Sydney. You waited two years before your house could be finished. So you lived with the family. At night, possums, ring-tailed, ran along the verandah ledge, looking like Disney cartoons.

There is a possum, brush-tailed, in the chimney in the study. I decide to call in an expert. Life here has been a succession over the years of possums hauled out of chimneys and taken down to the bush. Fruitless exercise. They usually beat us back up the hill to the house. This time a charming young possum man sets a trap. He will return and, with possum in cage, will wire all chimneys.

Possum imprisoned. Do we want it taken kilometres away and released in bushland, or returned to familiar territory? Always the idiot, 'Oh, bring it back.' The possum man's licence stipulates that where a possum is returned, new accommodation has to be provided. I am stunned at the thought, but happily agree. I can't wait to see what sort of apartment will arrive.

The possum returns with alternative accommodation — an oblong sentry box with sloping roof (Good if there's a snowfall?) and a round hole just big enough for a possum to enter. I think the odd Federation tile and earthenware chimney pot might be necessary to persuade the wily one that she is entering a chimney. We decide the oak tree is the best habitat, so the apartment is taken way up and attached. I feel the urge to shrink and move in myself. The cage contains not one but two possums. She had been concealing a baby. They are both hauled up and decanted. Divine.

My house is surrounded by trees – two liquid ambers, one huge fir, one immense oak, palms, ferns, two China pears... and a partridge...

Many times and over a number of years I had seen this house. Dropping children off at school I'd drive on to do some marketing, and though the direct route wasn't past the house, once I'd seen it I took to driving that way. There it sat, comfortably on its corner with its picket fence and its trees. There was a long, enclosed side verandah and a front verandah with a return. I couldn't see where that ended. I could see diamond-paned windows.

Once, a girl on a beautiful horse came out of the side gate. I felt that lovely surge of horse passion again. I'd so loved riding at her age – and later. I envied her her own horse.

The house came on the market. We were looking for something bigger and presented ourselves as potential buyers. It was out of our range. We didn't bother to go inside.

I still drove past, occasionally.

A year or so later, by now desperate for more space, the price came down and we walked through the front door. I found myself turning left – to the diamond-paned windows.

A few months pass. My father stands in the centre of the room – already my sanctuary – liking the new house, pleased we are settled, something also settled within him. In weeks he is dead. I drive to North Ryde and am ushered into his room at the nursing home by Matron. There he is. I bend and kiss him – 'poor key-cold figure of a king' slides, unasked, into my mind. No king, though. Just a private, proud, simple/complex man, incapable of harming, capable of being harmed . . . Ghosts abound in this corner.

These days the house has a high wall around it. From the street you see white wall, trees, old terracotta tiles, chimney pots and the long side verandah. It started its life in 1907. We have lived in it for thirty years. Just two of us now. Being in one place has been important. There has been no wish to re-live a peripatetic childhood. If the fates are kind, it is where I'll die.

In 1993 I was working on the Bill Bennett film *Spider and Rose*, in Mudgee. *Spider and Rose*, by way of being a road movie, was a very physical shoot. Desperate for a massage, I tried some of those recommended locally. Not brilliant. The crew kept saying, 'Wait till Julianne gets here,' – Julianne being an American they had met while filming on Easter Island. She had arrived one day off a South American cargo ship, and stayed till filming was completed, massaging here, massaging there. Julianne did arrive in Mudgee, and on the following Saturday evening I received the best massage I have ever had. This was real healing. I entered another realm and that night slept ten undisturbed hours. Unheard of.

The shoot ended and Julianne turned up in Sydney – I had the luxury of a massage at home. Again, bliss. When I dragged myself back from whatever state she'd put me into, Julianne was sitting by the diamond-paned windows, slightly distrait. 'There is a presence here,' she said. 'It is a late middle-aged man from some earlier time wearing a suit.' She assured me his name was David. Later, over tea, she began to experience the sensation of a presence determined to get a message through to me. It was David, again, having a busy afternoon. Julianne passed on the message: 'You must write.'

I stammered, a little bemused, that I was thinking of starting some research.

'No! No!' from David. 'You will know what to write.'

The moment passed. Julianne apologised, assuring me this seldom happened, but that since childhood she had experienced psychic moments. I am not a member of Sceptics so took it all in my stride, neither quite believing, nor quite disbelieving, certain only that Julianne was in an embarrassed and disturbed state. We sipped our tea.

August 1994. I have my contract with me. Robert Sessions of Penguin Books meets me at my agent Barbara Mobbs's flat, overlooking the Harbour. I look down through clear, light green water to sand and strands of seaweed. I sign. We talk.

This book is the result. I can always blame David!

PART ONE

ONE

I never acted at North Sydney Girls' High School. No one suspected I had any desire to; I barely knew it myself. Hearing Miss Farrell, the English mistress, read Shakespeare, particularly the Sonnets, had a profound effect on me. She was able to inspire a love of language and metre and the music of words that may have been the basis for what came later. But unrecognised then. Once, in class, we acted out one of the rude mechanicals' scenes in The Dream. I was cast as Bottom, and the laughs were certainly there. Not enough to really stir, though. Then something quite out of the ordinary. I was asked to deliver one of the two speeches to celebrate Empire Day on 24 May, something we all did in 1939.

I spent a distracted May holiday working on my speech, and come the day was prepared, but terrified. The other speaker, Veronica, was the top debater in the school. I had never debated. Empire Day was a big occasion. The whole school assembled in the hall; there was a row of chairs on the stage. Veronica and I waited in front of the chairs, and the staff processed in, gowned, led by the Headmistress, thin-lipped and formidable. I was ready to die. Miss Geer took her place in the centre of the stage, standing, glanced towards me, and said, 'The chair, Ruth!' I remember thinking, how kind she is, perceptive even, aware as she must be of my trembling knees. Gratefully I sank into it. A glance, this time of extreme coolness, was again shot in my direction. 'I mean, for me, Ruth!' This was the moment the entire school, staff included, exploded into laughter. As it subsided, I got on top of my agony and presented an impassioned speech of patriotic fervour which had the rafters 'ringing with sustained applause':

> Ruth told us about some of the great men associated with the building up of our Empire. Naturally, as her time was limited, she could only mention comparatively few, but she presented those to us in such glowing terms that we could not help but feel a thrill of pride.

My first review — from the School Captain, Pat Bartlett. Now, looking back, I suppose that occasion just might have set something stirring. Comedy and fire in the same bundle, even if inadvertently.

Odd, beginning one's memoirs mid-season Edward Albee's *Three Tall Women*, a play based, as it is, on the dying recollections of a 92-year-old woman. Well, I'm not 92 and we're all dying.

So, what am *I* remembering? Whatever the detail – or lack – my recollections, as opposed to those of the character I'm playing, have everything to do with how I *felt*.

What brings a play to life? What is the special alchemy? It differs each time, subtly, though the pattern may be constant. For me, it always starts with the highest of hopes, and a barely contained excitement. It begins with a gathering.

Three Tall Women rehearsals commenced on 22 May 1995, in the small rehearsal room at The Wharf, home of the Sydney Theatre Company – surely the most idyllic place in the world in which to rehearse, to work, to perform. A transformed finger wharf, it juts into Sydney Harbour on the western side of the Bridge. Sit on one of its verandahs and you feel you could touch that Bridge. A busy port, container ships glide past like apartment blocks, ferries crisscross, yachts dip, water taxis dart; sunsets are technicolour extravaganzas; fishermen catch fish right underneath you, and food and wine is handy if you're feeling flush at the end of the day – and if by some extraordinary chance you know your lines.

So, we gather. Pamela Rabe plays C, Pippa Williamson plays B, I play A, and Shane Nicholson will play the youthful son of our composite. Our director is Wayne Harrison, the director of the Sydney Theatre Company. Also present, Angus Strathie, designer, and Nick Schleiper, lighting; our stage manager is Michael Bader, assistant stage manager Katy Pitney, and, finally, there is Victoria Mielewska, who will bully us into the correct accents with the help of tapes of the late American poet Anne Sefton reading her work. These will be played endlessly in my car, alternating with a taped interview of an upper-class American elder lady describing the top families in America, their place in the scheme of things, who married whom and who didn't.

Rehearsals can always be relied upon to broaden one's knowledge. Staff from all the departments sit in on this first nervous gathering. We have a little speech of welcome, the set and costume presentation from Angus, a discussion, coffee break, then all not directly concerned with performance leave us to it.

We sit around the table and read Act I. We break and the three of us lunch in Cafe Tutu, attached to the Dance Theatre downstairs. We return and read Act II. Wayne decides he wants to concentrate on Act II ahead of Act I, and the faintest of warning bells sounds in my head. Act I is massive for A, and I feel I will need all the time possible to get on top of the lines. But, as ever, I'm charmingly co-operative. And anyway he's right – the play in many respects is Act II, Act I more a bizarre and, for some, disturbing, progression towards a stroke, preceded by a life story that, to me, epitomises wrong choices with their resultant pain. Albeit told from the comic perspective. Act II the play, Act I the vaudeville show, some feel. Not me, though, but Theatre, like poetry, is a free country and at times, again like poetry, completely subjective. Part of its charm and endless fascination. But Wayne's choice does pose an added strain.

The week is spent around the table analysing, delving deep into the special psyches of tall women – the problems, the traumas. I feel a little inadequate – I can't remember mine. Do I need recall therapy? The temptation, at times, to invent trauma is difficult to resist. Surely shooting up so rapidly between the ages of 16 and 20 must have caused angst. Perhaps the feeling was more akin to Alice in Wonderland in my case. Ridiculous instead of painful? Shooting up, I hasten to add, here referring to vertical extension not drug injection. Our discussion moves to the role of the Mother in life. Therapeutic.

Some weeks later I meet a young actress/singer who speaks of the difficulty of playing a deeply emotional role, how it can take over one's life, so that it becomes impossible to leave the role behind in the theatre – which, the thought flashes in unbidden, is its only place, surely? However, she's young and clever and possessed of a quite beautiful voice, and we chat amiably enough. I keep my thoughts concealed but hope that one day she will find a way to solve her dilemma or she's in real strife. Someone else joins us and starts speaking of the anguish felt at times by grief counsellors, and how grief counsellors themselves will sometimes be in need of counselling. I have a wild vision where a line of counsellors counsel each other, on and on, till we finally get to the last counsellor. He's alone – a tiny Leunig figure weeping, 'Where is *my* counsellor?' Or the last individualist meets the last counsellor and they fight it out.

We are rehearsing – four weeks' rehearsal for a play of such complexity is perilously brief, but standard procedure in this country. The saving grace, as always, is lots of laughs; Pamela, in particular, able to transform me from the blackest despair to a state of delight by a moment of inspired clowning. I want an evening where Act I is Pamela's moments strung together and Act II Wayne's anecdotes. This is all that should happen at rehearsals; anecdotes and clowning – work gets in the way.

The whole process grinds on. Victoria is picky about accent to the extent that one wishes to kill her, but doesn't because she is always right. There are the usual, mostly polite, discussions with Angus: 'No, that colour is not *quite* so good on me perhaps.' He is almost pushed to the edge. There are moments one wants to dive into the Harbour, other moments one wants to preserve forever.

A normal rehearsal period – almost.

The entire 'process' this time was accompanied by the shattering, mind-blasting noise of pneumatic drills performing Important Work on the wharf pylons – presumably undertaken to stop us and night-time audiences sinking without trace. Sometimes we retired to a space the size of a cupboard to escape the battle noises – often stage management would patiently move and mark up the other rehearsal room – hoping we were getting a little further from the epicentre and that our heads would stop throbbing, particularly poor Pippa's – a migraine sufferer from way back. The drills had an unerring instinct for nosing us out. Once we moved across to the Opera House in the vain hope that peace could be found. That, of course, was the day some major noisy restoration began *there*. I fell prey to the Never Again Syndrome, starting in my toes and working relentlessly up through the legs and torso to the head: 'With any luck I'll have that stroke right now and my dummy can play the part.'

There is no escape. Production week begins. We have the technical rehearsal, we have a dress rehearsal and we have four previews, one of which is good – and that's it. Opening night. Speaking personally, and that is what this is about, thank you very much, I have not experienced worse. The audience is vile, so vile that I receive a letter from the arts editor of one of our major publications apologising on their behalf. That's a first. In *Three Tall Women*, the character A has three or four long, rambling speeches describing an event from her past. These speeches are nearly identical. Dangerously so. Getting onto the wrong track can be disastrous. This opening night, of course, I do just that and in an instant am on a merry-go-round that looks as if it may still be circling come breakfast. I manage to fly clear eventually, thank God, and point the play towards interval, much to the relief of the other two on stage, who have been watching, fascinated. Extrication is just in the nick of time for Wayne. Out there in row D I sense he is about to open his veins. The second act comes as a blessed relief, and works splendidly. We take our curtain calls.

It all happens on adrenalin, and whatever the opening night crowd may or may not think, they will never notice the loop, or the recoveries or the near disasters. These are dealt with. In this business, ideally, one is never to be seen, even momentarily, at a loss, especially if one has been dancing on a tightrope for fifty years. Fall off now and everything would break. So you don't. Whatever the grief, the cure begins from performance two when the paying customers come and the real, untroubled work begins.

Three Tall Women played for 169 performances, eight times a week – with the exception of the return Sydney season when we played, luxury, just seven. It was sold out before it opened first time round in Sydney, and played to near enough full houses everywhere it toured.

Our happiest experiences, somewhat surprisingly, were Geelong and the Gold Coast. On the Gold Coast we played to over a thousand for each of the four performances. Something to ponder when the perception persists that capital cities are the natural, the only environments for artistic appreciation and awareness to flourish.

Yesterday, matinee, Gordon (Chater) came. Loved it. Got all the jokes, and wept. The audience here great – all 1200 of them. Muted – fluted – cheers . . . some brave souls stand as we line up. This matinee is mostly elderly, but we have some school groups as well. The perfect mix. We have found during this long tour that it has been a progression of involvement – especially from women of all ages, and the young – since Geelong, and the Monash matinees. It becomes quite overpowering. And next day Gordon writes a wonderful letter: 'If you never did anything else (but you will of course) your Tall Woman is an apogée.' He loved our composite. Said it was his mother. And Shane, who had not one word to say, moved him to tears.

I remember the ones who slept through *Three Tall Women*. They had a great night out and were completely untroubled. We were always happy not to be adding any burden to their lives in yet another example of the therapeutic properties of Theatre. The sleepers always woke up feeling marvellous, and their applause matched the most vociferous. Unfortunately, people who fall asleep in theatres are always in the front row. Mind you I might have dropped off, too, if subjected to Nick Schleiper's blazing white lights – a blaze that accompanied us everywhere we went. Highly effective, but a slight hazard to the front row. On stage, we usually managed to stay awake. One night in the return season in Sydney a young man sat in the middle of the front row reading a book, there being sufficient light to accommodate him. Backstage at interval we farewelled him with ribaldry and cups of tea. But he surprised us. There he was after interval, turning the pages till the end of the play.

People – particularly women, I suppose – will still stop in the street and grab my hand, and stammer out what Edward Albee's play meant to them. *Three Tall Women* meant a great deal to all of us, too. The very best thing about performing in a beautifully crafted play, and one that is, as well, written with the precision of a music score, is that, like fine music, it develops and becomes ever richer. More and more nuances are uncovered as the weeks and months progress; digging for gold, it is – and there's always a little bit more. The three of us turned tiny corners, shocked one another. It's that sort of play. And when Anita Hegh took over from Pamela Rabe for the return season in Sydney, the tiny changes provoked other discoveries. It never ends. Unless you become bored.

Over 160 performances. How many times does it all work for you? How many times do you think you've been even halfway good? Forget the connections with your audience – that's something else again. It's what you're paid for. How many times in a run do *you* really feel everything has worked? It's miraculous if you can summon up that handful, unbelievable when it's three or four. Most times it's good if it happens once. Just that once when you really think you might know what it's all about, when every piece of the jigsaw fits. It's what you keep looking for.

Opening night *Hamlet*, the Playhouse, Melbourne, in the Performing Arts Centre. We are performing *Three Tall Women* in the smaller Fairfax, part of the same complex. A woman arrives late for *Hamlet* and stands at the back through Act I. At the first interval she goes to claim her seat, which proves to be occupied. Discussion ensues, tickets are examined, and the occupant of the seat exclaims with a degree of astonishment, 'But you should be at *Three Tall Women!*' Snaps the woman, extremely irritated, 'I wondered when Ruth Cracknell was going to appear!'

Two

The first Cracknells arrived in Sydney in 1817 on board the sailing ship *Matilda*: Great-great-grandfather James and wife Margaret with 4-year-old Susannah. They settled in Sussex Street, and six more children were born in the Colony, one of them Great-grandfather Richard who, in the 1830s went north to Morpeth and then to Maitland. Maitland, on the Hunter River, was one of the first New South Wales country towns to be developed in the Colony. Richard was an accountant with the Maitland newspaper, the *Mercury*, which, with two others, he finally bought in 1854. He sold his interest to one of his partners ten years later, and 'did not afterwards go for any lengthened time into any regular business, having in fact acquired means of comfortable living'.

While he must have had an enviable time floating around from interest to interest, Richard also had a bakery to run, and

I imagine he was delighted to hand this over to my grandfather, Walter, as soon as possible, so that nothing from then on could impede his untrammelled progress through life.

My grandfather assumed full control of the bakery, added a flour mill, conducted a carrying business and bred draught horses. He rushed to join the Hunter Valley Light Horse in 1885 when there was a major war scare in the Colony – the Russians –, finishing up as major of the troop. The Major was active in The Lodge, Churchwarden at St Paul's Anglican Church, and ultimately the Mayor of Maitland – the very epitome of the prosperous country town bourgeoisie of the period. I never knew him, or my grandmother, an exemplary helpmeet from all accounts, but I knew most of my aunts and uncles – my father, Charles, had three brothers and six sisters. The elder sons left Maitland, eventually, for greener pastures, but also, I suspect, because they were unable to cope with Grandfather's autocratic conduct or his expectations.

It fell to Charles, the youngest child, to inherit the business, he being able to cope with the 'Pater' a little better than his brothers. Another reason, I have no doubt, was that my mother seems to have been the only one who was not in awe of Pa and was able to wrap him round her little finger. The three unmarried daughters, Edie, Birdie and Clara (sometimes referred to in composite as 'Edie-Birdie-Clara'), thought their Pa was God and worshipped accordingly. My mother knew he was human, and didn't. Three other aunts married, and I saw them only occasionally, but Edie, Birdie and Clara were to play vital roles in my life.

My mother, Winifred, also the youngest – of eight –, was born in Sydney in a terrace house in Jersey Road, Paddington just down from the police station. Her life was somewhat less structured than that of the Cracknells. Whereas Maitland was visiting cards and At Homes and tea parties and church and the Benevolent Society (Edie was President), and calm would have prevailed – just as long as they all kept on the right side of Pa – the Watts household at Paddington was noise, emotion, shouting, swearing, tears, laughter and fierce loyalties. Winifred's placid father, a gentle, book-loving salesman for a boot manufacturer, had sailed from Yorkshire as an infant with a mother who had dreaded the prospect and who died en route. His father remarried in Sydney. One unhappy childhood resulted.

My maternal grandfather went to Fiji for a time, and was finally re-united, by mail, with his grandparents in Yorkshire who were anxious for him to return to them. He decided to stay in Sydney and finally married Sarah Ann Goddard, who managed him and their rowdy offspring with a control based on the belief that calling a spade a spade was the way to 'keep on top' and 'stay ahead' – respectably on top and ahead, of course. I'm not disinclined to agree. Sarah Ann was the only grandparent I knew, and that was not for long – she died when I was 12. My memory of her is of an old lady, still with brown hair, sitting in a chair in the house in Kensington to which she and the four unmarried Watts 'girls' moved from Paddington, wearing an ankle-length, voluminous granny print dress made by daughter Bay, the dressmaker. She is clutching the housekeeping purse, listening, missing nothing, dropping the odd aphorism. 'Beattie, Beattie,' she would call to the aunt who was the housekeeper; though Sarah Ann could walk unaided, it was important to know where my Auntie Beat was every minute of the day – or night. Possibly the greatest wisdom Grandma passed on was 'Believe nothing you hear and only half of what you see'. All my Watts aunts, my mother and my own children absorbed that simple fact. To this day when told something on the greatest authority, my own secret reaction is, 'Oh really?'

Perhaps the only Watts daughter not to subscribe fully to the dictum was the eldest, Florence, but then she married the politician Archdale Parkhill, subsequently knighted, and such a philosophy is, perhaps, difficult to maintain in the political household. She was referred to by the others as Lady P. Florence had the same grounded resourcefulness as her sisters though; when my cousin, Bruce, was given an air gun as a birthday present she simply solved what was to her a major problem by wrapping it in newspaper, smuggling it onto the Mosman ferry and dropping it overboard in the dead of night.

The Watts's story, certainly my grandfather's, has a Dickensian flavour; my Cracknell side more of a Jane Austen bent. Miss Austen would have been completely at home sitting in the corner of the Rosewood Room in the family home in Maitland.

My Auntie Ethel Watts was a schoolteacher, specialising in music. She was the first singing teacher appointed to Government schools, and one of her early posts was at a school in

Newcastle. There she met one of the Cracknell 'girls', friendships blossomed and ultimately Winifred Watts and Charles Cracknell met, and that was that. To leave the hurly burly of Jersey Road, Paddington to go to the ends of the earth in Maitland must have seemed like banishment. Winifred wept. Fifteen years later, she would weep to leave.

Those first fifteen years of marriage were possibly the most idyllic of my parents' life together. My sister, Gwenyth, was born two years into the marriage; I arrived eight years later. A lovely, easy, companionable round of socialising and close friendships for my mother, a live-in maid, a community of interests for my father, a business that was his, ease and pleasure continuing endlessly, painlessly into the future. Holidays at Swansea, the lake, great food and cooking, my mother spreading to splendidly comfortable proportions, and the small child always on hand, watching, listening, happily sucking a lobster claw if the evening's entertaining encompassed a fish course. My big sister there whenever needed, already the prefect.

Flying through the air on Gwenyth's bicycle, legs spread wide, arms clamped around. Clamped around her for dear life. Clamped around her often, a baby koala, never wanting to let go. Sleeping next to her in the big oak bed, waking, alone for a moment, then wriggling over to the other side, arm snapping around. Eight years' difference in our ages, she remained, remains big sister, always just that space ahead, just out of reach. Absurd, when she's the most approachable of people; I just don't think that attribution of superiority to the seriously senior ever quite fades. Ask the baby in any family. We're always aiming to please. Always just that touch in awe, even at our cockiest – which for me was not infrequently in those early years.

And, most important perhaps, I remember once, when I was 2, singing a chorus of 'Rose Marie' at a little boy's birthday party. It was starting to get dark. There was a tiny spotlight that shone on my pale blue voile dress. I can't answer for him, but I loved that moment. The applause. The spotlight.

In the heat of those impossible Maitland summers I, along with other babies in other houses, was taken out at night in my pram, covered with net, and as the grown-ups gasped the only sound in all that heat, all over Maitland, was the crying of babies – night after night after night – until coolness returned. A drought in the first year of my life. Rain, ever since, a lucky symbol.

Hot, hot summers could be escaped by making the long journey to Sydney for reunion with the Watts aunts and Grandma. We had a car that superseded a beautiful sulky and horse. We had a succession of cars during my first dozen or so years: a Dodge saloon with a running board, a Chevrolet, and a car that had a dicky seat. Wonderful this one; I'd sit way up back in something the size of a boot (two comfortably, three with a squash), with a rug tucked all around if it was cold. The delicious feeling of proceeding through the night with an icy coldness brushing cheeks and every other bit as warm as toast.

We would set out, Mum, Dad, Gwenyth and infant me complete with the toys necessary for survival – something called an oomi, which had started life as a full-sized nappy but ended as a small square of frayed cotton the size of a lady's handkerchief, plus a fragment of celluloid with a thatch of hair attached. Either of these dropped accidentally out of the window would cause our fine progress to halt as everyone raced back to find one or other or both fragments, the absence of either promising a nightmare journey for the remaining long hours. We would bowl along, occasionally singing rounds of 'The Sergeant-Major' who endlessly proposed around the corner and under the tree, or 'Tipperary', or 'Pack Up Your Troubles'.

Finally, we would breast the hill north of St Albans and join the tail-end of the queue for the punt at Wiseman's Ferry. The slow crawl downwards could take an hour or more, but the excitement was maintained by the sellers of Smith's Crisps. Would they ever reach our car? Out of their wooden tip-top boxes came transparent paper bags of delight, filled with the crunchiest, most flavoursome of morsels, and at the bottom, a blue, waxed twist of paper containing salt, unravelled and sprinkled without conscience. At last we would drive on board. A chugging slide across black water, and if I was awake doubtless my father's strong arms held me as we gazed over the river.

Somewhere – Castle Hill? Pennant Hills? – would be the first sight of Sydney. A maze of twinkling lights. Fairyland. It caused such excitement, anticipation and wonder that I felt I might burst. A very early glimpse of ecstasy.

I have no memory of the rest of the journey to Sydney –

probably I was asleep — but our holiday destination would be Bondi, Manly or once a small flat in Flinders Street from the window of which I dropped a tiny rubber ball and watched, helpless, as it headed straight down a drain. The unpredictability of life was revealed in the smallest matters.

The quintessential Australian childhood. In and out of the water. Never taught to swim, never unable to. In Sydney, as I grew older, I was conscious always of the accessibility of water — calm water, choppy water, seductive water, safe water, dangerous water.

Judging the waves at Bondi, Maroubra, Collaroy, Newport, Dee Why, Palm Beach. Bilgola, romantic; Harbord always the best swim. Some waves allowed to smack in the face, others breasted just before the crest, others dived under before they took me apart, tossed me, and there would be an eternity when I felt I'd never clear the surface. Often I didn't, but ended the torment unceremoniously slapped onto the shoreline, full of sand, empty of air.

Balmoral was calm, beautiful, but I was never brave enough, like some, to swim, contemptuously, outside the shark net. Even in need of repair, the net surely provided some protection. I was brought up never to swim in Middle Harbour waters unprotected. Not even a foot in. My childhood swimming was shadowed by the tale of a young boy, less than knee deep in water at Sirius Cove, near where Auntie Florence and Uncle Arch lived, taken by a shark — sunrise, the water grey, then stained, red. Matching the sky.

So, to Grandma and the Watts aunts at Kensington. Lunches (cold pickled pork, chutneys, pickles, bread, sliced tomatoes, pudding, Beat's sand cake), served up on the enclosed back verandah, which had a long table and chairs and a stretcher bed where Beat slept. Grandma would be seated in the straight-backed leather and wood armchair above which was a picture called *His Head in a Whirl*, depicting a gentleman in evening dress, his head a spinning orb. On one side of him was a beautiful, coquettish blonde, on the other a sultry brunette. They were so beautiful, those two, their gowns so elegant. I could never make up my mind, over the years I visited, which he should favour. There was also a picture of a chained Hope trapped on a rock in the sea, trying desperately to extricate herself from her bonds as the water lapped ever higher. I gazed and felt anxious. At the far end of the room, under the windows, were low, built-in cupboards and above these, flush to the wall, a small set of bookshelves containing, among the French novels and the classics, a copy of *The Decameron*, which later caused me to view at least one aunt through different eyes.

Auntie Bertha had a bedroom, as did Auntie Ethel, and Grandma had the front bedroom. For the life of me I can't remember where Auntie Bay slept — another stretcher in the back room, I suppose. A minute kitchen contained a small marble bench top (responsible for perfect pastry), a sink with a cold water tap, and a small stove in the corner, difficult to get at. This led to the breakfast room with its round table and chairs and Grandfather's wonderful likeness above the mantelpiece; sidewhiskers, gentle, sensitive eyes. There was the formal dining room – three rooms designated for meals yet no bed-room for Beat or Bay – and 'the lounge room' with sofa, chairs and a wind-up gramophone, on which, every Christmas, Bay would play Christmas carols at full volume, the gramophone thoughtfully placed near the open front door for the benefit of the neighbours like it or not. I remember hearing Melba on the gramophone and Chaliapin and Florence Austral, Galli-curci, and Richard Tauber and Kirsten Flagstad and Wagner. Auntie Ethel was wont to murmur 'Ah, Wagner...' at odd moments.

There was a tiled bathroom with, luxury, a bath heater and a lavatory. Outside in the yard was another lavatory with a nail for the cut-up squares of paper (proper lavatory paper was reserved for the bathroom), and in the corner the big cast-iron pot with corn for the fowls who ranged free in the sandy soil of their enclosure, shaded by a lemon tree. There was a wide side passage – a carport today, probably – flanked by hydrangeas, and most delicious of all, a room under the house called Annie's room; dark, cobwebby, full of the unimaginable. It had a low door, bolted from the outside, so entering was fraught with tiny terrors, the most possible of which could be imprisonment by someone of that ordered household bolting the door which had been carelessly left open. Its floor was the sandy earth. I never quite knew what it housed, though it seemed brim full.

There was a black cat, Noah (saved from drowning), and a dog called Jip, from *David Copperfield*. And a canary in a cage on the back porch.

It was all so delightful, so warm, all sights and sounds and wondrous cooking smells. Occasional flashes of temper, and always the talk that never flagged. Except, later, when I stayed on my own and came to realise that one time in the day was sacrosanct and silent. Beat would sit on her stretcher bed, light a cigarette and gaze out of the casement window. No one ever spoke to her then; this time was not to be intruded upon. I have this image now of a strong, dark, aquiline face which seemed carved at these moments, no expression, no movement other than hand lifting cigarette to mouth, and then the gentle exhalation. I'd watch for a moment or two. What was she thinking? Who was she thinking about? No one ever knew. Perhaps that ten-minute ritual was the only thing that kept this frustrated, French-speaking intellectual – a member of Alliance Française and the Dickensian Society – sane in a house of women for each one of whom she was cook, washer-woman, housekeeper. The others worked.

I can't plumb Beat's thoughts. The bitterness and frustration and resentment that would accompany a similar situation today wasn't part of the climate. Simply, she performed her tasks, as the others did theirs. Housekeeping was what *she* did. Difficult to conceive of today, but this was the era when duty didn't sour, was performed without rancour. And perhaps because of this, my aunts had access to contentments denied today where 'happiness' equates with success, a success often achieved by a punishing self-aggrandisement. Perhaps it is we who don't have the trick of it.

At the time, I was fascinated by Beat's moments of

stillness. I wondered about all those thoughts of hers, and now I like to think of them joining Teilhard de Chardin's myriad grains, slowly ascending with the smoke to his 'noosphere', his thinking envelope surrounding the planet. I'd hate to think they were lost forever.

The house in Kensington was to be the centre of much of my life. A special corner that could be visited at any time. A place that could be relied upon to provide entertainment and occasional succour.

I had aunts in Maitland, too. There I am – sitting in Margaret Johnstone's kitchen. She's shelling peas, and I'm staying for lunch. I'm not yet 4. Auntie Maggie is, perhaps, my mother's closest friend in Maitland. Why am I there, alone? I can't remember. I remember what I feel, though – revulsion at the thought of eating peas. The gorge rises! The brain turns quickly. 'I can't stay for lunch with you: I'm not *allowed* to eat peas!'

The story gets trotted around, laughter over the mah jong table. I'm very much the centre of attention, the late child, no one my age, most of the children older.

I'm visiting my three Aunts – Edie, Birdie, Clara – who live some little way from us. My mother is doing something else, so I am despatched in a taxi. They fall on me. Tea, cakes, milk, biscuits on the Limoges plates. I converse and entertain and all is faithfully reported. And after afternoon tea I am returned, alone, in the taxi, to the house with the lattice on the verandah and the lawn all around.

A comforting place to be. Nothing to cause the slightest ruffle on the surface. Mild practical jokes in which my father joined with relish — I think he fancied himself a bit of an entertainer, certainly a juggler, oranges flying in all directions as he was, sadly, inept. He had a pleasant light baritone singing voice and a beautiful speaking voice. There was a musical society in Maitland. He sang with it. Auntie Birdie learned the violin from the nuns at the convent, but could not be said to be a fine example of their skills. This never deterred her from the occasional solo, and people were always kind. Probably, when I think back, my main impression of Maitland would be of music — light music, mostly, all the operettas and musicals. But *never* Gilbert and Sullivan, which I still loathe today as much as my mother ever did. She was always playing the piano. Although virtually self-taught, in childhood she had risen to dizzy heights, playing the class into school at Paddington with a rousing march. My most melancholy memory is of her playing a quite awful ballad called 'Marchéta' which she would launch into after I'd gone to bed at night. It was about 'departed love', and, rendered with great feeling in her tender mezzo, it aroused such anguish that I would rush sobbing to her side, begging her to stop:

MARCHÉTA

(a love song of Old Mexico)

Marchéta, Marchéta, I still hear you calling me back to your arms once again . . .

I still feel the spell of your last kiss upon me
Since then life has been all in vain.
All has been sadness without you Marchéta
Each day finds me lonely and blue . . .

My poor heart is broken
I want you Marchéta
I need you Marchéta I do

My father was a quiet man, and I can't remember him ever raising his voice. He certainly never swore. My mother was no stranger to expletives, and raised her voice a great deal. The main task of child rearing was, as was customary, in her hands, but I do know that on the rare occasions my father entered the lists and with the quietest of voices suggested I desist from something or other, I was stopped in my tracks. Whatever the quality he possessed, when used, it was unanswerable. He had it with animals, too, and without seeming to exert much effort could get them to do pretty much as he wanted. There is the grand story of one of the bakery cart-horses propping in the middle of Belmont Bridge, all blandishments and threats by the carter having no effect whatever. Summoned, dad approached the recalcitrant animal, took the bridle and whispered in the horse's ear. Horse moved off instantly and amiably.

Horses. Even before I read and saw *National Velvet* and emulated the heroine with leather belts tied around bed ends — this was

practice with reins, not early experimentation with S and M –
I had nourished a quiet passion for horses and riding. Stories
of Auntie Birdie riding in amateur trotting events added further fuel to my nicely simmering passion. Hard to imagine
Birdie, in later life, which was when I knew her, once being
quite so daring, but she was certainly the right size to don
jockey's silks. How jaunty she would have looked, leaping up,
grabbing reins and zapping off.

My dreams leaned more towards dressage. There was, however, a problem. No horse. Riding in early years was restricted
to holidays in the country when all available time would be
spent at a riding school. Invariably these establishments contained a number of patient, unexciting horses that carried
generations of school children, uncomplainingly. But in some
respects this seemed only a step or two up from riding the
ponies on the beach in the summer, or the elephant at the zoo.
One did learn the rudiments though. Like swimming, riding
was something I took to naturally, Birdie's genes triumphing.

One of those establishments, in rural Bundanoon, was
run by a gnarled and weathered old man who fancied the 12
year old and always had her by his side. My hand would sometimes be held – fragility trapped in corrugated iron – as he
persuaded me to rein my horse back to a canter at snail's pace.
The nearest I ever came to dressage, and how I loved that sensation, that stylish control. (Turning on a dime, as Geoffrey
Rush said to me years later after a particularly good night with
the interrogation scene in *The Importance of Being Earnest*.)

The very best of times, though, happened nearer home,

when, at around 14 or so, I became acquainted with the owner of another riding school in suburban Mowbray Road, Willoughby. I first went there with a friend from North Sydney Girls' High.

The owner of this establishment was equally gnarled and old, but of the feminine gender, I think. Her house was weatherboard, as was she, and seemed in imminent danger of collapsing into the dust that surrounded it. Dust constantly being churned up by the ten or so horses that dwelt in her suburban back yard. Stables, yards, chaff, troughs, bridles, saddles, horsey smells, hens, roosters. Heaven.

The back verandah with its wooden bench tops containing an array of empty treacle tins for screws, string, nails, buckles, bits of leather. The kitchen which was similarly stacked with rusty tins, jars, bottles, tea, sugar, flour; bridles, rope, strings of onions hanging from nails so that not a square inch of wall space remained; the meat safe. All bore a strong resemblance to the sets I walked onto later in *Ben Hall* or any of the other 'struggling pioneer' series the ABC were so fond of. Mess, mess, mess. Ordered mess, though. Like life.

I can't remember her name. I think there was a Mrs in front of it. If so, no bestower of the title was ever in evidence. She was stooped, thin, small, wore riding breeches and dusty, stained boots. Spoke little but had a keen, sharp intelligence glinting out of eyes that missed nothing.

Fortunately, I was a favourite in this establishment, as well, and was permitted to take out a horse on my own. A beautiful thoroughbred mare, Lady, who was our riding

My Cracknell grandparents, Mary Ann and Walter

My maternal grandmother, Sarah Ann; the only grandparent I knew

Standing, from left: Harold, Beatrice, Ethel and my mother, Winifred
Seated, from left: Bertha, Florence and Ada (Bay)

Standing, from left: my father, Charles, and Ray
Seated, from left: Herbert, Grandfather and Frederick

Winifred

Charles

Babe Ruth

Riding with my friend, Patricia Wilkins

Mother and my sister, Gwenyth, Sydney, 1940s

*Independent Theatre Drama School students — weekend in Blackheath.
Clockwise, from top left: Fay Grieves, John Kingsmill, Ruth,
Desmonde Downing and Diana Davidson*

Arms and the Man *radio broadcast, 1955.
Seated, from left: Sir Lewis Casson, June Collis, Ruth,
Dame Sybil Thorndyke and Sir Ralph Richardson*

Studio portrait taken for the Mercury Theatre, 1952

Gracious Living – *demonstrating the art of ikebana*

mistress's pride and joy. These were my halcyon days. As often as possible, Lady and I would head off through suburban streets till we got to Castlecrag, then along Edinburgh Road at a fast clip. Edinburgh Road in those days was just bush with a smattering of Burley Griffin houses. Wind down and down over dirt road, and by then it was just me, horse, old forest, wattle everywhere and when I pulled up, silence. Until the whip bird started. A sprig of wattle picked to make Lady look festive. Off again into the sharp breeze that took the heat out of the sun making its unimpeded way to my face. Lady and I alone in the world and loving one another. Finally, Sugarloaf Bay with a rowing boat or two. Dismount, give Lady a rest, lie down, munch an apple, gaze up at intense blue, feel the blessed sun, take a step outside oneself for a second.

A dozen years later I presented the first strange mark on my face to a skin specialist, and from that day on I was never again allowed to expose skin to sun.

THREE

When the decision was made to sell Cracknell's Bakery in Maitland and move to Sydney, we lived for a time in part of a house at the top of Inglethorpe Avenue, Kensington, which was where the Aunts lived. The house was alongside the steps and wide footpath that ran beside the monastery perched in splendour on the top of the hill ('They always get the best places.'). I could look over the fence and see the impressive bulk of the monastery and nearer the fence a high-rise of concrete, useful for bashing balls against. I once observed, fascinated, a man urinating against this wall — a function I'd not observed before. There would be other occasions, of course, when something similar would be witnessed, evoking little interest.

One occasion, however, I do remember. Paris, 1984. I had stayed on alone to study a one-woman play, *Machiavelli,*

Machiavelli, by John Upton. My days fell into a routine of breakfast at my favourite *salon de thé*: *'Non, non, non, non, un oeuf sur le plat.' 'Mais le menu dit les deux oeufs, Madame.' 'Mais je ne veux qu'un oeuf, s'il vous plaît.'* Occasionally I won. I would take my script into a little park at the end of Ile St Louis and work for the morning, then walk back for a light luncheon, more walks, dinner. All very civilised, and one could easily brush aside the odd, pallid gigolo offering his services in whatever capacity might be desired. This was simple to deal with and provided interesting conversation as one walked to the restaurant one had in mind for a determinedly solitary meal. Grave and polite, extrication at the doorway was never a problem.

Good fortune provided May Day during this time. A lovely day to be in Paris, much celebrated. Sprigs of lily of the valley handed out and the large tricolour at the Arc de Triomphe lazily moving in the breeze. (Why does it stir my sluggard sense of patriotism more than other flags?) As I wandered back across Pont Marie, there was a mime performance in progress, starring Pierrot. It was entrancing. The day itself was breathtaking; the sun shone and the light had that exquisite, shimmering quality that makes you want to stay in Paris forever. The actor's face was a white mask with sad, sad eyes and red lips. The performance was touching, bewitching. The Seine sparkled, the stone walls along the embankment basked in a golden richness. A moment that should never end. It did, of course. The performance finished, there was applause, the crowds drifted. I watched my mime, still fascinated, as he meandered across the bridge and down the steps, his object doubtless, a moment of reverie and contemplation as he gazed in the river. Searching for inspiration for our further delectation? Not on your sweet nellie. He turned his back and pissed loud and long on that sun-drenched wall, then, adjusting himself, sauntered off. Behind his soulful, vulnerable mask something else emerged, something swaggering, insolent, slightly aggressive. I didn't want him, I wanted the mask.

The stain faded ultimately, I imagine, and the soft rains of Paris do obliterate, but just then it seemed a melancholy end. Pierrots shouldn't piss on walls. Pierrots are magic. But don't trust them.

We stayed in Kensington for a time. Time enough for me to start school – infants – before we began our peripatetic journeyings from one side of the Harbour to the other. Chatswood, Bondi, Artarmon, Chatswood. Primary school years passed in a sort of dull haze. Willoughby Primary School was remembered in the main for my loathing of the sewing teacher, who seldom missed an opportunity to hold up my unfinished efforts in front of the class, my only completed garment being a pair of gargantuan bloomers. She exerted such an influence that she entered my dreams and tried to drown me in the basin that stood in the corner of the hell that was the sewing room. I still don't sew.

Except one occasion. Years later, in London, I took on a multiplicity of roles, including one with the unlikely name of Cool Cool Water, in a production of *The Pied Piper* on the West End. Trader Faulkner was the Pied Piper in a production that had both funny and dreadful moments – one where I was left saying four people's lines, plus a crowd reaction, to avoid dead silence on stage. I was allotted the comedian Jimmy Edwards's dressing room – we were playing matinees only. His fridge was padlocked. He obviously didn't trust Australians.

We were required to make our own costumes for *The Pied Piper*. Letter home:

24 November 1953: Here I sit in a somewhat crummy restaurant in Tottenham Court Road surrounded by Greeks eating enormous quantities of chocolate eclairs and all talking about me. I have just glared at them and they have returned to their munching. I am going out ... for another repulsive burst of sewing and have dashed in here after work for a quick bite ...

Repaired to Ladbroke Grove where lives my helper, and had a horrible night SEWING. I can't begin to tell you just how tired I am – I could scream, and if anyone so much as speaks above a whisper, I probably shall. And if ever I'm half-witted enough to commit myself to a production that entails costumes being run up by members of the cast, you may take me out and shoot me. I'm sick of tramping out to Ladbroke Grove to the sewing machine, I'm sick of hemming and cutting and pinning and tacking ...

Despite sewing, I was always top of the class at primary school, with little memory of how I arrived there, and I did have one or two staunch friends who made up for the girl who gathered up a group one day and marched them off with words directed towards me: 'We don't want *her* with us, do we!'

My great friend was Daphne Cotterill. She had serious, grey eyes and wonderful long, thick, blonde plaits as opposed to my short, thinnish, brownish hair. She lived not far away, and we spent a great deal of out of school time together. We didn't speak much; sometimes we carried books and cushions and my dog to the branches of the peach tree in our tiny orchard alongside the Californian bungalow in Mowbray Road, Chatswood. We might stay there all afternoon, reading and eating the peaches. Then I'd walk her part-way home and she'd walk me part-way back – on and on until we got sick of it. We had a similar dry sense of humour. Our heroes at that time were all the film comics, and we did a nice line in Laurel and Hardy impersonations. We formed our own Secret Society – two members only – held meetings and kept a book of rules. Daphne and I once wrote and performed a play in my backyard for the neighbourhood children. No beckoning siren, though. Merely play.

Our play didn't include dolls, however. I never really took to them. I had a pram, of course; in it lodged an exquisite creature. She was not a doll dressed for a christening, drowning in lace, she was a doll looking the way a doll should. She was impersonating a baby. A mask in other words, with unreal china blue eyes that snapped open and shut and an expression that never changed. I looked after my doll but my heart was not in it, if I'm honest. My favourite toy was a koala bear, which accompanied me to bed to the ripe old age of 13. Then he disappeared.

If only I could say that about my daughter's dolls. Mea culpa, mea culpa.

How can a mother send off said daughter's dolls after she has fled the coop? Reminded of this recently, more in sorrow than in anger, remorse flooded every pore. Particularly as I have no recollection of the event.

'I had the dolls in a drawer covered in their little sheets and blankets and you sent them away.'

'Heavens, did I?'

Silence.

'I'll give you a doll every birthday and Christmas.'

'I don't want a doll now, I wanted those ones kept. They were in the old cedar wardrobe.'

Weakly, 'I suppose I was tidying up! Anyway, there are a couple of dolls left. I saw them the other day.'

'NOT mine.' Pause. 'And the train set, too.'

'Nobody was using it, and it took up half the verandah! I kept tripping over it!'

Silence.

'I sent it to the Burnside Homes, for Heaven's sake. Imagine their joy . . . And the joy of the little girls who got your dolls!'

'Yes . . . I do tell myself that.'

Brightly, 'I haven't sent your wedding dress away!'

'I don't want that.' Mutter. 'I wanted my dolls.'

Daphne and I spent many holidays together with one or other of our families. I remember going to my Uncle Arch and Auntie Florence's Burradoo house, lent to Mother for the May school holidays. I remember a frosty, cold Empire Night with bonfire and fireworks and I remember the coronation mugs, one green, one red, emblazoned with the likenesses of King George VI and Queen Elizabeth, which held our steaming cocoa. (Who, today, even knows what Empire Day was?)

I holidayed with Daphne's family at Avoca Beach, north of Sydney. I remember sharing a wave with four sharks. Perhaps they were porpoises, but, no, we knew they were sharks and so did everyone else in the water as they scrambled in ungainly fashion for the shore. 'Save me, save me!' cried one man flopping in the shallows. We treated him with contempt.

Mother went to hospital for six weeks when I was 11, and I stayed with Daphne's family. They were Christian Scientists, and attending Sunday School with Daphne was obligatory. She became devout. We remained close. When she married I was her bridesmaid. Daphne's father was a jeweller. Many of the jewellers he traded with were Jews and the ones who were friends were invited to Daphne's wedding. Middle-aged and elderly men, with their wives. I was 20 and absolutely charmed by their courteous manner, their ability to converse with focused and courtly interest on a variety of subjects with one so much younger. I didn't have such conversations with the young Australian males of my acquaintance, and the Jewish gentlemen set a benchmark that evening not easily met.

Round about fourth class my family crossed the Harbour

again to live in Bondi. On my first day at Bondi Primary I was introduced to the girl who was filling inkwells. 'This is Ruth, who was top of the class at Willoughby. You'll have to look to your laurels, Louise.' A great start, but Louise took it in her stride; I remember that I didn't like Bondi, so I imagine the laurels were safe.

The Cracknell Aunts – Edie, Birdie and Clara – had come to Sydney by then. They had a small flat in a red-brick block in Edgecliff Road, Edgecliff, and that took my mind off Bondi, which I loathed. The Aunts took me to evensong at All Saints in nearby Woollahra, which I didn't loathe, particularly as the choir boys and I got older.

How the Aunts fitted into their flat I don't know. Edie had the main bedroom and Birdie and Clara shared a room which, as well as their beds, held an enormous old cedar wardrobe. They were slim, 'the girls', so careful and considerate movements around the tiny space enabled lives to be lived amicably. I loved it when they opened the wardrobe; chiffon scarves would droop, one drawer contained jewellery – trinkets, mostly. Bangles were in vogue, and Birdie, being particularly modish, had endless treasures. Sometimes I was given a scent bottle, sometimes little boxes were opened for me to see inside.

Birdie enjoyed taking me for a swim, and this made Bondi bearable. There is a photo somewhere of the two of us walking along the promenade – Birdie, the flapper still, I, in shorts and a straw school hat pulled firmly down, eyes on the ground, the reverse of modish. Birdie had a boyfriend, Jim

Webster, for years. He went to the war, he returned from the war, they went out together, year in year out, till he died. They never married. Jim had his mother.

We traversed the Harbour again to settle in Artarmon for a time in a boring red-brick cottage that had been built for us. The house may have been dull but the life was not, and the next few years were the most carefree, innocent and untrammelled of all. The days rolled endlessly ahead in a succession of quiet, sustaining joys.

I had my friends in the street. My very favourite was John who lived opposite, and Daphne was not far away in Willoughby. John and I rode one another's scooters, we confided in each other. We were great, great friends. Most days after school we would be together, or, with a gang of sorts, we'd wander off into the bush, climb trees, tell secrets, form and unform alliances, pass on the odd bit of sexual information, usually as schoolboy/girl wit or smut, about which I was snootily priggish. Sometimes I was the only girl in the group — true innocence, it seems to me, can sometimes be a protection.

I'd learned the facts of life in sixth class at Willoughby Primary School when a girl who probably finished up in social work felt it incumbent upon her to circulate her slightly askew knowledge in these matters. I promptly discounted it all, but curse today that I don't have a copy of the hot document. My relationship with John transcended all this nonsense. We were sexless. Real friends. I was even dragooned into his cricket team, but treated with disdain come the match and banished to the boundary to fetch and carry and throw. When I batted came a certain grudging respect. Fast eye, fast reflexes.

Once, my friend and I wrestled, half seriously, half choked with giggles. Our battlefield happened to be his parents' bed, and as we rolled, fully clothed, punching and elbowing, I did have a momentary flash of terror that perhaps I'd have a baby.

He who had the bulk of my devotion, fealty and anxious caring, however, was my dog, Laddie — as much the object of my passion as Bottom ever was of Titania's. He was a handsome, white Pomeranian, and, unlike most of the breed, a true larrikin with loads of personality. Mother liked to wash him once a week in foaming laundry suds when the wash was over, and finish him off in a Reckitt's blue rinse, just like the linen. He was always at pains to avoid this so a pretence had to be devised by Mother, who, having accomplished the large wash, then had to present a convincing performance of leisured idleness. In the middle of the busy Monday morning household chores, she would take up knitting, paper or book and sit on the rocking chair on the front verandah. Laddie would be watching all this from a safe distance, but could never resist racing over and leaping onto her lap. And that was the end of him! He was never bright enough to work that one out, but as she was irresistible to him, anyway, as to the rest of us, the result would have been the same. A lap is a lap is a lap. I loved watching his bath and observing his deep melancholy as he was soaped with Sunlight, rinsed off and then transferred to the tub of liquid lapis lazuli. Then out, and stand back as the furious shaking off of water started and the move in with towels as we energetically performed the only part of the proceedings he took any pleasure in. Brushing and the combing completed and an exquisite creature stood before us. For a second or two. Then, off, into a corner of the backyard, and a scramble under the fence through the easement. He'd be back within the hour, filthy. His perfect revenge.

Washing dogs, riding scooters, John, Daphne, sister Gwenyth home late afternoon all the way from Sydney High across the Harbour, Dad home, dinners, warm house, piano played. Lying in a bath looking out the window at a softly moving sapling; eyes down, gaze at the ridge in the plaster above the soap holder; disappear inside and Alice could wander in a mysterious, private world. Cross the Harbour to Aunts of one sort or another — round and round we went, and as long as we kept on doing it, the magic would stay.

Touch wood, don't tread on the cracks.

I'd seen the flight of magic first at the age of 11, when the centre of my universe, my mother, became seriously, painfully, dangerously ill. Much of my life was lived with the nagging fear that my mother would be removed from me. Anxiety took root. It has never left. Mum was an entertaining, warm, funny, magnetic woman who should have been on the stage. Not permitted in her day — not an acceptable occupation for the respectable —, but her personality and effortless gift for being the centre of whatever group she was in was one way in which the latent talent was allowed to flower. My own friends adored her, which caused me occasional pique, but not for long. I was as much under her spell as they were.

She sang, often in parody but sometimes a ballad, and certainly all musical comedies of an earlier period, with *The Merry Widow* pre-eminent. She cooked instinctively, given the lack of imagination in much of the contemporary cuisine, and presented the usual popular miracles of sponge, pastry and pavlova. And sausage rolls. Long, slender, elegant short pastry with a filling the special mysteries of which she unfortunately took with her. Of course, parties then always ended with a huge supper – my mother's, it was acknowledged, occupying some sort of pinnacle. I can only surmise that the competitive edge was sharpened in Maitland, where cooking was the one great area of creativity. She truly loved cooking. People of all ages flocked around her, like moths to a benevolent flame. The element of destruction was entirely absent from her nature.

One fatal flaw, though. A melancholy defeatism that, as my father's business prospects whittled away, gradually turned her into the semi-invalid that she was for the latter part of her life. That first hideous moment, when she was hospitalised for six weeks – always a private room no matter what the state of the family finances – was encapsulated for me in efforts to escape the sound of her cries. I'd flee to the far end of the backyard, hang over the gate, and pray for my sister to come home from school. Some of the agony was only heard by me. It would have passed by the time help arrived. That illness excepted, most of Mother's ills were psychosomatic. But what difference does that make? What made it all bearable, even oddly enjoyable at times, was that her humour and shrewd eye for the fake or pretentious never deserted her. She had a line in repartee that could somehow be maintained in the middle of an asthma attack as I might be endeavouring, stupidly, to get a cup of tea into her at 3 a.m. Like Noel Coward, she had a talent to amuse.

She also possessed a degree of toughness in her relations with us. Complain about one's treatment at the hands of some malefactor, her invariable response would be, 'But what did you do to him?' She had a healthy scepticism about one's tales of perfidy, too, sometimes carried much too far as in the morning I went into her bedroom to relate what had befallen me the previous day on the way to Grace Gibson's Radio Studio in Bligh Street. Mother was breakfasting in bed, Saos and tea on tray — meagre breakfasts always. In hushed tones I related how, as I was walking up Hunter Street from Wynyard, in broad daylight, part of a crowd, an approaching man veered towards me and jabbed his elbow painfully, and very deliberately, into my right breast. Painful, outrageous, and requiring the administration of brandy and sympathy when I arrived at the studio. Mother lowered the *Sydney Morning Herald*, looked at me a long moment till, finally, 'He must have been tall' she said, and returned to the editorial.

Years later, my elder daughter, Anna, 14 or so, walking home from school, was lunged at and grabbed in many places by a youthful pervert. She burst in on me in the kitchen with the news. Horrified, I said, 'Anna, what did you do?' maternal emotions surging through my long since recovered breast. She was fiery with rage. 'I told him to fuck off!'

'Anna!' I shrieked. 'Did anyone hear you?' My mother's daughter — priorities a little out of kilter.

FOUR

England declared war on Germany on a Sunday – 3 September 1939. Next day at North Sydney Girls' High there was an air of suppressed excitement. No one had any idea what was ahead, but for those of us at school it seemed the most important and, yes, exciting thing that had ever happened. Unreal, though. We *were* a long way away.

The thought that this war would extend for six years, that Japan would enter, that Australians would spend years in prisoner of war camps in Germany, occupied Europe, Changi, Japan, that great cities would be obliterated, that atomic bombs would destroy two cities and in two strikes change the world forever, that an entire race of people would face extermination – all this was unimaginable that spring morning. The excitement – mixed with just an agreeable hint of fear – carried us through that day and the following weeks until the routine of war took over. We formed Comfort Funds and knitted and made camouflage nets. We watched as many of our male, and some female, relatives joined the forces and embarked for unknown destinations, as some of our friends went to Canada to learn to fly if they hadn't already learnt here, and as they themselves started bombing cities and repelling fighter planes. And dying.

One cousin, Keith Dillon, went off, fought with the Australian Imperial Force in Greece and Crete, was captured and spent the rest of the war working on a farm in Germany where conditions in winter were icy, but never too icy for an Australian to insist on washing in all weathers from a lone tap in the yard. Food started running out. His post-war legacy was diabetes, and ultimately blindness and amputation. Another cousin, Tom Cracknell, was a commando in the islands to the north of Australia, where he was captured and listed as missing in action. We all spent the war imagining his life as a prisoner of war. Parcels were sent off through the Red Cross. In fact the Japanese 'hell-ship' in which he was travelling, steerage, was sunk by the Americans, and it was only after the war that any of us knew that he had been dead all those years. My other cousin, Bruce Parkhill, was on Rabaul, captured, but luckily made it all the way to Japan as a prisoner of war, where he got thinner and thinner...

We were still innocent of all this that Monday at North Sydney Girls' High School. Yet when the press reports of the bombing of England, and particularly London, came in, it was as if we ourselves were being bombed every night. When Japan entered the war we started building our own shelters in suburban backyards, reading advice on what to do in an air raid. Darwin was bombed, Broome had an encounter, we were losing ground on every front. Anything seemed possible as Japanese armies moved closer and closer. We kept buckets of sand handy for the incendiary bombs, and some of the younger school children were sent away to the country. And there was rationing ... ration books. Not really a problem, this, apart from butter for the cooks. Once, when young neighbouring friends of the Aunts in Kensington went on a country holiday, they returned with some butter for Auntie Beat. The girls raced in to see Beat, a favourite of theirs, on their return. Their lyrical descriptions of cows, meadow and pasture were cut short by Beat with an impatient, 'Bugger the scenery, where's the butter?'

I began reading American poet Alice Duer Miller's long, fervent 'The White Cliffs' about a young woman's love of England and her falling in love with a scion of the upper class and marrying and seeing him off to war and losing him. Alice Duer Miller seemed to speak for all of us in those early days as England burned. I read 'The White Cliffs' often at fund-raising occasions: 'I have loved England dearly and deeply/ Since that first morning, shining and pure/ The white cliffs of Dover I saw rising steeply/ Out of the sea that once made her secure ...' How completely and utterly 'English' so many of us were!

There were weekly gatherings in St Michael's Hall in Hunter Street in the city where we netted and netted — my sister, some friends, and Birdie, too, working feverishly, gossiping

— strange looking, rough camouflage nets. We wondered where they'd end up.

My last day at North Sydney Girls' High School I thought, at the time, might break my heart, leaving as I was one year too early, family finances being at their lowest. I had desperately wanted five years, as had been my sister's lot at Sydney High. I'd had three awakening years after the tedium of primary school, comfortably placed in the middle of the A stream with an academic bias — English, History, Maths I and II, Latin, French and Science — then in the fourth year switching to a commercial year, where to an easier ride with the academic subjects was added book-keeping, shorthand and typing. The French was commercial, nodding slightly in the direction of day-to-day office/financial concerns — not the poets or the writers! That somewhat spurned business training was to stand me in good stead later, however, when acting engagements were not always thick on the ground.

My friends in that fourth year were a delightful band, and, at least, we had a year of comparative ease and sociability compared to everyone else moving relentlessly towards the Leaving Certificate. It was in that year that my perfect front tooth was knocked out by a friend. We were trying our hands at hockey on the hallowed fourth-year lawn, and not being hockey players my opponent raised the stick to assault height and a tooth hit the sward. It was alarming — more so for the other party, I imagine — but her progress in life was unimpeded and she went on to become school captain and, ultimately, the mother of one of my

— mostly — favourite satirists, Patrick Cook. I hid away for a while, but not forever, and dentistry is a fine art.

From school I briefly worked at Farmers Department Store before taking a job at Ku-ring-gai Council. I had a first-aid certificate and was required to learn a modicum about air raid precautions. Local councils were an arm of the Emergency Services, and we took it in turns to man the phones where we knew the difference between a yellow and a red alert. There were many yellow alerts but only a few red, mostly false alarms; when they occurred the mouth dried.

On the night Sydney did have its brush with the enemy, I was at home in Chatswood, alone with mother. The siren sounded. Night time. We rushed into the tiny front garden (forgetting all my training the while), looked at the sky and heard a plane flying low overhead. Good sense prevailed, and I hauled my parent upstairs to our flat and thrust her under the table, which ages before I'd insisted be placed in what was the safest part of the flat. As in all crises I started to eat — celery, this time, stick after stick. Mother was safely ensconced and I was waiting for a phone call — I'm not sure why — that might say, 'Proceed to . . .' It didn't take long for my mother to crawl out from under with the statement that if she was going to die she preferred to do it on her feet, thank you. So we sat in the dark, blackouts in place, and made cocoa while we waited for the All Clear. Next morning we read about midget submarines. Was there a bomb or shell on Rose Bay? Or just depth charges in the Harbour? No, a ferry torpedoed in error.

The heroes throughout those war years, for me, were the

airmen. Not surprisingly, I suppose, when once role playing in my head with a script from the Saturday cinema serials, I'd fancied myself as a 'world famous flyer' – another Jean Batten, Amy Johnson or Amelia Earhart. Not that it was hard to adopt those flyers as the heroes. In those early days of the war, fighter pilots were the closest one could get to jousting knights, a true one to one encounter that didn't carve up battalions of the innocent in the process. I knew the names of all the most decorated and courageous of those early flyers who flung themselves into the skies, day after day, night after night, and shot down or were themselves shot down. A heady, glorious period when, for a time, the fate of us all seemed to rest on the skills and reckless courage of just a handful of young men. At the age of 14 I pictured them scrambling again and again into their beautiful machines – Spitfires, Hurricanes, though the Hurricane never quite as glamorous as the Spitfire. I knew how many aircraft the number one ace, Irishman Paddy Finucane, had shot down. I mourned, as inevitably one after another young pilot was shot down. They were my pin-ups.

In many ways the most extraordinary of these young men was an Australian, Richard Hillary. Educated in England, he learned to fly while at Oxford and was drafted into the Royal Air Force when he was 20. Hillary's life had been privileged, and his time at Oxford as enjoyable and stimulating as all those other Oxford luminaries who had preceded him: W. H. Auden, Stephen Spender, Evelyn Waugh, Louis MacNeice, A. L. Rowse. Hillary, though, lacked their particular passions, talents and political involvements. He was lighter, a rowing blue, and would have had little patience with the fires flickering away in those other quarters.

Early in the war, Hillary lost many of his friends and was himself shot down in 1940. Horribly burnt on the face and hands, he became one of the triumphs of the great pioneer of plastic surgery, Archibald McIndoe. No longer handsome, though. But certainly attractive, and always to women. Unable to fly, and continually pondering on why he had been spared, he wrote a book, *The Last Enemy*. Because of the book, he was persuaded to go to America to lecture and show reason why the American support of the war effort was essential – all this, of course, before Pearl Harbor – and became, in the process, the darling of the intellectuals and of one film star, Merle Oberon.

The Last Enemy struck a chord among intellectuals, among artists, and also among the more thoughtful of the privileged within England. Some of whom might once themselves have flirted with fascism. Those whose world was being shaken not just from above, but from its very roots. Arthur Koestler was one who took him up. Koestler's theory that we live life on one of two planes – *La Vie Tragique* or *La Vie Comique* – was something I related to when I came across it much later. One lives in one plane at a time without ability or desire to comprehend the other. Travel *La Vie Tragique* and remain trapped there until ready to cross into *La Vie Comique*. Then, the theory goes, there will be little patience for those travelling the tragic way. The travellers on each remain absorbed in their way to the exclusion of the other.

The escape from this exclusive journeying, Koestler

believed, would only occur in times such as war when both ways intersect and the travellers on each understand, at last, and turn their gaze towards the others. The high danger, excitement and tragedy of war lays down different ground rules. Hillary epitomised this convergence for Koestler.

Hillary himself was moving relentlessly towards his own death, forcing himself back into flying against all argument and persuasion. He opted for night flying, the most dangerous, and eventually did die, though in an accident, not in battle. A mystique wrapped itself around him. There was speculation about his end – was it suicide, conscious or unconscious? The odd book still appears, unwilling to let his shade rest. As if anyone could know... His portrait, painted by Eric Kennington, is in the National Portrait Gallery, in London, a face of piercing eyes and puckered skin.

For me, as a Romantic, Hillary inhabited Camelot, but then Camelot was a myth, and destined to disappear as a grimmer, uglier reality began to emerge. The world has been forced to look in the glass ever since, and, for some of us, at times, it is an appalling vision. But also in a strange way a fairer vision, perhaps. I found a fading piece of typescript from these times, written by John Gillespie Magee, junior:

> Oh, I have slipped the surly bonds of earth,
> And danced the skies on laughter-silvered wings;
> Sunward I've climbed and joined the tumbling mirth
> Of sun-split clouds – and done a hundred things
> You have not dreamed of – wheeled and soared and swung

High in the sunlit silence. Hov'ring there
I've chased the shouting wind along and flung
My eager craft through footless halls of air.
Up, up the long delirious, burning blue
I've topped the wind-swept heights with easy grace,
Where never lark or even eagle flew;
And, while with silent, lifting mind I've trod
The high untrespassed sanctity of space,
Put out my hand, and touched the face of God.

The poem seems, now, as if it might have come from another planet. But that's the way it was then — for some of us, at least.

Of course, I fell in love with one who perfectly fitted that romantic ideal. Three years older, extremely good-looking, wearing a uniform of glamour, son of close family friends . . . I waved him goodbye when I was 17, and what had started as a simple schoolgirl crush developed into a deep and desperate longing only ever alleviated by his infrequent letters. He went to England and became part of a squadron that went on nightly bombing raids over Germany. He was decorated, was heroic in that way they all seemed — those photographs of bombing crews in parachutes and jackets and helmets standing in front of their giant machines. Heroic indeed they were, and we didn't dwell too much on what it must have been like living under those clouds of bombs building up to a crescendo as the war neared its end in Europe. Our focus, my focus, was up in the sky with them, night after night, my emotional centre locked in the northern hemisphere.

When the unwitting object of my very private passion came home from the war we met again. A rather dry feeling as illusion gave way to reality and scales clanked heavily and noisily from eyes. He was three years older, I was three years older — schoolgirl had metamorphosed into young woman, and ten minutes of stilted conversation was all that was needed to show that we had nothing in common.

FIVE

The department store, Farmers, where I took my first job, was subsequently taken over by Grace Bros. Farmers had it all over Grace Bros. Fronting up to a counter to be attended to, even sitting on a chair if you please, beats finding and fighting your way through the racks any day. As an 'office' sort of person I was employed in the Staff Office, which was presided over by a small, middle-aged dragon. I was the junior and attended to all the more boring clerical tasks. The days seemed endless, but I wasn't particularly depressed, just inclined to revert to primary school mode – tune off. I lasted a month and earned one pound and ninepence per week.

It was wartime, and there were processions along the main streets of Sydney whenever soldiers were departing overseas. How we cheered them! Too much so, one day, for the small, middle-aged dragon. The mainly female members of the Staff Office were all hanging out of the windows waving and cheering when a cross voice behind snapped, 'Not so much excitement, Ruth! You're far too noisy.' I wilted.

That was the day, suitably squashed, I decided to test the Staff Canteen. In those days, canteens were mini versions of prison dining rooms. I entered this unattractive room, head a little elevated, and while noting there was a roped-off area, failed to see why. Head too high. There was one vacant seat on the far side of the room for which I made a bee-line, taking the direct route – straight across the roped-off area. The reason for the barrier became apparent in the split second it took me to hit the floor. There I lay, flat on my back, slap bang in the middle of a large pond of Irish stew.

The following excruciating minutes, while transforming me into a greasy length of total embarrassment, also planted a tiny seed in the unconscious connected to the actual *sound* of laughter and the realisation of what that laughter did for people. It somehow looped back to the agonising moment on the stage at North Sydney Girls'. It was confirmation, even if vaguely, of the fact that the victim/perpetrator need not necessarily remain just a figure of fun. At school, I'd been saved by an impassioned speech. This time I wrestled with the purely comic. Making people laugh held the potential for something else, perhaps. I wasn't too sure what, but there definitely was something lurking.

At the conscious level, I was ready to die. Kind people scraped me down and dried me off – along with their tears. I somehow made my escape and returned to the Staff Office to be met by the dragon, whose worst fears were confirmed. I think she would like to have killed me – the escutcheon of the Staff Office had been well and truly besmirched, with peas and potatoes, no less.

Charity finally prevailed and she ordered me home, telling me firmly to change out of my disgusting attire into a spare skirt of hers, which she kept in the office. Her bidding was done. The fact that she was extremely short added the final horror to the day, and I left Farmers in a miasma of shame wearing the first example of a mini skirt to hit Sydney. Extremely mini, just a degree or two lower than crutch. The fashion then was mid to low calf, and there is really nothing to recommend being some twenty years ahead of time.

My resignation was shortly thereafter tendered, and doubtless gratefully accepted, because I had gained a position at Ku-ring-gai Council. There I stayed happily for the next four years or so – and a touch luckily, considering I was nearly shot one day. The paymaster was making his rounds with the pay envelopes, and for some reason decided to show the gun that accompanied him on these rounds to an interested party. I was standing near him when there was a very loud bang. The stinging sensation in my right leg obviously indicated grave wounding. As I was sinking to the floor, the bullet was discovered in a nearby wall, and my leg recovered. The paymaster was not tempted to show his gun again. I don't remember too much being said about the incident, as one would expect on the North Shore. He was certainly not asked to hand the weapon over. This was one of several near escapes and goes some way towards explaining my belief in the guardian angel principle.

I was 17 when Marjorie Webb, a friend of my sister's, took me to a play. I had been to the theatre before, though had little recollection of it, even the pantomimes to which mother took me. There was not a great deal of theatre around at the time – the Tivoli, which was the vaudeville house, and the Theatre Royal, which mainly concentrated on musicals and importations. More serious theatre was left to the fully professional Minerva, which had opened in 1939, and to the Little Theatres – amateur in the sense that no one was paid, despite the fact that their ranks were filled with professional radio actors looking to get theatre experience. These theatres included Doris Fitton's Independent, Bryant's Playhouse, founded by Beryl Bryant with her father, George, in 1932, and the New Theatre. May Hollinworth's Metropolitan Theatre came a little later.

So when Marjorie Webb, agent of fate, took me to the Modern Theatre Players' production of *George and Margaret* in 1943 at the St James's Hall, she had little notion of what her kindly act for young Ruth would do. The St James's Hall was the church hall of the Church of St James in Phillip Street. It was not a true hall, being instead a perfect little horseshoe theatre seating two hundred or more. We walked up the steps into the theatre, took our seats, I looked around, and – snap! That was it. We watched as the tiny orchestra filed in to the orchestra pit – all six of them, including a small boy in short pants, an elderly man playing the flute and a spinster refugee from an earlier palm court trio. Men were in somewhat short supply just then in drab wartime Sydney. The orchestra played valiantly in front of a red velvet curtain, then, a flourish, and the curtain rose. A strange excitement gripped me.

George and Margaret was not exactly a play to set the world afire. It was only faintly amusing, but watching that cast of six or seven presenting a play with such relish filled me with an envy that would only be satisfied by getting up there with them. I could wish that the Paulian moment had been brought about by something a little weightier, a little more inspirational, than that extremely ordinary piece. *The Trojan Women*, say, or at least *Lysistrata*. But *George and Margaret* it was.

The Modern Theatre Players was run by Edna Spilsbury, London trained under the formidable Elsie Fogarty, who was voice teacher to the then greats of the English Theatre. A drama school was attached to the Modern Theatre Players and I joined with alacrity. Miss Spilsbury (quite some time before I addressed her as Edna) was an excellent teacher of the rudiments of acting. From knowing absolutely nothing, and possessed only of an immense longing, I progressed gradually to a stage where I could express myself without too much self-consciousness. And through her particular method of movement and mime I gradually acquired an ability to cross from one side of a stage to the other, and all the variants, without looking too ridiculous in the process. Miss Spilsbury excelled in voice training, of course, and little else of this standard was to be had in Sydney at that time. She had a studio in the old Palings Building in Angel Place. At least once each week I would ascend in the ancient lift to the fourth floor and make my way along a corridor with studios opening off each side. Right next door was Frances Scully's Academy of Dance. A glance sideways would reveal straining bodies attempting the impossible to the thump of the piano. One! Two! Three! Four! One! Two! Three! Four! One! Two! Three! Four! Again! One! Two! Three! Four! One! Two! Three! Four! Pale faces. Mothers seated around the walls, knitting socks for soldiers. In another studio, a singing lesson in progress. Somewhere else, piano practice. It was heaven. I belonged.

For the next four years I spent most of my spare time at the Drama School, graduating from class exercises and scenes to my first public appearance – an evening of one-act plays. I cannot remember what my play was called, but I was cast in a 40-year-old 'character' role (playing years older from the out-set) in a comedy. I heard an audience laugh for the right reasons for the very first time. A heady experience! One of the senior members of the Modern Theatre Players, and already an established radio actor, was Kevin Brennan. He came up to me at the end of the performance and proffered the first advice: 'Don't tread on your laughs.' Never to be guilty of it again. Then, small parts in the 'major' plays, and, one day, I was a fully fledged member of the Company.

At about this time I read J. B. Priestley's *The Good Companions*, and I felt one of them. Plays would travel to various halls and 'theatres' around Sydney. I remember going to Ashfield Town Hall, church halls and once we took the train all the way to Parramatta to perform for the boys at the King's School. Afternoon tea after the performance, tea and cakes handed around by boys with impeccable manners, and in the train on the way home the male lead stroked my hair. Miss Spilsbury later warned me of the threat that some actors could pose, and the dangers that abounded on all sides. I listened politely, and glanced his way with greater interest.

I left the Modern Theatre Players in 1945, realising that Edna could not provide sufficient stimulation once one passed the elementary stage. It had been a crucial and, in the main, rewarding experience. She had some excellent people in her group — it was there I first met the splendid actress, who became a good friend, Betty Lucas. Kevin Brennan went on to many fine roles in film and on stage and then went to England where he worked successfully for a number of years. And I still vividly recall a young comedienne, Sylvia Woods, whose timing, lightness and style I've not seen exceeded since, and seldom equalled. Born in the wrong time in the wrong country. Had she been born in America she would have been at the top of Broadway, or matching the style and wit of the American screen heroines who were my idols — Carole Lombard, Rosalind Russell, Katharine Hepburn. Sylvia taught me much, just by watching her. Nonetheless, it was time to move on, away from the delights, the friendships, the minor enmities, the too close attachments, the spiky jealousies, the blind loyalties of the Amateur Dramatic Society. They were replaced by Doris Fitton's rather more serious version of precisely the same at her Independent Theatre and Drama School. My last performance for Edna Spilsbury was as Mrs de Winter in Daphne du Maurier's *Rebecca*, in which my faithful, albeit unconscious, reproduction of Joan Fontaine's screen performance in the same role, caused high, if uncritical, praise.

Earlier had come the first radio engagement – August, 1945. It was proffered after months of writing for auditions, getting them, passing them, and then making the rounds and knocking on door after door. A singularly hateful occupation – until one stayed open. An engagement! A letter of contract! It was in a state of disbelief and no little terror that I presented myself at the AWA Recording Studio in Clarence Street. To this day, I can recall the sickly sweet smell of the whitewood lift that propelled me to the third floor. The sickly sweet smell was in danger of gaining another component that would have eliminated the sweet, so ill did I feel. I entered the Studio presenting the calmest of facades and was greeted coolly by Edward Howell, the producer. I may have been introduced to the rest of the cast – I was certainly presented to his wife, Therese Desmond, who was playing the lead in the series *Ask Anne Carter*. I was engaged for one of the episodes. Therese was 'grand', as were all the Radio stars of the forties. I don't think I spoke to anyone for two years. They all terrified me. Lyndall Barbour, Sheila Sewell, Thelma Scott, Neva Carr Glynn, Muriel Steinbeck, Queenie Ashton, Enid Lorimer – as far as I was concerned, they inhabited Olympus. Two years on, we were colleagues, but there *was* a hierarchy, and one had to make that climb up the mountain.

Ask Anne Carter was a dramatised version of an agony column. Letters flooded in with heart-rending emotional problems, which a cast dramatised once Miss Desmond, as Anne Carter, had read the introduction; the narrator introduced her, followed by an appropriate rise and fall of theme music. The episodes were uniformly and unrelievedly awful, but everyone got through them with maximum efficiency and a good deal of larking about. I remember that one actor struggled through his scene with someone else removing various bits of his attire. One of the greatest exhibitions of focused attention I can recall.

I received money — pounds, shillings and pence — for every episode, and as I was guaranteed five episodes per week in any of the many serials emanating from AWA, I felt brave enough to leave Ku-ring-gai Council. I was farewelled with a volume called *The History of English Literature* — a somewhat brief glimpse — and a volume of *Best Plays of the Modern American Theatre, 1944*, and considered myself launched.

My parents watched with faint surprise, ultimately, I believe, taking a quiet satisfaction in it all. But they weren't exactly turning handsprings.

Six

Radio was the one sure source of income for the actor in the 1940s and early 1950s. From that first engagement in 1945 I spent the next seven years gradually getting to a stage where I could be assured that work would always be there. As a cautious nature insisted that I have some other means of support, the years were also spent in a variety of office or secretarial situations. I persuaded stockbrokers, book publishers, furniture suppliers and barristers to accept my services in a purely part-time capacity, even though most of them felt they were in need of full-time assistance. It simply meant that I had to work at a pace stopping just this side of frantic, skip lunch and make myself as charming as possible. Working in Little Theatre as well added another dimension, so that any tendency to workaholism now can be sheeted home to those days. The barristers were the simplest. I would turn up with an empty notebook, sit down at the other side of a desk, cross a leg, fill a book, and as long as everything was transcribed within a couple of days they were happy. The stockbrokers were the most interesting and the most enjoyable, and I developed an interest in share transactions that a few years later would pay for a return trip to England and something to spare. All this additional activity was grist to the mill.

The one providing the best copy for an actress was the wholesale furniture supplier with premises in the basement of a terrace in Bayswater Road, Elizabeth Bay. As there was a brothel opposite, much surreptitious research could be carried out. My employer had a fierce, not to say unreasonable, temper, but by then I'd learned not to be concerned by unreasonableness. We had a good and mutually understanding relationship, and he was, I think, quite fond of me. While I was working with him his wife presented him with a daughter. She was called Ruth, but I can't claim any influence here. It was a fine biblical name, no more no less. Years later, during the run of *Three Tall Women* at The Wharf, I was going for a walk between the matinee and the evening performance. Approaching The Wharf steps I was vaguely conscious of a woman standing alone. She stopped me, and as well as talking about the play, to my great surprise said, 'Actually, I've been wanting to speak to you for years. You used to work for my father, I believe.' And yes, her name was Ruth.

My ability to deal with occasionally unreasonable, not to say vile, behaviour, was acquired in Radio. For quite some time I was fairly nervous of all the producers, most of whom seemed at times to behave like cranky children – with the odd notable exception. In their defence they were always working against the clock, and needed to get a set number of episodes out each half day. Any interruption to the steady flow induced panic on all sides. You were expected to get yourself out of any trouble during recording; mistakes were irretrievable technically. A young actress who apologised, as I did, at the very end of an acetate recording for a quite minor misdemeanour, could cause something approaching apoplexy. This I came to understand and with the gradual gaining of experience everything became much happier. Sometimes praise would even be handed out. Thus did confidence grow. My favourite accolade came from the legendary E. Mason Wood at Macquarie, responsible for serials and live hourly broadcasts of plays, who told me solemnly one day that I had the blessed gift of pausation. I've tried not to let that run away with me since, but, yes, pausations I am good at.

All of this – the minor explosions, the throwing down of spectacles – was part and parcel of Radio, and once the apprenticeship had been served, one was part of the gang. Occasionally, though, the odd bit of sadism crept in. Did something about me invite it? All I do know is that for the many months I was playing a leading role in a serial, a particular director managed skilfully to subject me to intimidation that occasionally bordered on minor physical abuse. No one else in the studio was aware of what was going on, but every week in the train from Chatswood I would go over all the scripts painstakingly and dread entering that studio. Until the glorious morning something snapped and I knew I was not going to submit any more. Not for so much as a second. I felt omnipotent. I was up there on Olympus. I played out the whole scene in my mind and, again and again, with glee, returned to the moment where I threw the script in his face. Never had my step had such a spring in it. I waltzed into the studio, barely able to contain myself, script at the ready. Well, of course my tormentor entered the studio and absolutely nothing happened. From that moment I was never subjected to his attentions again. He became a lamb, though forever loathed by me. And I can't remember being subjected to anything of the sort from that day on. The learning curve had been slow, but ultimately effective. Don't mess around with me!

Radio can be potent, particularly for the impressionable. The serials were sold all over the world, so that fans could turn up in the most unlikely places. I had one in what was then British Guiana. She was still at school and developed an obsession for the character I played in a serial written by my friend, Eleanor Witcombe. I grew to curse Eleanor for writing such powerful stuff. The letters, always addressed to the character, started slowly, grew to a flood, and the situation began to get out of hand when her mother turned feral. These letters were answered, irregularly, by me, with tact and coolness. The letters gave the unfeeling Eleanor the idea for another serial based on someone arriving uninvited on the doorstep from Uganda — a sort of twist to *The Man Who Came to Dinner*.

I eventually sought the advice of a psychiatrist I'd met at

parties. 'Simple!' he said. 'All you have to do is break the connection with the character. Explain to her that you are Ruth Cracknell. Your problem will be over.' I did just that and within the week received an equally passionate missive addressed to 'Ruth'. The psychiatrist whose advice I sought happened to be Harry Bailey, who was to practise deep sleep therapy at his Chelmsford Clinic some years later, so perhaps the fact that the solution didn't work shouldn't have surprised.

My most satisfying times in Radio were with the Australian Broadcasting Commission. There, directors could offer more than the purely popular entertainment that was the priority on commercial radio. The most exciting and innovative work in the country emanated from the national broadcaster, and I haven't changed my mind today. It is to be hoped politicians don't finally manage to destroy this unique and enduring asset. At time of writing they're having a pretty good stab at it. When I first started at the ABC my mentor was the wonderful director Frank Harvey. He was charming, erudite, gentle and because of these qualities, combined with a great knowledge of drama, was responsible for some very fine work. The director of Drama and Features, Neil Hutchison, was another who spurred me on and the plays we were doing – the Greek tragedies, Shakespeare, the Jacobeans, Strindberg, Ibsen, Chekhov, as well as the best of the modern playwrights, were both challenging and a joy. The ABC provided productions of the very best local writing, too; I first came across Douglas Stewart's fine verse plays while working there.

There were also feature programs and poetry, where one

met and was constantly challenged by the likes of Mungo MacCallum Snr, in the Features Department, and John Thompson, poet and a director of Features (and father of Jack). Poetry was always a favourite area of work and it subsequently turned me in the direction of feature writing. I remember a feature on the Russian poet, Akhmatova, for the ABC and in 1974, at the instigation of Martin Esslin, for whom I'd worked in Australia, I wrote and presented a feature on Judith Wright's poetry for the BBC, as well as one on A.D. Hope, in collaboration with the actress Kirrily Nolan.

A large part of my education in literature and plays came from those days at the ABC. At least a play a week. I played opposite the fine English dramatic actress Sonia Dresdell in a play called *Viceroy Sarah*, in which she played Sarah, the Duchess of Marlborough, and I played Abigail, her lady-in-waiting. This performance, not so long before I first went to London in 1952, elicited a very warm letter of recommendation from Neil Hutchison, which was a great help when I sought work at the BBC.

Whenever visiting actors were out here with a play, they would be approached to perform in one or other of the live radio plays, and for some reason always accepted. Why they would wish to work on their day off I'm not sure, but am grateful they did because it meant I had the opportunity, in 1955, of playing opposite Sir Ralph Richardson in *Arms and the Man*. He played Bluntschli, I played Raina. Dame Sybil Thorndyke played Catherine – a part I had played earlier at the Mercury Theatre – and Sir Lewis Casson played Petkoff.

This play was directed by Harry Harper for the Macquarie Network and was broadcast from their auditorium on a Wednesday night. So perhaps on this occasion their stage play had finished. I hope so. The actors, as usual, sat in a semi-circle, the microphone centre stage. On prompt side was all the sound effects paraphernalia, which was in the hands of Oscar Lansbury, father of Coral and uncle of Angela. He quite enjoyed a tipple, and, some thought, may have had a bottle stashed somewhere in his corner. If so, it never interfered with the accurate delivery of door slams or coconut shells to gravel tray.

This night we were all in place for *Arms and the Man*. In those days on Radio, live broadcasts were performed in front of an audience and the cast members were expected to be as glamorous as possible. Always black tie for the men. I was wearing something extremely beautiful created by Peter Hurst, the elegant designer on Phillip Street, who, tragically, died from an early cerebral haemorrhage. When I look back, it seemed it was an epidemic then. That night, I was suffering more than usual from nerves. The visitors all looked splendid, I'd found rehearsals tremendous fun, but had fingers well and truly crossed now. In the event all proceeded smoothly. It was a little disconcerting that Sir Ralph seemed inclined to wander every time he was not actually at the microphone. He would meander to the back of the stage, disappear behind the piano, immerse himself in Oscar's area, so that there was a degree of tension each time his entrance approached. He never missed, he just seemed incapable of sitting still. I remember him as extremely charming – not to say flattering! Word got back and I preened.

Years later, when I was in London, as usual I called Lionel Harris, who had directed me in *The Duenna* in Sydney in 1956. He was directing a television play at Ealing, with Sir Ralph playing the lead. I must come out and meet him again over lunch. Buoyed by Sir Ralph's earlier comments, I went. We had the most charming lunch and conversation, made especially memorable as I watched, fascinated, as Sir Ralph emptied his cup into his saucer and delicately raised it to his lips – just as grandma sometimes had. Lunch over, they walked me to the lift, farewelled me, and I watched in a happy glow as they wandered off. 'Now tell me again, Lionel,' I heard him say, 'just who *is* Ruth Cracknell?' These things keep one's feet on the ground.

While all this early Radio activity was proceeding during the day, my nights were spent at the Independent Theatre. When I started in Radio I was still a student of drama; by 1946 I had joined Doris Fitton's Drama School, attending one or two nights each week. The School would put on results of the work at various times throughout the year. It took quite a time before one graduated to a production in the Independent Theatre. Doris ran the Theatre autocratically, and directed most of the plays. Being cast in the main productions was the aim of all of us vying for attention and opportunity in the School. Finally, my moment came. I was cast in a musical play called, prophetically, *The Melody That Got Lost*. I was to play what would be termed in those days the character lead, and I even had an understudy. We proceeded smoothly up to the dress rehearsal day, which always occurred on the Sunday before the opening night mid week. At the same time I was understudying a radio play, the idea being, presumably, that the understudy would be able to rush to the microphone if one of the stars collapsed mid sentence, and take over. The men were covered by our director – or, at a pinch, I suppose, Oscar in sound effects. The understudy's presence was essential at that last radio rehearsal on the Sunday.

I thought I could just about time it and make the dress rehearsal at the Independent Theatre without being missed. Alas, no. The understudy was up on the stage by the time I arrived, grasping her moment. An actor's nightmare. I slipped quietly into the seat alongside Doris. At an appropriate moment I enquired whether I should now go up on stage. Miss Fitton turned an icy glare on me and said, 'No, Ruth. Not now – or ever.' I was sacked before I'd even started! The fact that the Radio engagement was professional, and that the Independent was entirely amateur made not a jot of difference. The financial arrangements may have been amateur, the discipline was anything but. I slowly walked out of the theatre, my friends on stage in a state of shock, their dismay stopping just short of striking on my behalf. Solidarity has its limits! The play opened with my understudy riding on a crest, but not for too long. The melody didn't just get lost. It disappeared. Quickly. Doris felt disinclined to give me another opportunity, but I remained at the Drama School.

It's worth mentioning here that many actors endure real

nightmares. They are part and parcel of being exposed night after night. They mostly involve trying to get to the theatre on time through myriad obstacles; arriving at the wrong theatre; coming prepared with the wrong play; turning up with the right play insufficiently learnt; or being the only one who never had a script in the first place. Struggling to make it all up in these circumstances is torture. The nightmares are unbearably real and one awakes with relief. My most inventive of these horrors concerned trying to get to a theatre. I seemed to be in a large estate of townhouses, terraces, tiny parks. Someone had been delegated to take me to the theatre. We were running late, of course, and this man insisted on reversing the whole long and complicated way with me hysterically trying to persuade him to turn the car around. We'd barely left the housing development when I realised the play would, by now, have been cancelled. I awoke in the proverbial cold sweat.

In the event, Doris and I made it up, and I was directed by her again, in *The Au Pair Man* opposite a very new John Hargreaves, and in Edward Albee's *A Delicate Balance* with Alexander Hay playing opposite me. Alex was a fine director in his own right, which was just as well as Doris's direction – towards the end – was, alas, not always the most inspired. Alex felt obliged to intrude, so we privately rehearsed, at my house, a scene that seemed way short of the ideal. By the end of the evening we had something that bore little resemblance to Doris's efforts and the new moves none at all. 'Are you mad?' I queried Alex. 'She'll never accept this!' One of Alex's inscrutable smiles. 'My dear, she won't even notice.'

Notwithstanding, I am second to none in my admiration for Doris's strength, determination, and continuing struggle to keep her Independent Theatre viable. During the 1930s, 1940s and right into the 1970s she presented play after play and was almost alone in providing Sydney's theatregoers with continuous serious fare.

I was allowed on stage at the Independent Theatre again when John Alden formed his Shakespearean Company, which was to perform there. Possibly due to Doris's recommendation I joined his company, understudying various roles and then graduating to one of the goddesses in *The Tempest*, Mariana in *Measure for Measure* and, finally, Goneril in *King Lear*. This was Alden's great success and was performed at the St James's Hall for six months, though not on every night of the week. Dinah Shearing was Regan, and Alden himself was Lear. The play had quite an impact on Sydney in those days, particularly the eye gouging scene. People would rush out – hopefully making the street before throwing up. This performance in 1950 was a turning point for me. A major role. I was 25, and in theatrical terms could be said to have arrived – eight years after that first venture into performance with Edna Spilsbury. It had taken quite a while.

John Alden was an English teacher with a passion for Shakespeare and a determination to form his own company for the purpose of presenting it. An unlikely dream in those days and finally only able to be realised with Doris Fitton's co-operation. She had the theatre, he had the experience.

Rough productions in some respects, got together on a shoe-string, but some fine actors. All who worked in Radio were delighted to have the opportunity to flex their muscles in this way. His designer, Alistair Roberts, knew what he was about and could also turn his hand to performance. He was a memorable fool in *King Lear* and Ariel in *The Tempest*. I learned much from Alden – both what to do on stage and what not to. Can one ask for more? I found him difficult at times, but I don't necessarily lay at his door the gnawing ulcer that was the legacy of my time with him.

My next theatrical involvement was with Sydney John Kay, a German Jew who had been touring Australia with a German jazz group, the Weintraubs, when war broke out. Adding insult to injury he and the rest of the group were interned. John was released in 1942, and during the 1940s established the Mercury Mobile Players, which took classic comedy to factories and schools. His most successful production was Molière's *The Imaginary Invalid*, with Peter Finch enjoying a huge success in the title role. In 1952 John Kay re-started the Mercury Theatre in its first permanent home, at the indispensable St James's Hall. His aim was to present European-style repertory theatre, rotating plays frequently, often nightly. He gathered about him a company of actors and – unheard of – paid them! To my knowledge, this was the first time actors performing serious theatre in what till then could still be called Little Theatre, were paid. The performances were of a high order, and it was in many ways the most interesting development in Sydney theatre at that time. I was invited to join the

Mercury, which I accepted with alacrity and gratitude. I already knew most of the other members of the Company – we were, after all, meeting in Radio studios –, but I did meet for the first time Gloria Payten, a German actress with a Greek father and an Australian/Greek mother who trained in Dresden, where she had lived during the war. Gloria arrived in Sydney with her mother and sisters in 1948 and was one of the first approached by John Kay. Gloria became my very good friend and ultimately my agent. I was with her International Casting Service from day one, and still am. Her death in 1989 left an enormous gap, and the whole industry mourned one of its most important members. Gloria's whole life was the business of performance and casting. Her extended family was the acting profession. She was a shrewd businesswoman and very lucky gambler, ideal attributes, of course, in one's agent. In her will she provided for a trust to be set up for actors and directors whereby the successful applicant is given the opportunity for overseas study. It is known as The Gloria Payten Foundation and Gloria Dawn Foundation.

I played in a number of productions with the Mercury, including *Arms and the Man*, and a twin bill comprising *The Comedy of Errors* and its source play *The Twins* by Plautus. My last play with the Mercury was Strindberg's *The Father*, in which I played Laura, the most challenging role for me to that date. The success of the production, and the knowledge that this was about as far as one could aim in Sydney at that time made up my mind for me. As with many other Australian actors before me, I decided the time had come to head for London.

SEVEN

I was given, among other presents, two dozen fine lawn handkerchiefs with hand-worked edges by Auntie Beat and Auntie
Ethel, when I left Sydney on board the *Otranto*. And a Collins
Trip Book with headings such as Date of Departure, Auto-
graph of Captain and Officers, Date of Return. There were
pages headed Itinerary (divided into columns for Date, Place,
Hotel). There was a page for Traveller's Cheque Numbers and
another entitled Gifts to Buy. There was Hotels and Restaurants Visited. And one, simply, Purchases. The only writing by
me on any of these pages is Date of Departure: 6 December
1952 – London:

> What a sailing! Numerous people – couldn't get into
> cabin so all my people entertained in lounge. Strain
> mounting throughout the 'party' and I found myself

wishing it was all over ... Then the gong and everyone is off. This is really awful! I managed to hold off
till saying good-bye to Mum. Am amazed and
touched to see Father shattered and also to witness
my sister's first tears (in my sight). Everyone was
wonderful and I love them all ...

I sailed with four friends, and the journey was looked on by
all of us as the adventure of a lifetime. All five of us lived at
home, and, holidays aside, it was the first time we had in any
real sense been parted from our families. In 1952 not only was
this the case with the five of us, it was the norm. Five maid-
ens setting off as if we had just left convent school. We were
innocent, we were unsophisticated, we were armed with letters
of introduction and were expected to communicate with the
parental home every inch of the way (as indeed, I wanted to),
caught as we were in the trap of obedience. We were all
expected home, sooner or later.

My travelling companions were another actress, Pat
Crocker, Maureen Hennessy who worked at the ABC, Paddy
Duly who was rich and idle, and Joan Spies whose workaday
activities I no longer remember. Along the route we gathered
Maev Holness, and this group stayed more or less together or
in contact for about nine months. Where possible, we still
meet – around Christmas, most now with children and grandchildren. There is only one missing; Patti, who died in 1992.

On board *Otranto* there were charming ship's officers
guaranteed to turn heads and break hearts. To and from

Marrying Eric, 1957

Anna, Jonathan and Jane on the beach at Mollymook, 1965

Anna   *Jane*   *Jonathan*

1967

Rehearsing A Cup of Tea, a Bex and a Good Lie Down, *1965*

The 'America's Cup' routine from But I Wouldn't Want to
Live There, *with Gloria Dawn and Lyle O'Hara, 1967*

I'm Alright Now, *with Reg Livermore, 1967*

Studio pose with crossed toe, 1967

Jocasta in King Oedipus

Just Ruth, *the one-woman revue I wrote, 1977*

London year in year out must have presented a recurring pattern that stopped just this side of total boredom for them, but their good manners were unfailing; they were mostly amusing companions and I imagine there was the odd compensation along the way. Also on board was Eric Phillips. He was travelling with his sister and mother and they had plans to live in London for two years while Eric continued his path in electronics. I saw Eric on and off over the next six weeks, but not noticeably more than any other of the young men on board. Had any then prophesied future marriage for us, we would both have thought them barking mad, but something perhaps did begin during those six weeks.

Shipboard life for all who made the pilgrimage 'overseas' in the 1950s was, at times, like one long cocktail party, which could be my reason for an aversion to these today. It seemed exciting at first, but by 22 December had apparently started to pall a little even then:

> Shipboard life enters into a somewhat monotonous
> pattern after awhile and I feel no inclination what-
> soever to list every day's doings much in the manner
> of a country town social register. Sometimes it's fun,
> sometimes it's boring. The best things on this ship
> are still the things 80% of the people never see. Sea,
> sun, wind, weather in all its moods, the 'feel' of this
> lovely ship . . . This is perhaps a cloudier time of the
> year than some with the result that the face of the
> sea is constantly changing. Sometimes it will be its

brilliant Reckitts blue, then shades of grey will appear and the whole surface as far as one can see is chequered and variegated most beautifully – blue, dark blue, light grey, steel grey, with here and there patches of putty colour where a truant sun has just caught hold of the edge of a grey patch.

Much more of this and I could have undertaken copy for the travel brochures.

I suppose it was inevitable that I should have been called on to organise the ship's concert. The most remarkable memory from this activity is the day I was in deep discussion with the Entertainments Officer over running order and deletion of the proving-to-be-completely-hopeless items, when one of the kitchen staff ran amok and attempted to rape and possibly knife a young woman in our close proximity. The fact that we were barely aware of what was taking place (at one time the woman actually fell onto the seat I was occupying, and I politely, but vaguely, moved up to accommodate her) speaks volumes for our dedicated focus on the matter in hand. Kitchen hand was duly, if violently, brought under control on the deck below us – by now I was giving the intended victim a little of my attention – and thrown into the lock-up, which was alongside the hospital. In the hospital at the time were Eric's mother, his sister Gwen and two others who had been badly burned when a launch blew up in Colombo. In addition to their own major troubles, they now had to cope with the ravings of a maniac not two feet away and separated by just one thin wall. The tropics are always dicey.

The only act I remember from the concert was an impressionist and magician, European, with an elegant presentation that stood him head and shoulders above the rest of the talent.

In the event, one occasion on board *Otranto* eclipsed everything. On a limpid late afternoon I found myself on B deck and my companion was the very tall, very good-looking Ernest Grauman – the elegant worker of magic at the ship's concert. I was not unhappy to be there. The novelettish atmosphere was in no way unacceptable. 'I leaned towards him. I had never seen such sensitive, tender, intelligent eyes.' His first words, after pleasantries, veered the wrong way, horribly the wrong way: 'On the day war was declared,' he said, very calmly, 'my grandmother opened her veins in the bath.' Steaming brightly, merrily through the Mediterranean, just through the interesting, historic and very fascinating Suez Canal. There was no escaping the eyes, no escape from the next half hour:

That afternoon Ernest Grauman came up and started talking to me – at first about trifles and then suddenly, and I guess without either of us realising it, I heard his life's story. I felt ashamed and unhappy. He is of course Jewish which I hadn't realised till then – Czechoslovakian, and a member of a fine and revered family who ran a seventy-year-old exclusive business in Prague. He told me something of the history of the Jewish race – how for centuries they had been unable to perform any trade or manual work which meant that they became either professional and intellectual men or businessmen. He told me a little of his family — musicians, scholars (one, an uncle, one of the most famous Shakespearean scholars alive and a translator of the works into German) — and he told me something of his early life, the music he listened to, chamber music evenings at his home. Came the rise of Nazism he left and heard nothing more of his family throughout the war — he was in the Czech battalion in London. He had little hope but returned after the war to try and see what he could find out about the thirteen members of the family he had left behind. There was no trace whatsoever, nor of the seventy-year-old business. They might never have existed, his family — no one knew anything. He told me of a Czech captain who accompanied him who got word that his parents were in a certain concentration camp. He piled a jeep with blankets and provisions and set off, only to be told on arrival that the Germans had injected their veins with petrol the day before. He was talking all this time without bitterness of any kind, but with a sort of hopeless resignation. He's had so much, so very much . . . he's just trying to find somewhere he can settle, happily, away from the constant, subtle humiliations (where there is no outright cruelty) that seem to follow the Jew wherever he may travel. He told me how the Czechs in his battalion would roam round at night beating up all the Jews in the same battalion, but how they left him strictly alone (6 ft). He is at present living in Cardiff with his wife and small daughter – safe and secure but still not happy. But could he ever be?

The days, the weeks passed. The cocktail parties, the dances, the deck sports, the reading, the writing, the idling. And one moment of serious culture. On board was a very young Malcolm Williamson, and he asked me to join him in a recital in the B forward lounge. A couple of hundred people turned up and the nerves grabbed. Never volunteer, never volunteer! I read Australian poets among the Shakespeare and the Yeats, Malcolm played Goossens and Ravel among the Beethoven and Chopin, and we were joined by a classical singer, Harry Nairn. No one left. The concert was followed by Landfall Dinner, which may or may not have been significant. Malcolm and I kept in touch in London for a time. From memory he worked at Boosey and Hawkes, and began the steady journey upwards towards his current eminence as Master of the Queen's Music, and fine composer.

It had been six weeks completely cut off from the real world. Away from the passengers there were moments of splendid, nourishing isolation . . .

EIGHT

Arriving in London it was as if every reference point was familiar. A monopoly board come to life, all the reading of the preceding twenty or so years making virtually every street and square and garden familiar, but so much more vivid now that one was a part. I was a tourist/traveller for a few months only. Then I was a Londoner. By July of 1953, I had moved into a basement flat on my own and by October of that year I was the only one of the original five travelling companions left in London. At last, at long last, I emerged from the chrysalis and ventured into my own identity.

At first it was a non-stop dash from one end of London to another and an engorgement of theatre that threatened to unhinge at times, sitting at the back of the Gods and occasionally going without food to afford tickets. But not always uncritical. Donald Wolfitt's production of *King Lear* didn't please and I don't think because of my own involvement with the play in Sydney – rather something to do with the fact that even to my possibly inexperienced eyes I was very much aware that here was an actor/manager who seemed determined to surround himself with the inferior. Much later I read the delicious comment that 'any actor who worked with Wolfitt always spent his whole life behind a pillar'. I had obviously been aware of something amiss. But great strength and power. On the other hand I was swept away by Pamela Brown in *River Line* and beside myself with *The Way of the World* with John Gielgud, Eileen Herlie, Paul Scofield, Margaret Rutherford... *Julius Caesar* at the Old Vic was fine, except for the women whom I castigated as 'shocking' (displaying, as they were, a style of acting I regarded as vapid). Lyn Fontanne and Alfred Lunt in a Coward piece called *Quadrille* provided 'magnificent acting. I almost feel I will be satisfied if I never see another performance, for this surely was perfection. Fontanne looks wonderful, she must be 60 or more but looks an extremely youthful 40 on stage – she is charming, witty, warm, scintillating – I could go on for hours.' The sets and costumes were by Beaton: 'I have now seen the height of acting perfection.' This was the first play I saw in January 1953, and as regards performance (if not the play) obviously set a high standard.

There were other, perhaps more important, discoveries. I took myself to the tiny Arts Theatre for a performance of *The Seagull* with Beatrix Lehmann as Arkadina. It was, surprisingly, my first contact with Chekhov in Theatre and came close to wiping everything else out of my mind. What I thought that night hasn't changed forty years on, namely that a fine production and performance of Chekhov is the very best of times in a theatre. Certainly, it's the most human.

The performance, however, that had me reaching for superlatives was Margot Fonteyn's. I saw her when she was dancing at the height of her powers and wrote home about it on 27 February 1954. A very ardent fan letter, I suppose:

I shall tell you about last night, which was an 'occasion'. I went to my first Ballet at Covent Garden and my first glimpse of Margot Fonteyn. There are one or two things that stand out in a lifetime as quite unforgettable experiences – a Queen crowned, one's first glimpse of England. Heidelberg in Spring (for me) and, I imagine, entering Sydney Heads. There are many theatrical 'moments' which are exciting or moving, but none, to my mind, has been an 'unforgettable' experience on a par with those other things.

Fonteyn is sheer magic, and it is a magic a little hard to describe. I have never seen anything like it on a stage and I am still dazed from the exquisite memory of it. She is the idol of London, without a doubt, so that one goes to one of her performances with a tremendous feeling of expectancy and excitement. It was, as I have said, my first trip to the Garden, and that in itself is quite wonderful. A beautiful, glamorous, Royal theatre, with atmosphere like no other theatre I have seen. The tiers, the elegant boxes, the rose-coloured furnishings, the tiny lamps all along the tiers that light up slowly and fade slowly, so that the darkness is held off for an instant by hundreds of tiny rose lamps; the Grand Staircase; the paintings.

An audience at a Fonteyn Ballet is tense and emotional, and hardly able to wait for the first glimpse of her. The ballet was the entire *Sleeping Beauty* – Prologue and four Acts. The orchestra started. We listened – we waited – and the curtains drew up (wonderful curtains that pull up and fall down in folds) to such colour, lighting, costuming and general fairytale enchantment that one has never seen before. It was a feast! The sets were spectacular – going back for miles, seemingly; spacious, ethereal – pillars, steps and castle receding back, back to a misty nothingness – so high, so broad. The costumes were magnificent – the elegance of the 18th century that no succeeding century has got anywhere near. The dances – the gavottes and minuets, village dances and fairytale cuteness.

We watched the Prologue, where the Good Fairies bestow their blessings and the Bad Fairy makes a crashing entrance in sulphurous smoke in a chariot drawn by six monkey monsters, and places the curse.

Then we saw Act I – the entire Theatre on the edge of its seat, waiting! We approached the Moment, the corps de ballet indicated up stage . . .

the music whipped up to her arc – and there she was
– the merest glimpse of a powder puff whiteness as
she ran through columns at the back of the stage –
a sharp nervous burst of applause at the first sight
of her – then she was off stage, and making her first
true appearance to dead centre and a burst of real
applause. You can feel the entire Theatre catch its
breath as she stands relaxed – hands, arms, feet,
body, quite perfect – a tiny, fragile ballerina in a pool
of light against a rich, elegant, colourful background. She smiles ('I'm going to enjoy this as much
as you are') and she dances. I can't analyse her dancing – I only know it is the most perfect thing I have
ever witnessed, that it's ethereal, that it is light as
swansdown, that it is fast as a whip crack, that it's a
flower unfolding and growing before your eyes, that
it's the most fragile, breathtaking thing I have ever
seen – that, in short, it is magic . . . Never have I so
wanted something to go on forever.

The Sleeping Beauty has many solos and pas de
deux (the male dancer, Michael Somes, was awfully
good) and at the completion of each, there is a
shout from the audience and she, or she and he,
takes easily six curtains. Of course, it's all rather
tough on the rest of them – they do all tend to look
like baby elephants after her (and they're not).

Even apart from Fonteyn, it is probably the
most spectacular thing I've ever witnessed on a stage.

The Lilac Fairy floats on a river in a massive shell, with a sail – forests grow and the palace when the Prince wakes her, is spidery, overgrown, eerie and wondrous to behold.

What a night! I don't think I ever want to go to the theatre again.

At the final curtain, I thought the place would go up. It was like a football crowd – they (she and Somes) took curtain after curtain and she finally took one with house lights all up.

I keep remembering bits of it. One moment where she dances with just one fiddle accompaniment – a lovely violin obligato to her dancing. It was like watching music.

To see her just walk across a stage is to have seen something. And the worship all round her – from her slaves out front, from the orchestra, from the other principals, from the corps de ballet.

I swear she's not human. I don't think the crowd waiting at the stage door would see her. I should think she flew off on a broomstick.

Also, in those early days in London, my actress friend Pat Crocker and I went to see the recording of a radio show – The Goon Show. I duly reported home, 'It was quite fun, hilarious in spots, with one particularly good comedian – Peter Sellers . . . ' (Thank God I approved.)

I had been offered work by the Dundee Repertory Theatre almost as soon as I arrived in London. I had decided, however, to take a complete break from acting for twelve months, at the end of which the urge arose again and I auditioned for the BBC, the Old Vic and the Royal Shakespeare Company. So I stayed firmly in London, not wishing to abandon surfeit for the comparative drabness of earnest theatrical fare in the provinces. Staying meant I had to find alternative means of keeping the wolf from the door. The first of these alternatives offered employment with the publishers Batsfords, a fine old family publishing and bookselling house, established in 1843. To give an idea of the flavour that permeated the Batsfords I entered in Mayfair 110 years later, here is part of the foreword to the book by Harry Batsford, one of the then directors, which the firm brought out to celebrate their centenary. The book, *A Batsford Century*, is edited by Hector Bolitho.

The story is of 'little' people, to whom we may be happy to belong, who have gone their quiet ways in patience and steadfastness. Like them, I am British, business and bourgeois, and intensely and equally proud of all three . . . Commerce is not, as some term politics, 'a dirty business', but the touch of union that knits the whole world kin. Once in the Suk at Marrakeesh in Morocco I chatted long to an Arab leather-worker, and we found that as producers and sellers we had much in common; we shook hands warmly and parted with mutual understanding and esteem. My father once broke away for good from an old family who spoke of trade disparagingly; now it is the younger generation which is in danger of bondage to snivelling shibboleths and flibbertigibbet phylacteries: that there is something sordid or soiling in producing, buying and selling.

If our story is set deep in the soil, it is equally rooted in craftsmanship. My little uncle Herbert once sent me as a boy to hunt up an electrotypers' foreman called Tijou, to see if he were akin to the great Jean of that name, master smith to William III, and noblest of ironworkers in England. It is a joy to study the richness of an old textile, to thrill at the tiny, delicate scrollwork of a watch-cock, or become intoxicated over a Wren church interior. We have always been linked with historic work in stone, wood, metal and plaster, and it has been our privilege to discover and illustrate it, and to have met and worked with such modern craftsmen as Starkie Gardner, the ironworker, George Bankart, plaster-worker and plaster-lover, and above all Fred H. Crosslley, medievalist architect, designer, writer, and photographer of lovely work. We have thus been rooted in England and English life, even if we have accepted books from abroad, illustrated the work of many countries and sent our products all over the world . . .

This, then, was the Batsfords whose solid and charming door I walked through. The Batsfords who were responsible for fine, well-produced books, with an emphasis on architecture and specialist books and possessed of a quality list of authors. It was housed, when I joined them in my humble capacity as general stenographer, in a tiny, elegant Georgian house in North Audley Street, just around the corner from the American Embassy.

Batsfords was the perfect environment in which to study the English class system at work, but at the more gentle end of the spectrum, where everyone was accorded his true place and worth. It had a gentle, civilised strata going from Mr Brian (Cook), and Mr William Hanneford-Smith, both directors, through to Mr Francis Lucarotti, the production manager, for whom I mainly worked, plus a discreet waft of womanly support throughout the enterprise – engaged in the main in secretarial or organisational activity. The legendary Harry Batsford I didn't know, but I relished the descriptions of him roaming round the countryside with enormous vigour, getting damp and eating pilchards out of a tin with a steel ruler.

Today, the North Audley Street house has had a complete refit and turned itself into a not particularly exciting showroom for women's fashion. Racks of clothes replace the solid tables where piles of books lay. No bookshelves line the walls, the stairs have been long since blocked off. A modern plate glass shop front sits uneasily below the simple Georgian first floor, which is all that remains of the old place. The new owner and his charming sales assistant cater to the Arabian population of this part of Mayfair and the owner had heard that his boutique had once been a bookshop...

Among the people who worked in Batsfords was a brilliant secretary and organiser, Fay Jenkins, who became a very good friend. Fay was Irish, but totally upper-class English Catholic in style. Witty, outrageous, she knew nearly everybody worth knowing in London, had parents living in a flat near Hyde Park, and herself shared a flat in Knightsbridge with four vacuous blue bloods, which establishment was described by Fay as 'the only place in London where you will find five virgins under the one roof'. When I finally met this lot I felt, with the exception of my delectable friend, that their status would remain quo for quite some time. Their gentlemen friends – I met them when we went to tea with Mummy and Daddy in Park Street (Daddy a retired Major, Mummy attractive and determinedly flirtatious) – simply didn't seem robust enough to effect any change. I remember we went for a walk after tea to Kensington Gardens, most of the group at pains to ignore the colonial, and when we got to the Serpentine everybody decided, 'We should go for a row!' When it became apparent that the ladies would have to do all the work while their escorts dragged languid fingers through water, I politely extricated myself.

Fay herself I adored. She was an expert guide with a fine eye, a great lover of London, and a frequenter of every gallery and bookshop the great town possessed – much in the same way that John McKellar loves New York. These people are invaluable – their love and knowledge lead down byways and around corners and into buildings that most inhabitants of either city have never noticed in a lifetime of living there. I am in their debt, and knowing them adds a rich patina. Fay, sadly, I lost touch with, but the time spent with her, and the correspondence that lasted for a while after I returned to Australia, were delectable. There is a tiny Roualt in the Tate, her favourite painting, which is a constant reminder. I always hope to find it.

Fay's weekends were spent in the country of course, and the whole atmosphere surrounding her was Wildean. In turn, she was quite fascinated by an Australian she couldn't pigeon-hole. By now, I was more English than the English and had lost all trace of my native accent. This was deliberate, because it was made plain that any hint of an unwanted diphthong or flat vowel would preclude work within my own profession. On the BBC not a hint of the regional, much less Australian, was permitted. It was standard upper class, educated tones, or nothing. The actor and television personality Roger Climpson told me that when he went to the Royal Academy of Dramatic Art the first thing to be dealt with was his accent. Painful, painful work until not a trace of the original Midlands sound remained. These days as I see my youngest grandchildren watching television, I marvel that their accents escape the unlikely mix of regional English, bastardised Cockney and American. Somehow they do.

My accent by mid-1953 was standard English and I fitted very well into the quietly bookish atmosphere of Batsfords. I began eating 'sophisticated' food at lunch time — German frankfurts and sauerkraut. Unlike Heidelberg, which I had visited just a few weeks earlier, where the staple fare seemed to be sausages, pancakes and maple syrup, and chicken in the rough. I stopped spending time in Lyons' Corner Houses. I frequented a chic cinema in Curzon Street, learned to fling garlic on what passed for steak when grilling, found Italian restaurants in Greek Street and bought fruit from Cockney barrows in Soho, when Cockney was unadulterated and the best sound in the world. I wondered how I would ever again fit in back home at 14 Railway Street, Chatswood.

My other venture into the workplace, and a much more serious matter, was with a business slap bang in the middle of the rag trade in Tottenham Court Road. It was rag trade itself, a Jewish establishment, exporting and manufacturing, the main export being cotton textiles. It traded under the name of Henry Susskind and Company. The managing director was Henry Susskind — a millionaire who did very little work, according to my immediate boss, Mr Trockenheim, who did *all* the work. I was engaged as a dogsbody/secretary — or such was my impression — but ended up able to manage the show and, due to later, tragic circumstances within my family, came within an ace of making commerce my career.

As it was, at Henry Susskind and Company, I was thrown in at the deep end, Mr Trockenheim simply taking it for granted that I could handle anything. He was an extraordinary man. A Polish Jew, his first wife had died in a concentration camp. He had a daughter, I think from this marriage, and had remarried. I should not like to have been the second Mrs Trockenheim. Unfailingly courteous and polite, he, neverthe-less, seemed edged in black. He had a brilliant and fast brain and his great, and only, recreation was bridge, which he played most nights at a London club, losing or winning, but mostly winning, very high stakes. He was short, balding, and not the least bit attractive — until, all too rarely, he smiled. Then he became the most attractive man in the world.

Mr Henry Susskind was large, imposing and benign, and there was a son who was meant to be gainfully employed. Young and slightly feckless, the son's main aim in life was to drive in as snappy a fashion as possible his beautiful light blue Sunbeam sports car — preferably with something equally snappy alongside. He was quite engaging and we got along splendidly, especially as he viewed me as the older woman to whom he could turn for advice as his various amours turned sour. No tension in our relationship whatsoever, but I was always enormously grateful that he was not frittering away his time in the Trockenheim domain. I might have killed him. There were two wonderful packers, one a young Cockney of dangerously swift repartee, and an ancient dust-coated venerable, complete with jaunty beret, who, in a previous life, had been an officer in a White Russian regiment. It was incongruous to see him heaving boxes and cases onto trucks, and extremely touching to observe the way his Cockney friend unostentatiously got to the heavier items first. Serge's great love was music, and he conducted a choir at an Orthodox church which he insisted I visit. 'If you love music,' he said. I went one evening and sat alone, completely hidden from view, as the choir rehearsed. Nothing much since has eclipsed that wave after wave of perfect sound swirling around the must and dust and grimy stone.

I worked hard for Mr Trockenheim, which may or may

not have been a good thing. After a few weeks he left for a business trip to Europe, firmly stating that I could handle things perfectly. Left with no alternative I rapidly learned the intricacies of letters of credit and bills of exchange, all involving huge amounts of money — or so it seemed to me. I negotiated this wilderness by developing an intimate relationship with a man at the Westminster Bank, who would painstakingly take me through all difficulties, assuring me that I wouldn't actually bankrupt the business. Our relationship was purely telephonic, but I have seldom had greater need of male strength and succour, and was eternally grateful that it was never withheld.

My other, not so reliable, support during Mr Trockenheim's absence was young Susskind, who was very sympathetic, quite useless, but at least able to provide the occasional cup of ill-brewed coffee. His heart was in the right place, though, and he took pity on me to the extent of offering the occasional lift in the snappy Sunbeam.

When my employer returned he was delighted and later had no compunction about leaving me again when he took an even longer trip to Burma. He brought me ivory.

I enjoyed myself at Henry Susskind and Company. I worked long hours, but had complete freedom, and could even absent myself for the BBC work that started to roll in towards the end of my time there. I enjoyed wandering around the Tottenham Court Road area, so different from the elegant Georgian squares and streets near Batsfords, and became an habitue of all the bookshops in Charing Cross Road; wandered through Soho, the West End, and Bloomsbury, and enjoyed the few talks I had with Mr Trockenheim that did not solely encompass business. His great piece of advice was not to waste money on inferior clothes: 'You have limited resources? Save up until you can buy something worthwhile. I only had one suit for years when I came to London. Nothing else. I lived in it. But it was of fine quality. Remember!' When he knew I was leaving, he took young Susskind and me to Prunier's for a smart lunch. I had escargots for the first time, and sampled half a frog leg, and the wine was so much more exquisite than any I could have afforded. Trockenheim! What an absurd name.

By July, 1953, it had become apparent that more permanent accommodation had to be found. Sharing the bed-sitter, complete with gas ring — even when the population was floating — began to wear thin. So the word was put about with various other Australians, and on 12 July 1953 I arrived at 12 Fairfax Road, Swiss Cottage NW6, phone number Springfield 1856. This, surely, was an address for Julie Andrews — had we known a Julie Andrews then. (A little later I went to Golders Green to hear one Julie Andrews perform in something called *The Boyfriend*. After that, the world knew.)

Number 12 Fairfax Road was a crumbling old Victorian house, which had the inevitable basement, and the inevitable basement was to be home for the rest of my time in London, give or take. I had one large room with a sofa bed, built-in cupboards, gas fire in a white-painted fireplace; parquet floor with a couple of rugs, one comfortable chair, one cane chair with cushions, two dining chairs and an enormous mahogany table that was to come in very handy at Christmas when the entire household, plus extras, was accommodated for a splendid meal:

CHRISTMAS DAY 1953

Grand Turkey à la Fairfax
Pommes de Terre Roties à la Penni
Petit Pois au Tin and Opener
Carrots Glacées à Eunice
Oignons Rotis au Greesi Keesi
Sauce du Pain à la Cracknelli

Pudding Noel Enflamme
Sauce Cannelle à la Cracknelli

Café noir   Café au lait
fromage   biscuits

That evening, after the day's eating and drinking, we engaged in a Christmas frolic I imagined would be charades. In the event, the complicated and mind-stretching activity turned out to be a precursor to the popular game Theatre Sports. It arrived in Australia some decades later – but we started it.

The basement flat opened onto the walled garden with its huge pear tree that I watched through four seasons. There was a kitchen all to myself, an attic at the very top where luggage could be stored, and a walk up a couple of flights to the shared bathroom. After the bed-sitter, I was in heaven.

The household comprised, on the ground floor, the tenor

Ereach Riley, who was performing with Sadlers Wells, his wife, Penny, and infant son, Timothy; up to the first floor where resided architect Peter Keys and wife Eunice, plus son, Anthony, and in the top small flat another architect, Brian Bona. They were all Australian, all in London for further study, or possible fame and fortune, and Penny and Ereach had been in London since 1948. The ensuing fifteen or so months were to be the most vital and important of my life to that point.

Near neighbours were Guy and Joy Warren – he a painter, she the potter. The clash of ideas (and personalities on more than one occasion), the wit, the breadth of their interests and knowledge were like a draught of a hitherto undisclosed elixir. My own family was politically conservative – the majority of my new connections were somewhat left of centre. The political talk now was different from anything I'd been used to and I was fascinated. For one thing, no one had two heads. I'd never actually met a Labor voter, which may be difficult to comprehend at this remove, but they were simply not thick on the ground in Sydney's North Shore in the 1950s. I was embraced, made a part of, led this way, that, buffeted, and in the process found the essential me, made the discovery that this was the milieu I belonged in. It had been a long hibernation. Having an affinity with lizards, let me say when the eyes finally open it's been worth the wait. Contaminated for all time, I was. Halleluja! For me, the person, it equated with me the actor walking through the doors of the St James's Hall all those years ago. My golden time.

NINE

The holiday time, the discovery time, the great occasions, the mint new experiences for the Australian in the United Kingdom, ebbed and flowed, and for me included my first trip to Paris. Paddy Duly and I flew there together, and one of the first things we did, oddly enough, was see Chaplin's film *Limelight*. I had arranged to meet a close Sydney friend, Betty Vidal, then working for the Americans in Heidelberg. Betty was a recovering tubercular patient, and her fits of manic energy were exhausting, but guaranteed to make sure the maximum was accomplished on any given day – or night. My mood in Paris was bleak, owing to a temporarily ripped heart, and the sentimental *Limelight* strains accompanied me everywhere I went whether I wanted them to or not. And proved invaluable years later when the music was used as accompaniment for my favourite revue sketch, *Dining in a State*, a long mime piece with a melancholy, not to say bleak, subtext. Everything matters. Nothing wasted.

No matter what the mood, of course, one's first visit to Paris is a landmark. I couldn't believe how beautiful it was. The city has never lost its particular magic, it never lets one down. Dangerously close to perfection, Paris. It rained most of the time during that visit, which didn't improve the melancholy. I remember I wrote a poem. A terrible poem. But the value of a manic friend is that exhaustion guarantees sleep at the end of the day.

I travelled to Heidelberg after Paris and stayed with Betty. It was spring, it was heartbreakingly beautiful, and I began to mend. Another poem – this one a slight improvement.

Heidelberg in 1953 had an air of unreality. It seemed suspended in time – everything on hold till the Americans went home. The Americans themselves seemed caught in an odd, out of joint time. It was party, party, party, always the same people, with an additional mix of whoever happened to be passing through. One felt that some of them would be lost forever. Europe had ensnared them, even if that Europe, for them, was defeated Germany. They were like flotsam in an environment of culture, history – good and evil – civilisation and learning stretching back for centuries. Certainly this was so in Heidelberg where the student and the professor still strolled, deep in conversation, along the Philosopher's Way. There was a strange mix of a defeated, at times bitter, race, leaping into recovery with the Marshall Aid Plan so that everyone there seemed smarter, cleaner, brighter, than the inhabitants of the still struggling island I'd flown out of. In Heidelberg, at any rate. One might meet someone whose father had been in a concentration camp because his writings had been anti-Nazi. Another who'd been thrown into a labour camp by the Russians at the age of 16. Others who must have fought in the war (Don't mention the war! Don't mention the war!), and were now working for the Americans. And students. There were battle-hardened Americans, and some very innocent ones, who all seemed to have one thing in common. They wanted to be liked. They were pulling Germany back into circulation with massive funding and aid, and expected, somewhat naively, that everyone would be grateful.

There were a few Australians working for the Americans too, enjoying a lifestyle that was sophisticated in a way undreamt of in Australia, and that provided opportunities for travel all over Europe, the Middle East and North Africa. (We turned up everywhere in those days.) They got through their work, they met in clubs, pubs and restaurants, seemed to stay up all night, and I'd be left to recover while they got through the day's work. Or maybe this pace was just turned on when the visitor blew in. All of this frenetic activity in the midst of a town of charming physical beauty with its architecture preserved (Heidelberg was untouched by war), its river and its hills covered, when I was there, with apple blossom, magnolia, pine and poplars, and new light, spring growth.

On one day I was taken to Baden Baden by way of the Black Forest and Wildbad. Baden Baden, being in the French zone of occupation, was full of chic French, shopping for jewellery, clothes, leather. And I visited a casino of delectable style, glamour and opulence, which bore little resemblance to the tawdry palaces that proliferate today. Luxurious, elegant Baden Baden. Coming from London, my mouth hung open; the victor and the vanquished.

I left Heidelberg at 1.30 a.m., after more dining and dancing, and was farewelled by a mildly raucous group who sang sentimental German ballads as the train pulled out. 'Auf Weidersen' undid me, and bleakness returned.

And the next day I saw the war. I saw Cologne, from a train window. I had never seen anything like it. We approached the station slowly. Nothing intact. There was devastation . . . devastation . . . turn your head . . . more devastation. In a few gutted buildings, people appeared to be living in a room or two, but for the most part . . . empty devastation. An endless procession of stark ruins. The Marshall Aid Plan hadn't extended this far. Not yet, anyway. I could feel myself getting older.

I returned to London via Amsterdam. How smug and boring Amsterdam seemed after Heidelberg. The self-satisfied Dutch were the reverse of the polyglot mix I'd left so recently. I took a trip along a canal or two. The commentator was quick to point out how much cleaner their canals were than Venice's. I thought the filth of Venice would be more to my taste.

My arrival in Amsterdam had not been auspicious. Crossing the square from the station a bag burst open and food – delicacies from Heidelberg – spilled out on all sides. The Burghers were quick to assist, and I made my way as best

I could to the lodgings where I would spend a night or two. An unprepossessing door at street level. I pressed the bell. The door swung open, mysteriously, revealing a narrow flight of stairs leading to the first floor. At the top of the stairs waited a German Shepherd mastif.

'Come in.' I presume this was what the dog said. It was, after all, Dutch. I climbed the steps with a mixture of feelings – none of them reassuring – and as I got to the top the dog courteously stood aside. Around the corner sat the proprietor, at a desk, and we conducted our business in English. I was shown to a room no detail of which remains with me, but I have no doubt it was spotless. The proprietors turned out to be very helpful. I was directed to the Rijks Museum and Rembrandt to lift the spirits.

Canal trips, wanderings, cakes, and a restaurant that night where I would be eating my only meal for the next thirty-six hours. I felt I'd chance a good meal and recklessly spent all on 'Biftek Tartar'. Tartare was not in my vocabulary. The raw meat, onion and egg slop was obviously an error, so I imperiously sent it all back to the kitchen to be cooked.

Next day, on the train to Ostend, hunger pangs were beginning to strike. By the time I reached the third-class saloon on the boat – destination Dover – I thought I may not last the night. Interminable it was, and spent sitting bolt upright trying not to collapse on the shoulder of the man alongside. Odd snatches of desultory conversation didn't improve matters. Next morning I stood in line for breakfast and was defeated by the discovery that this was not included in the price of the ticket. Now my guardian angel went into overdrive. My chaste companion of the night insisted on paying. This was one of the best meals I have ever had. I can still taste those sausages, feel the texture of the dark brown gravy, recall the succulence of the bacon, the creaminess of the mash. Thus does genuine hunger elevate the humblest fare into the heady realms of haute cuisine. And all for the exchange of my phone number. The fact that I was out every time he phoned over the next few weeks was unfortunate. But I told myself that gratitude is all the purer for having no strings attached.

How different Amsterdam is today — street lights, erotica, avant garde theatre, all the extremities, but still very tidy.

Travel has always played a major part in my life. Whenever the opportunity presents itself — infuriatingly seldom these days — it's throw everything in a bag and off. For an addicted traveller, living in London was ideal. One could radiate. Weekends provided trips of exploration that ended with my being fairly knowledgable about much between Land's End and John O'Groats, and quite a lot in between. Soon after arriving in England, four of us — Maev Holness, two men friends and I — did a monumental camping journey up to and around Scotland, travelling in an old London taxi that brought most communities to a standstill and caused articles to be written in local journals. It was enormous fun, and the moments of tension as evening approached and no suitable place had been found for the 'pitching' ceremony were, in retrospect, more amusing than our placid moments. My demands were regarded as unreasonable, requiring as they did a package of privacy, the picturesque and peace. A high-flying plane was sufficient for a site to be rejected.

We travelled in June. I pressed daisies from the banks of Loch Lomond in my diary. At our northernmost resting place we experienced something akin to twenty-four hours of light. We loved it, despite the piercing cold in the middle of summer. We bathed in an icy mountain stream ('bubbling along at the foot of our plateau. Banks covered with fern, foxgloves and wild rose, and the air filled with bird song made it the most delightful bath . . .') and fell completely under the spell of the vastness of the high places. Glencoe Pass and Glencoe itself were shrouded in mist, and the atmosphere the day we were there, with few others about, was overpowering; I was suddenly, and rather embarrassingly, ill.

Decades later, going back with my son, Jonathan, it was difficult to recall that first impact, any such overwhelming engulfment being quite unlikely in something that now has all the amenities, and guided tours and souvenir shops and postcards. The palpable atmosphere of 1953 has vanished – the ghosts at last laid to rest by sensible tourism.

During my time in England, I came to know most of the home counties through visits to friends, which included lovely times in Oxford. Penny and Ereach had an old Ford, and cathedrals and great houses could be viewed at leisure. I loved the wildness of Cornwall and was proposed to by a red-headed boatman of Viking descent wearing a gold earring long, long before they were trendy. How extraordinarily different life could have been – Wellington boots, thick sweaters and oil-skins. He felt I would be adept at polishing the brass.

There was a solitary journey to Dublin. I remember arriving on board the steamer with my third-class ticket firmly in hand and, as I rested bag in the stern among roistering, drunken Irish and contemplated a night in their company, it seemed too close to spending a night on a Sydney footpath outside a pub at closing time when closing time was 6 p.m. Familiar territory that I'd not brushed past since sailing through the Heads and had no desire to re-visit. I slipped back to the ticket office and paid the extra for the first-class saloon, recklessly letting tomorrow take care of itself.

Entering that saloon was a ridiculously different world. I have never, before or since, come in contact with such quietly polite, charming people. They couldn't belong to the same race, could they? Even the children were unfailingly charming to their elders, as elders were to them. I sat up all night and amused myself wondering if perhaps this group, most now in their comfortable berths, turned into raging roisterers in the privacy of their own four walls, and the ragers in the stern became models of decorum. They must have had some point of similarity.

If I'd thought England provided rigid delineations of class, it wasn't in the race with Eire. In those days, walk down O'Connell Street, do battle with the cold wind as chaff and manure whirled about, risk being knocked down by tearing, barefoot boys in too large overcoats, turn a corner into Grafton Street – and Alice is in another world. Understated tweedy smartness, beautiful hotels, shops – a little Paris.

I was staying, for my four days, in something very down-market in O'Connell Street, but had been invited to dinner by Maev's relatives in one of those undisturbed Georgian squares. We dined in a lovely Georgian house, somewhat frugally, again in an aura of exemplary grace ... served by a maid who could have attended Lady Bracknell.

My host was the Master of the Rotunda. He was an obstetrician of note and spoke seriously, among other matters, of his distress when, during his rounds of the wards, he might pass a mother and her perfectly healthy baby, and then, almost before he'd left the ward, would hear the cry 'Doctor, Doctor! My baby!' The lovely baby would be dead. He knew the mother had smothered it. He also knew why. She could well live at the top of a tenement with eight other children and no running water closer than the communal tap six floors down. I do remember asking him how he could bear it and his joyful reply 'Oh, but I just love babies! And I've seen more good things than bad.' I don't remember how far we progressed in a discussion on the merits of contraception. My host and his wife were charming, kindly people and they accepted a situation – not happily, but realistically – upon which an outsider, perhaps, had no right to comment. We moved to dessertspoon and fork, and the talk moved this way, that. My mind kept drifting up squalid stairs to a Hogarthian nightmare. I imagine, hope, things are considerably different forty years on. I envied my hosts their degree of acceptance, their certainty of the rightness of the pre-ordained. Along with Bernard Shaw, I was certain of nothing.

Some other charming Dubliner took me for a drive to the 'featherbeds', that expanse of soft, soft heather. We ended up high on a cliff top in County Wicklow gazing down on a milky English Channel, St George's Channel, the name irritating my companion a little. Everything soft — rain, underfoot, argument. Even when argument was anchored in fierce certainty.

TEN

I had been invited into Berkshire for the weekend by friends who lived in a wonderful jumble in a comfortable old house – children, animals, rambles down country lanes, sherry by the fire. This weekend the highlight was to be a point-to-point, the hearty, horsey activity that has horses and riders careering all over the countryside followed by a mob of people on foot who by instinct and some knowledge know where horses and riders can be seen, and where, most importantly, they will end up – all flecked with sweat and wild of eye. The horses as well. A good time is had by all as everyone struggles across ploughed fields in the freezing cold, insisting there is absolutely no better way of spending an afternoon.

This Saturday, 15 March, the Ides, in the middle of the ice and furrows, someone, tired of the mindlessness of it all, had opened his paper. On the front page I glimpsed a photograph of a crashed passenger plane, burning. I knew that my brother-in-law, Bill, had been flying to Singapore on business round about this time, but any flick of unease was dismissed, and we headed for home and hearth. There we learnt that a British Constellation had crashed on landing at Singapore on 13 March. Again, the flick. Again, dismissed. We discussed the tragedy briefly and moved onto other topics, and the evening passed in the usual happy muddle. On the Monday morning I was farewelled at the station and seen into one of those dog box carriages where six or so people share and stare for the journey. I settled back and the man opposite opened his paper. On the back page, clearly in my vision, was published the list of all who'd been killed in the Constellation. My eye went down the list, but I knew, long before I arrived at it, that my brother-in-law's name was on it. There it was — Sparling, William.

The train rattled on. And no escape from the dog box. Oddly comforting in a way. Nothing possible to be done just then, except feel the numbness. At Waterloo, Penny was waiting, and the comfort and tenderness and the practical took over and got me through that day — and the others.

And much later, how extraordinary, when it hit, to recall that Bill, whose catch phrase in any ridiculous situation had always been, 'Beware the Ides of March!' should ultimately have met, slap bang, the moment of heeding his own light-hearted warning. His funeral took place on the Ides. Also, much, much later, to hear that a fortune teller had once said to him, 'Well, you won't be killed in a car crash . . . '

The crash had been even more painful than most. The plane had burst into flames after it overshot the runway, and it was a while before anyone at the airport could find the key to the shed that contained the fire-fighting equipment. There were press photos of some of the crew, who managed to jump to safety. None of the passengers escaped.

So, for my sister, stark tragedy. Their son, David, was 4 years old. Everything, as it is at these times, in a state of upheaval. And a little later, the decisions were made and I decided to leave England and return home. But not before going into the BOAC office to pick over the remaining few, charred, belongings of the passengers. I have no recollection of whether or not I found anything of Bill's.

On a ship again. This one big. The *Orsova*, and it's her second voyage out. There's a cricket team somewhere. I'm up on the deck again, in the stern, watching the wake, discarding a few bits. It had always seemed to me that one is freest on board ship. Somehow, in the middle of an ocean, it is as if no one will ever reach you. Safe and secure. But look over the side in foul weather and the security can suddenly seem illusory. Perhaps that's the attraction.

The last months in England had passed with a high-speed melange of work with Mr Trockenheim, work with the BBC, auditions – at long last – with Stratford, with a slender hope dangled enticingly, convinced as I was that this represented the start of my career in the English Theatre. My ultimate goal.

Then. And from Mr Trockenheim strong persuasion for the setting up of a branch of Susskind and Company in Sydney. This last was considered very carefully – I even suggested my sister join me in the venture – but, ultimately, thanks, but no thanks.

There was a journey through France, Italy, Austria with Penny and Ereach and Timmy. We parted company in Germany and I went for one more time to Heidelberg and farewelled and exchanged addresses and promised always to stay in touch.

Then, before I knew it, the basement room was packed into cases. I stood there and let the pear tree fill my room with its strange, greenish-white light for the last time.

And it was over. A small, vital band was saying goodbye on the railway platform, a few presents were pressed into hands, and then onto the train. The worst of the tiny deaths over. Sydney was waiting and who on earth knew what else.

PART TWO

Eleven

The *Orsova* was pulled into Port Melbourne and stayed there, as was customary, for a night or two. I spent this time with friends Joan and Alan Swinbourne, whom I'd last seen in Cobham, Surrey, where they lived for a couple of years while Alan furthered his Army career. When I came back on board there was a message posted up from one Eric Phillips, commenting on the extraordinary coincidence that he should be on the *Otranto*, which had berthed right alongside while I was with the Swinbournes.

The *Orsova* set out on the last leg of her voyage home. I stuffed the note in a pocket and forgot all about it – and Eric – until *The Duenna* opened at the Phillip Street Theatre in Sydney in 1955. Every night, waiting in the wings, I would say hullo to Eric, who happened, again coincidentally, to be lighting *The Duenna*, an activity he could fall into easily when someone needed a break. Eric's passion was theatre. He had a fine knowledge of lighting and he enjoyed the challenge as recreation from his rather stressful activities as an electronics engineer with AWA. Every night, 'Hullo, Eric.' Nothing else.

Comedy strides in mysterious ways its wonders to perform! The canny, brilliant English director, Lionel Harris had come to Sydney to direct *The Duenna*, a play by Sheridan, which had been set to music by Julian Slade. The name role was comedy, pure and simple, and to my amazement Lionel had offered the part to me. Aside from that first one-act play for Enid Spilsbury at the Modern Theatre Players, I'd played very little comedy – a bit of Shaw on stage and some light comedy in Radio. *The Duenna* was comedy at times edging towards farce, so Lionel must have been either extraordinarily perceptive, or guilty of momentarily taking leave of his senses.

Gordon Chater played Isaac Mendoza, and the first day of rehearsal was my first meeting with someone who was to become an indispensable friend and colleague though, oddly enough, we appeared together in only three productions – *The Dresser* and *The Importance of Being Earnest* making up a trilogy of outrageous moments for us, all off stage, fortunately. If we'd ever lost control on stage I would have to have been carried off on a stretcher. I have been responsible for breaking up other actors on stage, quite inadvertently, but seldom guilty of losing control myself. When this does happen, it tends to be remembered!

The very worst, or best – depending on the point of

view – of those occasions occurred in the Phillip Street production of John McKellar's revue *A Cup of Tea, a Bex and a Good Lie Down*. We were playing to full houses and the management got just a *tiny* bit greedy and threw in an extra performance on Christmas Eve, which a very small number of people attended, everyone else being sensibly engaged in office parties or last-minute shopping. So we had a minute audience, one of whom was a solitary drunk taking the weight off his feet in an aisle seat. The number we were engaged in at the time, leading up to interval, was called 'Theatre Party' and was completely dependent on a full house with two or three of the cast being out in the audience. The ridiculousness of performing this sketch to fifty people, scattered, when each word pointed up our inability to find a seat, suddenly got the better of me. Unfortunately, I was standing next to the drunk when disaster struck. The next five minutes were spent trying, first, to gain some sort of control and, having momentarily done that, to get the offending, and in the circumstances senseless, line out. I failed. Time and time again. It was agony for me, sheer heaven for the audience and, I might add, everyone backstage as heads began to appear round the curtain. My main support came from the drunk who every time I attempted the line would kindly urge me on to greater endeavour: 'Go on, love, you can do it!' I was close to swiping him with the shoe I had in my hand and can remember retreating into the foyer at least twice, bent double, tears streaming down and in very real danger of apoplectic collapse. My fellow performers were quite useless. I think Gloria Dawn simply decided to sit down, let out her unforgettable guffaw occasionally, and leave me to it. All recollection of how that eternity was brought to an end now eludes me. I have no recollection whatever of ever getting past that first word, but must have, I suppose, as we obviously arrived at interval sometime before Christmas Day.

The Duenna was a delicious piece for the return to comedy. I got to wear a false nose, an unnecessary addition some would feel, but a degree of exaggeration in the comic areas was more than happily accepted by our director. Much was made of a long piece of chiffon I wore, which developed a life of its own, and Gordon and I certainly pushed things to the limit. He was quite wonderful and outrageously funny; we had a duet, which we enjoyed to the full – and beyond. Withall, it stayed a disciplined and attractive production, due to Lionel Harris's complete mastery of wit and style. His direction was very much to the point. I have an acute memory of him giving notes in the stalls after a dress rehearsal, summing up with the longed for words 'Well done!'. We preened. Long, long pause and then, 'Boring . . . but well done.' The next run proceeded like a firecracker.

It was one of the more divergent casts I've known, swinging from the extreme of extraordinary innocence in our soprano to total would be licentiousness on the part of our dancer. No, 'Would be' doesn't do justice to the situation. Tommy Merrifield, a New Zealander, was in a class of his own. And, to be fair, capable of diversification, too. Along with dalliance, he found time to discover the classics by way of comic books, diligently passed to him, possibly even read to him, by the main object of his affections at that time, she herself a serious classicist. He was a beautiful, sensual dancer, who drove women wild.

However, the very best thing about Tommy, apart from his Pan-like beauty, was that not only was he a firm believer in extra-terrestrial visitation, but he had himself once witnessed an unidentified flying object in New Zealand. He watched it, he said, for some time, 'hoovering over a domineering mountain'. Visiting New Zealand many years later, with husband and three young children, I thought of Tommy many times and kept examining the dominance on all sides, praying for something similar. Alas, no.

The same Tommy eventually went to England, discovered a talent for sculpture, and is these days sought after by corporate and other collectors to the extent that he is very, very successful and doubtless owns a whole library of first edition classics.

That grand opera singer, Geoffrey Chard, played the baritone role in *The Duenna*, and in off-stage behaviour was as dull as I was. The tenor, though, along with singing gloriously, became the object of yet another's determined lust. All in all, seldom a dull moment. The fact that Lionel's nickname was Pixie may have had something to do with the midsummer madness that attended the entire run.

Bill Orr, who was responsible for the Phillip Street revues, saw *The Duenna*, and asked me to co-star with June Salter in the revue *Cross Section*. A bit hesitant — this was a major change of direction — but after a modicum of persuasion the offer was accepted. We were to open in the second half of 1957. Eric was again to do the lights because the regular Phillip Street lighting man, Arno Leinas, needed a break.

When we opened, I didn't bother greeting the lighting man. I lived with him by then, our wedding having taken place about a month before — leaving just enough time for a mere ten days away alone before we both became extremely busy.

A knight in shining armour, Eric galloped forcefully back into my life late in 1956, picked me up off the ground, dusted me, steadied me, and it didn't take long for us both to realise that this time we'd better hold on. Which we've been doing consistently, with all the ups and downs, for over forty years. As my mother had said one day, 'Wouldn't it be funny if you married Eric Phillips?' It had taken quite a time, but like fine wine benefited from the delay. He is my greatest fan, and our life stimulates him and works because we are both focused very firmly on what we do. He is absolutely supportive in that he values what I do, as I value what he does. We are equals and that never changes, though I believe I rely on his judgement more than perhaps he needs to on mine. He is a crystal clear thinker. I can't even understand the basic principles of electricity. On a fairly regular basis Eric, painstakingly, tries to explain the process — at the most elementary level. It so far eludes me. I don't understand how it gets from its source to the light globe. I am like one of James Thurber's female relatives who suspected electricity was leaking all over the house from the plugs. Eric has lived with this.

Over the years we have been aided by household help —

at times, in the early days, much of my salary disappearing in that direction. That help has been absolutely indispensable and treasured. It has allowed the seams to stay stitched. I am profoundly grateful, and so is Eric. The Florence Nightingales added a richness. And still do. Enjoying the benefits of household help didn't seem extraordinary to me. For the first few years of my life I had, after all, been raised in a household where a live-in maid was considered essential.

TWELVE

The Phillip Street revues changed the face of Theatre in Sydney. When Bill Orr established his Revue house in that delectable church 'hall' he had the assistance of partner Eric Duckworth as manager and Paul Riomfalvy, who made up a triumvirate that kept this extraordinarily successful venture bubbling along through the 1950s, 1960s and into the 1970s – though when the Anglican Church sold the site and that beautiful theatre was pulled down, Phillip Street Theatre moved to Elizabeth Street. There was a later period in Kensington in an old pub, The Doncaster, and Bill finished his Revue days at Manly, running the Manly Loft till his retirement.

I'd heard about Phillip Street in London. That first revue, *Top of the Bill*, caused sufficient stir and was such a hit that the revues from then on proceeded from strength to strength with a creative team that had obviously been waiting for the correct moment to spontaneously combust. Writers John McKellar and Gerry Donovan, composer Lance Mulcahy, who also played one of the pianos opposite musical director Dot Mendoza – as did Ray Cook –, and Jim Wallett, too, with his lovely melodies, costume designers Peter Hurst and Frank Mitchell, designer Robert Lloyd; all were set to go. Another who provided some of the early music was Peter Sculthorpe. There was no running out of steam for a couple of decades. Later, Sybil Graham would take over as musical director.

Some of those who flaunted their stuff over the years with Phillip Street were Gordon Chater, Jill Perryman, Charles Tingwell, Max Oldaker, Ron Frazer, Margo Lee, June Salter, Lyle O'Hara, Barry Humphries, Reg Livermore, John Meillon, Bettina Welch, Diana Davidson, John Ewart, Gloria Dawn, Judi Farr, Barbara Wyndon, Wendy Blacklock, Noel Brophy, Donald McDonald, the last going on to become a successful playwright. Backstage, there was Pat Carter, dresser extraordinaire, and Bunny Ewart in the box office. The most delightful of times. Friendships developed and stayed intact, Bunny becoming one of my closest friends till her untimely death in 1978.

John McKellar became the principal writer, Gerry heading off to London to continue his other profession – dentistry, of course. All good dentists went to London. They were highly sought after, being more up to the minute than many of their English counterparts. And funnier! By the time *Around the Loop* opened in 1956, the revues were the hottest ticket in town, and runs of twelve months or more became the norm. Bill went out of his way to create stars, making the simple connection, still not made by some, that the public would flock to see those who both glittered and delivered. Australian names were up there in lights. People flocked.

The main joy of the revues was that Sydneysiders could see themselves reproduced right up there, night after night, before their very eyes. The writers caught the moment, caught the vernacular, and Sydney responded with sheer delight. They were heady days and in my view started the real turn towards an Australian Theatre before the rest of the country, and governments, caught up. And at least a decade ahead of the celebrated Pram Factory in Melbourne. From Phillip Street on, Australian audiences wanted to see themselves and their world. This was the fateful moment, and all who enjoy and respond to our own drama and performance today, and all who provide it, should pay tribute. The country owes Bill Orr and his merry band a mighty debt.

Cross Section followed on the huge success of *Around the Loop* and was set to run for a year or more. June Salter and I worked together as if made for each other, and years later that rapport made for a highly successful duo in *Lettice and Lovage* at the Sydney Theatre Company. Comedy duos are rare worldwide. I was blessed with a second, much later, with the unlikely teaming of Garry McDonald and me in *Mother and Son*. That particular combination changed my life, but was undreamt of in 1957.

We all had a marvellous and hectic time in *Cross Section*,

the cramped dressing rooms – one male, one female – providing an exemplary level of repartee. In addition to June and me, the distaff dressing room sported Yolanda Rodrigues and Dolore Whiteman and Rhonny Gabriel. The men's contained Antonio Rodrigues, John Parker, Peter Batey, Noel Brophy and Reg Livermore. Dot Mendoza was the musical director, who as well as her other accomplishments could start a round for herself on entering the stage by the simple expedient of clapping her hands behind her back. A strategy that never failed.

Life seemed paradise and set fair to continue so forever. Eric and I had a basement garden flat, completely ramshackle, but opening out onto a sloping garden among the trees above Sydney's Parsley Bay and looking straight across the Harbour to the Zoo and Clifton Gardens. We felt the atmosphere was pure Italian Riviera, and beginning our life there was a blessing. We would drive home from the theatre – frequently stopping at the Cross for deli food. We were both working very hard with two jobs each (I was fitting in Radio during the day). I remember one night when the moon was blazing and we were moved to stroll in Rushcutters' Bay Park. We tripped over a large mound of rags near the stormwater drain. The mound swiftly metamorphosed into the grand Sydney eccentric, Bee Miles. We hurried away. I was not to know that the bundle of rags would have such personal meaning later.

Nearly six months into our marriage, Eric was sent to America by AWA. He was away for three months, and not long after he'd gone I confirmed that I was pregnant and wrote him the news. His telegram of delight from middle America had to suffice until his return and he thus cleverly managed to avoid three months of morning sickness. My sister Gwenyth bore the brunt of it as I phoned her every day with a progress report.

I continued in *Cross Section*, visibly swelling, and finally called it a day at about five months. There was only one dramatic moment when I fainted, gracefully, at a curtain call, and it was worth it, really, to be swept up into Antonio's arms. Being a dancer he managed it with a fine combination of grace and strength, and coming round swathed in Peter Hurst's seaweed green chiffon, head hanging upside down and surrounded by a horseshoe of fascinated audience members, was interesting and faintly pleasurable. Yolanda and Antonio Rodrigues were two dancers in the American Kathryn Dunham Company and had opted to stay in Australia at the completion of that tour. It was our great good fortune to acquire them. I remember picnicking with them a couple of years later. There were two small children then, one intensely white, one intensely black, providing a marvellous photo opportunity.

On the way to the Telluride Film Festival in August 1996, Eric and I spend a few days in New York, and, over lunch, a friend asks if I'm ever recognised there. 'Only by Australians,' I say. We tell him of the young, aspiring Australian actor who fell on me outside the theatre where Al Pacino is in preview with Eugene O'Neill's *Hughie* – the photo, the charming chat. Back on 6th Avenue I make purchases in the pharmacy and am in the act of putting wallet into bag, on the sidewalk, when a passerby stops, calling out in delight, 'I know you!' He is black. He wheels back, and says delightedly, 'You worked with my parents!' Antonio and Yolanda immediately re-surface. (Not difficult when I'd been writing about them just a few weeks earlier.) We have a conversation that veers back and forth about the extraordinariness of coincidence. To say both Eric and I are stunned by this particular coincidence is an under-statement. We talk about the picnic years ago — we are a tiny group of joy, excitement and mutual recollection. He tells me that Yolanda is dead, the year before, and I have time for a tiny moment of grieving before finding myself lending him money, which he will 'of course return to the desk at the Wyndham'. And as light begins to dawn and his eyes turn cold, and he points out twenties in the wallet, I allow myself to be divested of most of my money. We count ourselves lucky that I still have a wallet and that two ageing Australians didn't end up in the gutter with blackened eyes. He'd struck the per-fect confluence — someone occasionally recognised in the streets of New York and with a history that included working with two dear black dancers. Six degrees of separation...

The highest praise I ever received from my mother was after she'd seen *Cross Section*. We were walking out of the theatre in a companionable silence when she turned with a look I knew well: appraisal, affection... and something else just lurking perhaps? Surprise? She passed judgement, 'You're quite funny!', and turned away.

A Cup of Tea, a Bex and a Good Lie Down is probably the

revue most remembered by Sydney; the title having not a little to do with its great success. It was very pertinent to the Sydney of the day. The taking of a headache powder was routine, particularly for the over-worked or frustrated house-wife, and this habit was succinctly encapsulated in John McKellar's inspired title. Three decades later, when speaking in Melbourne at an occasion honouring Australian women of achievement, I took as one of my subjects Professor Kincaid-Smith, Emeritus President of Medicine at Melbourne University. Her research work, finally acted upon in 1979, established the connection between the taking of headache powders and the commonest form of kidney failure then rife in Australia. There was a grim underside to the title which we of course never suspected – too many powders with the cups of tea induced a very long lie down indeed, at times on dialy-sis machines. And frequently a lie down from which one never got up.

My two favourite revue numbers were 'I've Never Known a Moment Free of Pain', dedicated to hypochondriacs, from *A Cup of Tea, a Bex and a Good Lie Down* (a number that John McKellar unkindly and quite incorrectly suggested was mod-elled on me), and 'Dining in a State', from *Cross Section* – a long mime piece showing a lonely, unsophisticated woman trying to cope with a menu in French, a patronising head waiter, and a large and very elaborate hat. Unsuccessfully. The piece was partly taken from life. One day on the train I was perusing scripts and lifted my gaze at a providential moment as a woman rose hurriedly from her seat. She was wearing a large and elaborate hat. She got to the door, which was partly open but stuck. She struggled with it for what seemed an eternity. All efforts to make it accommodate her hat proved fruitless, and as the guard blew his whistle she did the only thing possible. I watched, fascinated, as she squeezed through in the nick of time, the beautiful creation folding around her face. I could have helped but didn't. I wanted to know how she would save herself — always for me one of the more fascinating aspects of the human journey.

None of the problems with headache powders troubled our shenanigans with *A Cup of Tea, a Bex and a Good Lie Down*, of course, and we moved smoothly and happily, but with the usual trepidations to our opening. Sybil Graham was musical director, and others in that cast were Gloria Dawn, Barbara Wyndon, Judy Roberts, Reg Livermore, John Ewart, Donald McDonald and Kevan Johnston. A very young Reg Livermore, I remember, already exhibiting a precocious flair. My first meeting with Gloria, too, and I can remember feeling more than a little nervous, and in awe, her brilliant reputation having preceded her. Also, she had been nurtured in vaudeville, and I had come through strictly legitimate Theatre. So we met, each knew the other without effort immediately and we became very good friends. A mutual respect that spread out beyond the theatre and never left us. It certainly didn't me. She confessed, later, that she'd been equally nervous about the meeting. I watched her and learned much, not the least that if you're *that* good, top of the class you might say, not even the slightest warm-up is needed. Stand in the wings, look gloomy, slouch, groan, and then sweep into that circle and make instant connection with a rapt audience that is grabbed by the throat and never allowed to escape. John McKellar, who I think was responsible for suggesting her for Revue, did have to face the fact that Gloria's immutable dictum, expressed by her stern phrase, 'I never work blue!', required that language had to be properly circumspect in every number or sketch she took part in. Vulgarity, yes; even faintly foul language, no.

Many moments of that revue linger. I remember the number John Ewart and I delivered – he as a vicar, I as an English dowager – singing and playing our way through 'Anyone for Croquet'; I remember Kevan and me dancing a wild tango, choreographed by him, which ended my 'Love Goddess' number (a housewife's wild fantasy); I remember Reg Livermore's Swan Upping, punting his way down the river in straw boater; I remember 'The Red Roofs of Sydney', a duet between John and Reg; and Donald and me sitting on a bench, staring straight ahead, attempting, painfully, to recall someone with the uninspired name of Enid McInerney, plus a tribe of equally dull and unmemorable people from the past. A classic sketch on non-communication.

As with everything, Revue changes. For me, the perfect example of the genre today was revealed during a visit to the Tilbury Pub to see Jonathan Biggins – plus Linda Nagel and Phil Scott – in the most pertinent and brilliant observation of the whole catastrophe of Australia circa 1997 that one could hope to see. In Jonathan Biggins we have our irreverent prophet. An evening outrageous, but totally targeted. Also, unbelievably, combined with elegance. Rare. There *is* life after death. With Phil Scott and Linda Nagel, this view of the contemporary is like a beacon in an increasingly dark world.

The last of the big revues for me, and my favourite, was *But I Wouldn't Want to Live There*. This again brought together Gloria and me, and the additional cast member was Lyle O'Hara. An all-woman cast. Unheard of. Only three of us and the three of us the 'stars'. I'd first met Lyle at the Independent School, all those years ago. I seem to remember us having difficulty with an unexceptional piece on the Brontës of Haworth, and the not very enlivening text meant we were in real danger at every performance. We mostly controlled ourselves.

So there we were: Lyle, Gloria, Ruth. The revue was put on at the Phillip Theatre at its new location in Elizabeth Street in October 1967, and we were blessed, if that is the word, with a revolve. It was a technically difficult show, and controlling this tricky side of things was Sue Natrass who is now the general manager of the Victorian Arts Centre and destined to take over the running of the Melbourne Arts Festival in 1998. We had the best! The three of us did indeed revolve the whole night, so it became a matter of stepping off, donning bits or switching costume entirely, stepping back on again as a revolve went past, and being, in the process, extremely fleet of foot – or lose one! We covered the gamut of John McKellar's characters which is saying a lot, and the only trouble we ever got into was once during our number based on Sydney's new revolving restaurant. We were 'dining out' and were supposed to revolve into view, sedately, at the top of the number, but this night, making her one error in a five-month run of miracles, Sue pushed the wrong button, and the three ladies braced firmly to travel in one direction suddenly found themselves in each other's laps going the opposite one. As all control vanished in a flash, the copybook was badly blotted. As I've said, when it goes, it goes.

I remember with absolute clarity the number that had us as bizarre hippies taking over the orchestra pit and pushing the musicians aside as we clambered in after marching through the audience to the strains of 'When the Saints Go Marching In'. In control of the pit we continued the number with Gloria magnificent on trombone, Lyle handling percussion and myself on double bass with a, fortunately, simple base line that if pushed I could reproduce today. This wild activity tended to, as they say, bring the house down. I always felt restricted on my double bass and envied Lyle her wild freedom with percussion and tambourine. One day . . .

The number that personally caused the greatest hell was my monologue with three Pekinese dogs in tow. The whole sketch was based on the premise that people turn into their pets, so I was clad in a large Pekinese coloured fur and hat. The other two had to struggle as a cat and a hen, but as I was always too busy with my own nightmare I paid them scant attention. One of the dogs, named Fang, was my cross for the full five months, partly because he was too clever by half. I'd be waiting downstairs in the dressing room, and as the music cue approached, all the dogs, but particularly Fang, would become very excited. They obviously regarded the number as theirs with myself in the role of supernumerary. I'd grab their leads and head to the wings, wondering what hell Fang had in store for me that night. As long as I subjected him to my gaze throughout the monologue, he behaved perfectly, but the minute my eyes were off him, which let's face it is sometimes necessary if you wish to include your audience in the fun, he would swing into his upstaging role with relish. He could lie on his back and look appealing, wave his legs or just look at the audience and pant, and I would know from the delighted 'Ahs' in front of me that something was going on. The second I glared at him he would resume his previous state of inno-cence. The other two dogs were in my arms – I wasn't game to let all three roam – but the nights Fang would decide to crawl under a sofa, getting him out could add minutes, particularly if the other two dogs decided to help.

On the nights Fang behaved himself, the two in my arms would get above themselves. A glare from me would occasion a melting swipe with a tongue across my face, which mostly produced a round from the audience and encouraged the dogs to even greater excesses.

All these activities had to be incorporated somehow into the words. Not easy. Each time the number was over I was ready to strangle all Pekinese within reach, but, happily, by the next evening, as I passed through their quarters, their extremely winning ways would again triumph. I, too, would melt.

There is a saying in this business in Australia: 'Never act with animals or Jacki Weaver.' I keep doing both. I've appeared with cats, dogs and the odd horse. The pinnacle was my one television appearance in *A Country Practice*, when the producers obviously decided to test me. I proceeded through the whole episode with seven assorted dogs attached to a shopping trolley. Is there something in my curriculum vitae, undetected by me, that indicates animal training? Sadly, I find it difficult to say no. The latest was a baby kangaroo. And there was a pigeon, a cat, parrots and numberless dogs, all, I might add, at the same time. I once played a whole scene as Launce in *Two Gentlemen of Verona* on all fours, haranguing a dog, a situation I don't believe the dog, Shorty, ever recovered from as we were nose to nose. On that occasion, *I* made *him* nervous.

Despite Fang, I really loved *But I Wouldn't Want to Live There*. It seemed, to me, to contain some of John's most original writing and the novelty of a three-woman cast was both challenging and rewarding. We were thrilled the day film star James Mason, passing by, decided to see us. He came round and told us what he thought . . . which fortunately was pleasant! But, for all *he* may have thought of it, this revue was not as popular as some of the others and ran for just five months. Phillip Street revues were supposed to run forever.

The real bonus was that the three in the cast, a tricky number, got on so splendidly. This time it wasn't Three Tall Women – more One Tall Woman, Two Short. And it was delicious.

After *Cross Section* ended for me, and shortly after the birth of Anna, I was approached by Mungo MacCallum Snr, at the ABC with a suggestion that I write and appear in five-minute fillers, which would be played before the 7 o'clock news. Prior to that, viewers watched ducks meandering down streams and Mungo thought it might be time for a change. This appealed very much and I wrote a series of sketches called *Gracious Living*. Television was in its infancy and was stuffed with experts on all subjects, showing, with sweet smugness, how inept the rest of us were. I thought I should join them.

So instead of ducks, there I was demonstrating flower arranging, cake icing, baby bathing, sari donning, ikebana ... there was nothing in which I was not expert. At the beginning of my demonstration. By the end it would be mayhem, and so far as I was concerned it was no holds barred, but, of course, when desperation took over, as it always did, it had to be with the utmost graciousness. I was, after all, meant to be setting a standard. It was after that series that the experts disappeared for awhile, but they're a hardy breed. They keep returning. The phrase 'gracious living' now appears in the Oxford Dictionary, but I still claim I invented it.

The five minutes proved popular and they were fun to do, but the recordings have disappeared along with so much else from the black and white days. As I wrote them all on the backs of bus tickets and bills they've disappeared thoroughly. The odd photo turns up occasionally.

Gracious Living kept me in touch with performance during the difficult early days of baby caring – kept the mind turning. I was always profoundly grateful to Mungo for the suggestion.

Daughter Anna was born on a tempestuous Thursday, Lear on the blasted heath having nothing on Sydney that day. Jane, two years later, Jonathan, three years on from Jane, also decided to make entrances on tempestuous Thursdays, all three prepared to accept that their parents' wedding day, also a tempestuous Thursday, was the style to aim for – and all, too, delivered by an obstetrician whose name was Macbeth.

Our children have always led very private lives, first our own wish, and when the time slipped away and they were grown, it has become very much their wish. So not much will be said about them in this book, beyond saying that they are the central core of my being, that their presence has always seemed, and still does, miraculous, and that they are the cause of the *greatest* pride. Nothing surpasses it. The fact that we can, husbands, partner and all, sit around a table and entertain and satisfy one another – mostly – means that Eric and I have done something right in the process. When I look back, I suppose the quality we hammered in over and above all others was manners – and manner. They've graduated in that department summa cum laude, and are, as bonus, all possessed of an irreverent humour. What more can one ask? Other than in the fullness of time the due presentation of the next generation, which has already started. Six new treasures, Madeleine, Rebecca, Oscar, Isobel, Alex and Celeste – six at time of writing – make one know what immortality is all about.

When Bill Orr was running the Music Loft at Manly he decided to commission John McKellar to write a revue the title of which would be *Crackers*. No prizes for guessing who would be in it. In fact Bill Orr persisted in calling me Crackers from the early Revue days, and Patrick White added to this by making me Dame Crackers. (That is the only reference to Patrick White in this book. I had promised myself that this would be the one biography/autobiography/tract to emerge of recent years without the obligatory references to what Patrick said to me or what I said to Patrick, but this passing reference seemed apposite – and unavoidable. There, I've done it.)

With me in *Crackers* were Ross Higgins and Tom Oliver. We had a lovely time together except for the anxieties that never completely left Ross and me. We are equally neurotic in the matter of enclosed spaces with, to us, unsatisfactory exit provisions should there be a fire emergency. Our respective neuroses are always on the *qui-vive* for a fire – or an air raid – or a tidal wave. The Fire Department and other authorities were completely satisfied with the arrangements at the Manly Loft, but Ross and I set our own standards in these matters. Our problem was that this revue was cabaret style. Our backs were to the wall in performance – I hasten to add in a literal not a figurative sense –, and the audience blocked our way to the stairs, our intention always being to be first out in any hazardous situation. We wandered around gloomily in what could be called wing space, and were only satisfied when we'd placed a coil of rope near the open loading dock so that, in the event of an emergency, we could at least rope ourselves and precipitate a swift exit to the street 20 feet below. I believe we also had a bucket of water at the ready, but what that was for other than to throw in the face of someone who might beat us to the rope I'm not sure. I don't think Tom was included in our plans. Our fears were somewhat assuaged by these preparations, but there was always just that undercurrent throbbing away beneath performance which added sparkle. The eyes would flick nervously from side to side at times.

That said, the show was a delight, though as with most things I've been in the fine detail seems to elude. I am so in envy of other actors who can recall chapter and verse every role they've ever been in; pages of Shakespeare can be summoned up without effort. Around dinner tables I'm reduced to the odd nursery rhyme as the competition hots up.

I seem to remember an energetic chorus of 'Hello, Dolly' and a parody of Helen Reddy's 'I Am Woman', with me climbing a step ladder in an impersonation of Margaret Whitlam, if that doesn't strain credibility too far. I'm not sure what our duets or trios were about, but audiences were always delighted and happy, none more so than the Sydney producer Eric Dare, when he visited. He had had a great success at the Bijou Theatre in Balmain, with Reg Livermore performing his extraordinary Betty Blokk Buster creation, and it seemed to him that a change of pace, i.e. me, would be all to the good.

This was how, in 1976, I appeared in a specially written one-woman revue called *Puttin' on the Ritz*. John McKellar was to write it and it was to be directed by Peter Batey, who had directed many of the Phillip Street revues.

Puttin' on the Ritz had some wonderful material, though some of it alarmingly bizarre, for instance an impersonation by me of James Cagney as a pest exterminator. Sometimes one can be guilty of throwing caution to the winds. I was on stage all night, moving in and out of diverse characters, accompanied by an orchestra popular at the time called The Palm Court. They were dressed in a slightly send-up version of a *fin de siècle* ensemble and were grouped behind me. Probably the first mistake. Technically it was a nightmare, and the sound system was never mastered. Many different versions of mikes were attached to me in various places, none proving adequate, until my kind husband had one flown specially from Melbourne. By the time it arrived I was almost ready to accept a megaphone and quite impervious to what was being done to me by whom with what, which is why the technician was able to strap an extremely large, phallic, heavy object to my inside thigh without demur on my part. To even walk was a minor miracle.

Opening night started with the orchestra and me in position behind the velvet curtains, unable to hear any cues. My main attention was directed towards quelling the rising panic behind me, every musician looking like a rabbit caught in headlights, which is the look one wears when there is no guarantee of communication from the nerve centre. Curtain up and the night was proceeded with, the technical hitch at the top being remedied in the very nick of time. But despite that momentary stroke of good fortune, by the end of the night we didn't need a psychic to predict that we might well have a disaster on our hands. The mix was irretrievably wrong, with some areas working, others quite definitely not. No blame to be laid anywhere. Just one of those things.

Eric Dare decided after a week to put up the notice, but this, he said, would not be proceeded with if houses improved. I was by then writing some material to replace areas that would never work and had hopes that we might just turn it round. Without warning, two days after the notice went up, the show was pulled. I received this news in a phone call from a friend as I was leaving for the theatre for that night's performance; she'd tried to book seats for the night, but had been advised the show was cancelled. Someone had neglected to tell me about it. I went to the theatre and commiserated with the orchestra.

When something as deadly as this happens, there are differing responses. For me, it was shock. Clinical shock. Not nice. But one recovers, and my recovery was aided by a trip to London, where Kirrily Nolan was ensconced in a Sotheby's Works of Art course. She and I collected a number of antique prints, which were to form the nucleus of the shop that Eric and I intended to open. In four weeks, I returned with the booty and began to recover my nerve.

THIRTEEN

The recovery was aided by an offer from Colin George to go to Adelaide in 1977 for his first season there as artistic director of the State Theatre Company of South Australia. His words to me: 'I want to build the first season around you.' He offered me the role of Ranevskaya in Chekhov's *The Cherry Orchard*, Mrs Candour in Sheridan's *School for Scandal*, and he wanted me to finish my time with him with a one-woman revue, to be written by me, with two additional pieces by David Williamson and Alex Buzo. The one-woman show was an extraordinary expression of faith by Colin, and when it finally opened, my recovery was complete.

Colin gathered around him a group of actors and writer, Ron Blair, who was to be the assistant director. Some of those who would be unable to stay longer than one season were invited to become Associates of the Company and would thus maintain a link for as long as the Company existed. I was one of the Associates. I think we all hoped Colin would be there in Adelaide forever, but nothing is forever, and in the event Colin's time finished in 1980 when he returned to England prior to taking up a position as Dean of the Acting Academy in Hong Kong.

His time in Adelaide was a golden time for the State Theatre Company, bearing in mind that Adelaide has always been a notoriously difficult city for a subsidised theatre to succeed in. It *can* be done, but it's a devil of a job. With his skilful mix of classics and new writing – with an emphasis on new Australian writing – Colin managed to persuade Adelaide to support its own Theatre. There was a vital, confident atmosphere, and when I left after that first season, I never lost the feeling of being an important member of the Company. Colin inspired loyalty, and we were his to a man and woman. He instituted his own brand of warm-up sessions, and while never a lover of these sometimes too earnest gatherings, I was surprised to find myself contributing with the utmost enthusiasm and enjoyment. Colin led us into many areas of exploration of both texts and ourselves and to my knowledge no one put up any resistance. He is a Quaker and that particular quality which is shared by all Quakers permeated everything he touched. A little glow, and always beneficial to warm oneself by. I think he is the nicest person I have encountered in theatre.

The pattern for me in Adelaide was to rehearse *School for Scandal* and write as much of the revue as I could manage, play *School for Scandal* and rehearse *The Cherry Orchard*, open *The Cherry*

Orchard and rehearse *Just Ruth*, the name Colin had decided would serve our purpose for the revue. I lived a brisk half-hour's walk from the theatre complex and I've never been fitter. Working night and day was just what the doctor ordered, and the wonderful company of actors contributed the loveliest of memories, professional and personal.

In that first season, I remember, among others, Kevin Miles, Leslie Dayman, Dennis Olsen and Ted Hodgeman, Daphne Grey, Ron Falk, Brian James and Dorothy Vernon. I remember some recent diplomates from NIDA – Rebel Russell, Colin Friels and Michael Sibbery, testimony to Colin's astute eye, as Rebel is now a film producer, Colin highly successful in film and television and stage, and Michael one of the leading players at the Royal Shakespeare Company.

We sometimes spent Sundays together and considered ourselves a bit of a family. Notwithstanding, I still enjoyed retreating to the solitude of my lodgings. Sometimes Eric would fly in for the weekend, and I remember my son Jonathan turning up for part of the school holidays – image of a 14-year-old boy flying a kite with dedicated focus in the parklands opposite.

Finally, we opened and we were a success – for Adelaide, one could say a resounding success. I remember Dennis Olsen's beautiful Loparkin and Ted Hodgeman's Firs in *The Cherry Orchard* and the glacial, dripping wit of Daphne Grey's Lady Sneerwell in *School for Scandal*. I remember the difficulty Ron Falk always had in getting through an early scene in *School for Scandal*, with my Mrs Candour making mincemeat of the list of those to be gossiped about – I would always manage the first nightmare names, but it was anybody's guess what would come out when I got to Lord Spindle, Sir Thomas Splint, Captain Quinze and Mr Nickit – sipping cups of chocolate the while. And Ron's shoulders heaving. Ron insists I was no better, years later, in Simon Gray's *Close of Play* when I listed the children in a different order at every performance, and frequently re-christened them.

A deliciously stylish and outrageous *School for Scandal* it seemed, with a superb set by Rodney Ford, the English designer Colin persuaded to join him in Adelaide. There were false boxes constructed on the prompt side of the stage and opposite prompt, filled with caricature Restoration Revival men and women, the women spilling bosoms in all directions, like blow up Cruickshank or Gilray cartoons.

The Queen was paying a visit to Adelaide at that time, and during her tour of the theatre complex she was to catch us 'rehearsing'. We rehearsed the dance in *The Cherry Orchard* for an entire morning to be sure of presenting her with a whirl of colourful spontaneous activity as opposed to a silent and possibly glum group of thespians, as can happen. The door to the stalls was finally thrown open and a tiny figure in yellow gazed at us for a moment and then departed. We got on with the real rehearsal.

Years later I did indeed meet the Queen at a luncheon at Yarralumla in Canberra. Eric and I were blessed with a driver who'd done this sort of thing many times before and he delivered us to the door with perfect timing. We beat the

Queen and Prince Philip by a just comfortable margin, but being virtually the last to enter the reception area the Queen found herself face to face with me. The conversation proceeded in very stilted fashion until the voice said, 'And where do you mostly work, Miss Cracknell?' 'Oh . . . where the work takes me, Ma'am.' And smiled. In a flash we were in the middle of a quite animated conversation on the difficulties of touring. The Royal Yacht had been delayed because of an incident at Aden, and the business of wardrobe and what to wear was becoming a problem. Backwards and forwards we went for a time, two old pros in perfect understanding of the difficulties of being on the road . . .

The season advanced. We'd had successful openings with both the plays and I moved towards opening night of *Just Ruth*. I had resurrected some of the pieces I'd flung in panic into *Puttin' on the Ritz*, the rest were completed, and I had the two sketches by David Williamson and Alex Buzo – Alex's a particularly surreal sketch, David's bleak and gripping. Colin had wanted me to perform Samuel Beckett's *Not I* as a sort of curtain raiser, but I resisted, or my guardian angel smote me firmly. The thought of coupling Beckett – even one of his short plays – with a night of Revue would have been beyond my resources.

So, *Just Ruth* stayed as its own entity, and, thank Heaven, worked. I can't remember much about it, but I do remember it closed with an old, fragile lady walking along a tightrope holding a sunshade. It had delightful music, with Sybil Graham at the piano, beautiful, round smiling face beaming up at me and guiding me through every moment; and it had the skill of Michael Fuller's patient choreography, as well as his perfect, patronising performance as the Head Waiter in the mime sketch *Dining in a State*. It began in an ordinary way: 'My name is Ruth. I was born in Maitland . . . ', and meandered and scooted and jumped its way along. There was talk of a tour, but I'd laid my ghost and a three-week season was all I wanted.

FOURTEEN

If one had a dollar for every time someone asks 'What are the highlights of your career?', one could possibly retire forthwith. Every aspiring 15 year old, every journalist ultimately asks that question. This one can always be plucked out. No one will argue. It has that hallmark quality, if for no other reason than the eminence of the man at the helm. *King Oedipus* was the play, Sir Tyrone Guthrie the man.

In the decade preceding our meeting I had done considerably less in theatre as babies were abounding, and anything accepted had to be very carefully thought about. The decade started for me with a performance of Hugh Hunt's production for the Old Tote Theatre of T. S. Eliot's *Murder in the Cathedral*, with Robert Speight as Beckett, which opened in Sydney for a short run and then went to the first Adelaide Festival in 1960. Ron Haddrick was in this production, as were Dinah Shearing and Patricia Connolly, the last two and I taking on the roles of leaders of the chorus. This was the first time I had met Ron, and it was the beginning of a long and happy association in Theatre, which caused one radio announcer to introduce us, erroneously as it happens, as two 'who have been playing with one another for years'.

Some time early in 1970 I had met Robin Lovejoy at a party, where he mentioned the *King Oedipus* production. Robin was the artistic director of the Old Tote Theatre. I had known him for about twenty years. We trusted one another, which may have been the reason that when he was dying he asked that I speak at his funeral. What escape was there ever from a Lovejoy direction?

In the event, his funeral was quiet and private. This is some of what I said, in celebration and thanksgiving for his life, at the memorial service held for him at the Sydney Opera House:

The actors present here today owe Robin a debt. His roots were in Australia. He didn't remain in England. He returned. As its artistic director, he was the guiding force in the Trust Players in the late 1950s and 1960s, that splendid forerunner to all the major subsidised drama companies in the country. His belief in the ability of Australians to perform in their own theatres and to provide work of a high order was second to none. Every production he was connected with was fired with a belief in this country's artistic viability, the result of this belief was to be seen in theatres across the land in those days. Here it will be remembered at the incomparable Palace Theatre, subsequently destroyed – and the Elizabethan Theatre at Newtown. The fact that we are here today in the Drama Theatre of the Sydney Opera House is tribute to his success as a champion of this particular Australian dream that progressed from strictly amateur beginnings, in the 1930s and 1940s, to the professional strength that applies today ... it is significant, of course, that we are in this place. Robin Lovejoy was responsible as director of the Old Tote for the opening season here in 1973 of *Richard II*, David Williamson's *What If You Died Tomorrow?* and Jim Sharman's production of Brecht's *The Threepenny Opera*. The turmoil of those days, bringing anything to fruition in an uncompleted, untried space, where if one owned a car gaining admittance was only marginally simpler than scaling the Berlin Wall. Well, full circle, eh? The turmoil of those days, the ultimate resolution of the problems, artistic and technical – the most sophisticated equipment contained legions of gremlins – was the responsibility of the man we honor today.

The designers present are in his debt. As well as his own acclaimed gifts in these areas, as head of Design at NIDA for so many years, Robin had an enormous effect on all who passed through that Institute. I know his encouragement has been unstinting and I do believe that the high standard of design in this country, the innovative quality, the energy, are due in no small part to students' contact with the extraordinary imagination, the encyclopedic knowledge, the sheer practical ability of the man we honour today.

And directors are in his debt. Not only those who passed through NIDA when he was head of Directing, but all who ever attended any of the vast number of plays and operas over the years that bore his stamp. Fashions change, new styles emerge, but the essential integrity and creativity and damned hard work that were part of every Lovejoy production are constants within our profession.

One of his favourite words was ambience. We all knew it. I think I've only come now to understand its true meaning. Ladies and gentlemen, the ambience of Robin's going was golden indeed.

When Robin was working in theatre, there was not the same diligence as there may be today in recording achievement – or the reverse. The reference to ambience was there because it seemed to be the one word Robin was unable to omit from any rehearsal. At some stage we would all be reminded that our main task was to create that 'golden ambience', which all audiences had expectations of entering every time they took their seats. They should be offered nothing less. We trusted audiences themselves were aware of their own lofty expectations! Whenever the phrase appeared word of it spread around dressing rooms and the acting fraternity like fire, golden fire I suppose, and we all took great pleasure in reporting its latest manifestation.

Anyway, Robin's right.

Back in 1970, Robin knew I'd been working sparingly in Theatre since the birth of my children – the two Phillip Street revues being the main undertakings – but he mentioned that the great Sir Tyrone Guthrie was coming out to direct *King Oedipus* for the Old Tote Theatre and perhaps it was something I should think about. It was to be a new adaptation by John Lewin, which the writer had sent to Sir Tyrone, and which had so impressed him that this was the version he would be using. I was somewhat overwhelmed by the suggestion as Revue had dominated the 1960s for me! In Robin's defence, he and I did go back a long way. Ron Haddrick, who had had years of experience with the Shakespeare Memorial Theatre Company as it was then known, was the obvious choice for Oedipus.

Some to-ing and fro-ing, and a few months later I found myself in a large barn in Dural, northwest of Sydney, in the freezing cold, tossing a small beanbag at Ron, who tossed it back. And thus we spent a morning, under the eagle eye of Mechtilde Harkness, who was charged with making sure our breathing and voices were in top condition. It seemed a slightly pointless activity but I went along with it and made the appropriate noises. It was good exercise, and bizarre activity has never alarmed me.

In the fullness of time, we began the actual rehearsals. These were held in one of the buildings in the Sydney Showground, then the legendary home of the Royal Easter Show, before Fox Studios moved in. The building used was akin to a Literary Institute hall, with all attendant drawbacks. I seem to remember a black drape dividing the space roughly two thirds/one third. I had met Guthrie, of course, and been approved by him, and we'd all read his notes on the production – his view of Oedipus, his philosophy, the need, in his view, to incorporate elements of opera and ballet within the concept –, but this was moment of truth day. We were shown Yoshi Tosa's set and costume designs in this curtained-off section, as well as the designs for his extraordinary masks – great, mysterious creations awaiting expression. Oedipus and those around him, the protagonists as opposed to chorus and humble citizenry, would be wearing grossly built-up shoes so that with our larger-than-life-size masks, our crowns and headgear in place, we would represent the natural rulers in a larger-than-life-size play, a play that Guthrie thought the greatest ever written. A short play, but close to perfection for him. Those of us who would be wearing the kingly costumes were under no illusion as to the difficulty and discomfort they would present, but were all excited by the challenge. There was a speech from Guthrie – oh so brief, he didn't believe in them – and then it was work for those called for that first day. Those not rehearsing returned to the set and costume designs, emitting small sounds of excitement and appreciation, when from the other side of the curtain came a mighty voice: 'Quiet!' There was instant, frozen silence. We crept away.

In all the time he was with us that was the only occasion I ever heard Guthrie raise his voice. And it was the only time anybody ever again relaxed from total focus.

How to describe the rehearsal period? Fascinating to watch him mould the chorus, like watching a sculptor, a shape emerging as he moved people gently, adjusting this way, that — all so fluid. Guthrie had worked with Ron for some time before rehearsals commenced, so Ron was very sure of his direction. In a way everything else was being built around this central column — Oedipus, the King. I don't now recall any of his directions to me. It's as if a lot of the time one was left to develop the personal journey oneself. I do remember working one day on the great central scene between Oedipus and Jocasta, the guts of the play, but we never dwelt on it again: 'Don't wear it out, don't wear it out!' The dominant memory always is the shaping of that giant sculpture peopled by nobles and peasants, the doomed rulers inhabiting an Olympian pinnacle. We wore practice masks, and our shoes as soon as they were available. Our movements became slow, gestures broadened.

All that focus within the room, and none more focused than Judith Guthrie, sitting, watching, ready for his occasional swift glance. It was as though he were awaiting her affirmation, or checking to make sure she'd seen an actor at a moment especially pleasing to him. She always had.

I remember having lunch with them both in nearby Centennial Park, sitting on the grass, and the talk that always confirmed, re-inforced, Guthrie's view of Oedipus. There was a perfect symbiosis between them — equal, complementary. Standing next to her one day in the rehearsal room, seeing the tears streaming down her face. 'It still affects you?' I asked. 'Oh yes.'

Guthrie summed up Oedipus's dilemma as a man asking, 'Who the fuck *am* I?' He was the first I'd heard use the word without any hint of aggression. It gained a certain style, but was still faintly shocking that first time.

I remember, with delight, an over-zealous member of the crowd asking, 'Sir Tyrone, what is my motivation at this point?' as the crowd ebbed and flowed, driven, driven by the fates. The answer whipped back, 'Pestilence in Thebes!' I remember my surprise when Jocasta was in need of a line in a crowd scene — 'Write it yourself,' said Guthrie. 'You're a writer.' That Old Tote program didn't say Sophocles' *King Oedipus*, adaptation by John Lewin, additional dialogue by Ruth Cracknell. Never mind . . . injustices abound. Over and above everything else, I remember Guthrie's wit, misunderstood by some, but taken to by me as duck to water. I could never get enough.

We talked about jam. He had started a jam factory in Annagh-ma-kerrig in Northern Ireland, his home, which employed nearly forty people. He was passionate about trying to ease the terrible unemployment situation there. Did I know anywhere in Sydney where he could export his jam? I took him to a smart boutique in Wahroonga owned by a somewhat eccentric Irishwoman, Rosina Hayes. There were Guthrie and I in a trendy shop on the North Shore seriously discussing the prospects of jam importation. It seemed an ideal outlet, filled as it was with Irish tweed and Celtic adornments. He seemed satisfied. The groundwork was laid.

King Oedipus advanced to its opening and in the process I got close to both, particularly Guthrie. This is always the problem, for one knows parting is inevitable. I had a wild moment of hoping it wouldn't be permanent, for he asked me to go to Belfast to play Ranevskaya in *The Cherry Orchard*. 'She should always be played by a comedienne,' he said. This to his Jocasta!

We opened. It was a Sydney 'occasion' which meant, in those days, dress up and black tie. Guthrie was conspicuous in a navy suit, not caring for the sort of formality that Sydney so loved then. I was just a little sad to see he'd swapped his sand-shoes for proper shoes. We all lined up when the performance was over to farewell him, and reserve took over – a necessary protection at these times. He looked very handsome. We said goodbye formally. We were now in the hands of his assistant, the American, Dr Jean Wilhelm.

In the event, I didn't make it to Belfast, nor did the jam roll onto the docks. After we finished our Oedipus tour, Eric, the children and I went travelling around New Zealand in the May school holidays. Gazing at the magnificent scenery in the South Island, nervously checking on the dominance, the mind would occasionally wander and dream, linger, for instance, on Chekhov's *The Cherry Orchard* in Belfast, ponder on ways and means. One of us switched on the radio. Item number three: The death of Guthrie. I found it impossible to believe; he'd seemed the epitome of health and energy when he'd been with us.

I felt cheated. I wanted more. It was just beginning . . .

Later, I read that someone in Annagh-ma-kerrig had described his death with the words 'A great tree has fallen'. The metaphor seemed apt. Apt and personal. It still does.

Rise above! This was his constant refrain in the face of all difficulties. That phrase rang around the world and will always be associated with him by those of us fortunate enough to have worked with him. Those of us still alive. All I know is he touched me in some very deep sense. Put a mark on me – like a Japanese printmaker.

King Oedipus had its season in Sydney at the totally inappropriate Clancy Auditorium at the University of New South Wales, which had caused even Guthrie's optimism to plummet when he first saw it. But 'Rise above' reasserted its rightful place within him, and he somehow managed to convey Thebes with such soul-reaching conviction that not many who saw the production will forget. He always said he didn't want people to experience a wallow of emotion, but rather that Oedipus be with them forever, so that at odd moments through life it would surface, unbidden. The fundamental 'Who am I?' dilemma. Like all great Theatre, particularly tragedy, it had the impact of music. As it unfolds, there is the inevitability of the final, awful, resolution. In this case, death and blind banishment.

Ron Haddrick was majestic – in every sense. The masks added another dimension and I couldn't reach *him*, only approach Oedipus. There was a barrier to any comfort or connection in the human sense. Oedipus and Jocasta were 'other'. And yet the masks *did* gain expression, and some will swear they saw tears falling.

There was Ron Falk's extraordinary Tiresias, pushed to the limits in a costume that was all decaying, giant bird. In the days when I read reviews I recall this Tiresias being described as a geriatric Bondi seagull. An absolutely delicious image – but perhaps with a whiff of sourness about it? Guthrie was an eminent figure, and British to boot. Unacceptable to some.

Guthrie was the first, as far as I can recall, to present a classic text as though emanating from the land where the story was being told. The townspeople were encouraged to be plainly Australian. This was confronting to some. Barry Lovett as the old shepherd, for example, did seem to have overtones of a prize merino – in costume at least! Oedipus everywhere. Ancient Greece and modern Australia intertwined.

We took Oedipus to the Princess Theatre in Melbourne in a heat wave, where fires ringed the city and roasting winds blew in. Donning those massive costumes and putting the masks in place was not good – the reward always the journey for the audience. Movement was slow, gestures broad and measured. Giant other creatures. So hot was it that I remember playing bridge during the day. My host had electric fans under the table and offered basins of cold water for our feet.

The tour also took in Canberra, Perth, Adelaide. In Perth we had the sheer joy of playing in the Octagon at the University, a perfect Guthrie-advised design, the design where all his productions belong. The other production he did in Australia was *All's Well That Ends Well*, which had just finished playing when we arrived with Oedipus. I remember Frank Thring stayed on. A crowd of us were going to lunch with the painter, Robert Juniper. We were being given details on how to get to Robert's for lunch and he turned to explain. 'Don't tell *me*,' I uttered in dismay. 'I have no sense of direction.' 'I could see that,' the Thring voice rang out, 'from watching you on stage.' Frank and I became and remained good friends, possibly because I always fed him good lines. Lovely times in Perth. It is one of my favourite places, full of wonderful women – Elizabeth Jolley, Janet Holmes àCourt, Elizabeth Durack, Dame Rachel Cleland, and my dear Eve Akerman. Must be something in the water.

In Adelaide, we had malevolent heat. There we played in the neo-Gothic Bonython Hall – narrow clerestory windows, no real wing space. Entrances from the opposite side of the stage necessitated being led all around the auditorium – up one outside aisle, along another, down the final. A long journey, or so it always seemed. We played mostly matinees to accommodate schools and there was no air-conditioning, nothing to modify the fierceness of the sun beating through the windows. Rise above! Rise above! Small talk in dressing rooms was reduced to a minimum. Ron Haddrick's party trick after a performance was to remove his T-shirt and squeeze out a tumbler of precious bodily fluid. He grinned constantly as he got more and more emaciated.

Playing tragedy is never a hundred per cent tragedy, of course, nor does one dwell all the time with the gods. There were occasions when the beautifully directed and modulated chorus seemed to contain a non-Sophoclean line: 'The mind boggles...' flitted in and out sometimes; and I remember

Oedipus once in Melbourne laboriously moving into the wings and back again, when chorus work permitted his absence, so he could obtain the latest test cricket score. Cricket is Ron's other passion. He was once a player. Told me once he loved the sound of the applause.

Best of all, I remember receiving a letter from a fan in country Western Australia who said she had listened to me over the years on Radio and she wanted to let me know she would be travelling many, many miles to see this *King Oedipus* so she could finally put a face to the voice she knew and loved.

So the costumes, the masks, the boots were finally packed away. The great beings disappeared into a wardrobe skip. I just hope someone has had the sense to keep them.

In June 1996 I visited The Wharf for various matters, including planning my husband Eric's 70th birthday celebration. I met Alan Edwards, and complimented him on his performance in *Galileo* at the Drama Theatre. Talk turned to Guthrie and how in awe of him Alan was. They had met during the season of *King Oedipus.* Guthrie asked Alan had he seen it. Alan said yes and was asked what he'd thought. He wondered if he could lie to 'God' but decided for the truth. 'Sir Tyrone, I'm afraid I didn't like it.' A pause. 'But did you dream about it?' 'Well, yes. I went home and had nightmares.' 'Ah!' said Guthrie, touching him lightly on the arm before turning aside.

FIFTEEN

Being alive means that one faces death – if not one's own then the near ones. Surrounded by all those women when I was a child and growing up meant that there were many painful farewells. At times I felt like Blanche Dubois in *A Streetcar Named Desire*: 'that endless procession of deaths'. I remember some of the dyings vividly – the funerals less so. They eventually blended into one, all taking place in the inevitable and inadequate funeral chapel, the service conducted by someone unknown who didn't himself know the one over whom he was mouthing platitudes. While not lacking in spirituality, no one in the family seemed to have been a regular churchgoer, which does bring disadvantages at the tag end. Or used to, before funerals became less stilted.

I do like funeral stories though. My favourite, not even topped by writer Geoffrey Atherden's bizarre funeral episode of *Mother and Son*, in which Maggie Beare accidentally tips oranges into an open grave, is Dorothy Parker's experience when she and two friends entered the dreaded funeral chapel some time ahead of other mourners. Their desire – it was a close friend who had died – was to gather thoughts and themselves, in peace, and thus aim to be in some sort of control with the advent of others. In her fraught and absent-minded state Mrs Parker managed to activate the machinery that sends the coffin gliding to the lower reaches. Suddenly, an empty chapel! No dearly departed, no coffin heaped with flowers. With no other course possible, they quietly crept away, and history doesn't relate how the situation was retrieved. When I'm depressed I cheer myself up with that story.

The funerals, then, are best forgotten, but the many deaths are not so lightly dismissed. One after the other – they deserve some chronicling.

Auntie Bertha, for instance. I remember taking the tram to Kensington and going into that house, where, mind hurtling backwards, a sudden memory of going there on the hottest, windiest day in the world, dragging myself up the path onto the shrouded front verandah, ringing the doorbell and being met by a nearly naked Bertha – the pink milanese singlet *just* providing respectability – who intoned with fury, 'Like a blast from hell!', before disappearing into the bathroom where she resumed her prone position on the tiled floor, leaving me to my own devices. Bertha always took hot weather as a personal affront from the Almighty and was not amused. Possessed of a red-headed temper, she could be relied upon always for a good laugh, particularly when it was unintended.

Not today, though. I went into her room, where she was propped up in bed like a dying queen, sunken face, eyes staring, voice breathless, whispering one or two words before air needed to be gulped in. 'Hullo.' Head bent close to catch anything. Finally, 'How is your mother?' I reported the latest asthma attack. 'The poor thing,' between struggles. 'She suffers so.' Never a moan about herself, still a skeletal grin struggling through at times. And so gallant she looked, so gallant she was. I said goodbye, knowing that that was that. The heart didn't have much more energy left.

Bertha had been preceded by Auntie Ethel, but that sneaked up. I'd embraced her in hospital after an operation, no anxieties there, just the smiling warmth of the hug. Then the operation turned sour, and suddenly, unexpectedly, off trotted Ethel, grey tailored costume, large velour hat, walking stick and all.

With Beat it was the phone call early one morning from Bay, panic in the voice. 'I think she's gone.' And you don't know which is worse — the sudden, or the protracted, where at least there's some opportunity to adjust.

Those stalwarts of my growing years, irretrievably vanishing, vanishing. Into the funeral chapel again and again. On Father's side, Edie, the churchgoer, was finally released from the chair she was tied into in a nursing home in Bondi, still smiling gently whenever visited, even when blankness had replaced an all-consuming, endearing interest in the minutiae of everyday, dispensed over the teacups. And Birdie, too, after a coronary, losing it and able to communicate only smilingly and foolishly for the remaining years. Watching that disintegration now sends one frantically in the direction of the cryptic crossword or the bridge table, both guaranteed to provide the mental equivalent of a workout at the gym.

Bay and Clare were the survivors, Bay maintaining a wicked mischief till the end, Clare proferring calm acceptance of whatever or wherever life placed her. Actually, it placed her in a Home for Retired Anglican Gentlewomen, where she managed to persuade some other Retired Gentlewoman to do her washing for a very small sum of money each week, and where she obtained complete freedom of the shared bathroom by rising at 5 a.m. The lino on the floors, the evening meal at 5 p.m., the pill before sleep, the 'company', the tiny feuds among everyone else, all taken in her stride as if this last period of life was the most comfortable and enriching of all. She visited among nieces and nephew, was a never-failing delight, and when she was finally dying, patiently, and with a matter-of-fact acceptance of the end (or was it delight at the prospect of being re-united with a fully restored Birdie, always her favourite), I determined that she should die with a glass of champagne in her hand on her 93rd birthday. All arranged, she cheated us by departing with as little fuss as possible on her birthday eve.

Bay's last years were possibly the happiest of her life. A companion (who paid a little rent) shared the house at Kensington, and she and Bay were as delighted with one another as a couple setting forth in early marriage. One's 70s may be a long time to wait, but life for those remaining years was devoted to Bay alone and Bay's needs and joys, possibly for the first time. As I say, a long time to wait. Aside from a battle with typhoid in youth and a haemorrhaging ulcer in her 20s she'd never had a day's sickness, till at 81 she got stomach cancer.

What a hot, hot summer it was in 1961. My second daughter, Jane, was born in the December of 1960, but farewelling Bay took precedence that following January. Drive out to Kensington. Take turns at fanning her as she lay on the bed, front room at last. Brandy, occasionally. I'd just experienced birth and the joyous outcome of the naturally swelling womb. Bay's swelling stomach was an obscenity. Fan, smile, hold a hand. Then one evening, she said to Eileen, the companion of the last years, 'I think I'll go to hospital.' The ambulance arrived, and Bay didn't hang around. A few short hours and she was dead. My sister and I were beneficiaries – just the house. It was all sorted out, went on the market, and was quickly sold.

A major part of my life finally over. Not an unusual story, of course, or was it? The nature of the women involved, their crowded life together, and the fact that they managed all of it without ever seriously falling out perhaps does make it unique. For me it certainly was. I also know that they've never completely left. I'm not one for past lives vis-à-vis oneself, one's more than enough, but the recently past lives of others I do believe in. I have to. They float by constantly.

And what of that death, the vital, the pivotal one? From the time I'd arrived home in 1954, the London adventure finished, my mother seemed to go from one disaster to another.

Prone to allergies, an asthmatic from menopause, with a recurring winter battle with bronchial pneumonia, a digestive and alimentary tract that had virtually packed up. Today her life could have been different. There was not the knowledge, then, of what makes a person ill, what the psychological causes of an illness might be. There was little interest in the mental states of people, unless they presented as barking mad. Mum presented always as an amusing, charming, stoical woman who just had the ill fortune to be cursed with one physical problem after another. Partly true. Also, it needs to be said that some of the medical solutions of the day contributed somewhat. Fix one problem and create the conditions for another. But much could have been prevented if Mum's underlying anxieties had been plumbed. She was a master at concealment. Put simply, she didn't weather gradual decline in my father's fortunes. One of my earliest moments of shocked awareness that things weren't as carefree as I'd believed was coming home from school one day and finding that my money box had been opened with a tin opener. There it was, gaping on my bed where it had been hastily discarded. It was easily and smoothly explained away as the momentary lack of the ready when someone appeared on the doorstep. But as the car was sold, then the house, and we began the slow descent into ever smaller accommodation, it began to dawn that things were not going to improve. Nobody explained, nobody complained. I left school a year early. I knew any money that I might bring in was desperately needed, and simply accepted the fact. I think my philosophical bump was a little more highly developed than my mother's. She suffered –

but oh so quietly. Sometimes, on coming into a room at twilight, no lights on, there would be a barely discernible figure gazing out a window. Switch on the light, the mood would vanish.

My father went from his own business to running a company that was finally declared bankrupt. He proceeded to commercial travelling and finally to doing a course that enabled him of all things to manage one of the migrant hostels that sprang up after the war. He always lived on site, but not with my mother, who opted out of that adventure. So, still like the commercial traveller, he would go to Villawood or Bathurst for five days, returning at the weekends. He adapted to his decline with a deal of grace – and a deal more acceptance than she could muster.

Long after they were both dead, I remember giving a talk – a fund-raiser at The Wharf – and a woman came up and said, 'I've always wanted to speak to you. Your father was the director of the migrant camp I lived in when I first arrived in Australia. I was required to work at the camp and I had a baby, and I don't forget his kindness in making my hours as short as possible. Always precise about insisting I had enough time to feed the baby. Your father was a fine man.' The nicest thing that has ever been said to me at one of those occasions.

Those camps were unbelievable. Refugees arrived from who knows what horrors – 'reffos' they were called, there's always an appropriate name – and then found themselves in a barren camp somewhere in the middle of nowhere, surrounded by barbed wire. The unfathomable workings of the collective government/bureaucratic mind. The ones who got my father *were* lucky.

My mother's illnesses prospered. Much of my time after arriving home from London was spent in nursing. The asthma raged unmercifully most nights through winter, compounded as often as not by that dreaded bronchial pneumonia. The cups of tea were useless, but at least a gesture, and I do remember one or two good laughs as her impatience at my new role of carer exploded into wheezing expletives. We were never short of a laugh.

She also managed to develop some pretty hefty gallstones (operation not advised) so monotony could always be averted by a good gallstone attack. And because an earlier antrum operation (useless) had left her without a sense of taste or smell, death by asphyxiation was equally possible. Many's the occasion I'd rage into her room on coming home to a house full of gas fumes. 'Would you kindly check all the gas taps before retiring? Too much to ask?' Paper lowered. 'Oh, sorry.' Not exactly Maggie Beare, but an occasional glint in the eye, which I subsequently managed to reproduce.

I was well versed in the various manifestations of Mother's lousy physical state. Still, it was a surprise the day I arrived home to find that this tidy housekeeper had retired early after a bridge game without clearing up afternoon tea. A right mess on the traymobile. And what *had* she been doing? Chucking coffee over the walls? Brown stains and splashes, not very efficiently wiped. In the bedroom a ghostly reclining figure, white as death. 'Sorry, love, I've been so sick. I tried to clean up.' Off in the ambulance and a stay in St Luke's Hospital as long as it took for the haemorrhaging ulcer to calm down.

Which is how I came to be caught in the fridge.

Travelling from Penshurst Street, Willoughby, where we lived above the chemist shop, with excellent views into the kitchen of the Italian greengrocers next door – where occasionally the greengrocer would run amok with a knife –, all the way to St Luke's Hospital Potts Point where mother was ensconced in her private room, plus whatever work was happening in my life at that time, left little time for domesticities. But like my mother I can't operate in a messy environment. So this night, early in the week, after the return from St Luke's, I decided to clean the fridge. The model was one of the old Silent Knights, which were produced by Sir Edward Hallstrom from his Naremburn factory. Extremely efficient, and an exciting day it was when it took over from the ice chest. But cleaning it was a major undertaking. All the contents were on the kitchen table, and as the defrosting was taking an interminable time, impatient as always I decided to give it assistance with a sharp knife, working away on either side of the ice-cube trays. My arm went into one of the cavities quite easily, and then refused to come out. No matter what. I pulled and pulled and the more I pulled, the more wedged I became, and very swiftly entered a state of unadulterated panic. My father was at Villawood and not due home for four days, by which time I was sure I would have starved to death, all the food on the table being *just* out of reach. As was the telephone. Then the ludicrousness of the situation struck me, as I stood there, unable to sit down, arm firmly pinned and getting colder by the minute. A ridiculous situation, a tall upright figure, arm extended horizontally, ending inside a fridge. Incapable at that moment of realising that the ice would ultimately melt.

I began to laugh, I began to cry, convinced nobody had the bloody-minded sorts of situations forced on them that I did. Nothing would have persuaded me to shout for help. I really did prefer death to revealing myself in this dilemma. I even pictured a ride in a truck, fridge attached, to some un-welding establishment, the populace pointing and jeering. Eventually, I decided to calm down and think. Which was what finally led me to stretch with might and main across the kitchen table, stretch my fingertips to their limit, and with relief discover that one finger, with concentration, might just curl over the rim of the butter dish. Release became a possibility. Many strenuous efforts, and, at last, success. Grabbing a handful of butter I smeared it all over the frozen forearm and with immense gratitude slid out of the Silent Knight and flopped greasily to the floor. I don't believe butter has been used for precisely this purpose before, but as a commodity it obviously has limitless uses.

I watched my mother becoming frailer. One day she said, 'Do you notice life moving swiftly? It's rushing by.' A momentary chill. She had been thrilled when Eric and I married, and the first months of our marriage, in addition to all that meant to the two of us, also started a dialogue with her which was, and remains, one of the remembered delights of my life. We spoke for quite a time every day on the phone; relaxed, funny, perceptive conversations. There was no friction with Eric, because she was devoid of possessiveness, which is, I suppose, the sure mark of the emotionally secure. Thrilled at the prospect of another grandchild, and for the first time relatively free of illness, it was a halcyon time. One of those times that should be endless.

Then, six months into pregnancy, Dad rang – a Sunday night. 'Your mother has just had a gall attack.' Words I'd heard over and over, and taken in my stride, but this time I knew with clarity that my mother was dying. We drove to Willoughby and I could scarcely bear to enter the bedroom, where she lay, breathing with some difficulty. Her doctor ordered her straight into hospital – this time a ward at Sydney Hospital in Macquarie Street, where she was swiftly transferred into 'recovery'. The pancreas had by now packed up and that was that.

The next day we were all there. I had a cold. 'Don't come too close. I don't want to catch it.' Each stage in the process moving relentlessly towards the inevitable. 'Would you like us to get a minister?' someone asked. 'No,' I shouted, for she herself didn't know she was dying. Why confirm it for her who didn't need to know. And she died, Bastille Day, 1958. Just three months before Anna was born. When I finally allowed myself to be engulfed by grief, after the funeral, I kept thinking, 'How could you, just at this minute? How could you! Talk about upstaging!' She was the one, I suppose, to whom I had most wanted to present that child.

Years later, Anna, whose second name is Winifred, mentioned that the early years of her life were spent in the certain knowledge that sometimes her maternal grandmother was present. Anna never spoke about it at the time but was conscious of this presence. It was a highly comforting presence, and was always associated in her perception with laughter. Well, that would be right.

The others float in and out, round and round. When my mother slides in it's always preceded by 'The Merry Widow' waltz. I can be immersed in something, oblivious to the world, and, for no reason, the tune slips in and I know she's around.

I always loved it that Winnie in *Happy Days* signed off with that melody, but unlike Beckett's Winnie, my Winnie never had to ask 'Tell me, was I ever lovable, I mean, really lovable . . .'

SIXTEEN

In the early days of his directorship of the Sydney Theatre
Company in 1990, Wayne Harrison and I lunched. The talk
ranged over many things, including the difficulties, the odd pit-
falls that always seem to lurk. It was also, hopefully, encouraging.
Then Wayne asked if I would play Winnie in Beckett's *Happy
Days* in his first season. This came as a great surprise, but I
remember accepting with alacrity – possibly because my concerned and cautious remarks to him were not matched by a
similar flow of the same in my direction. But directors know all
actors are mad and seldom pause to count the cost of a venture.
There was to be quite a bit in the playing of Winnie – as much
in the physical as the emotional. Regardless, the joy and challenge
of playing the role took precedence over all other concerns,
despite the fact that Beckett has devised what can only be called
a refined piece of torture for his two players. But then he always

manages to do this. Ask those who have inhabited garbage bins, or appeared as just a mouth. A commando course before essaying him would not go amiss.

The director for the *Happy Days* journey was Simon Phillips and the designer was Mary Moore, who created a splendid and, of course, frightful to inhabit, mound for us. Wonderfully atmospheric, it gave the impression of rising out of a salt pan in the heart of the land. Alan Penney was cast in what must surely be the most thankless role in modern theatre – that of Winnie's husband, Willy.

In Act I of this extraordinary play Winnie is buried to the waist. Act II presents her buried to the neck, and Beckett specifies that only her eyes may move. One is forever grateful for the absence of a third act. Mary Moore, being a kindly soul, thought it would be helpful to contact the great Beckett exponent, Billie Whitelaw, regarding at least one of the technical difficulties. Did Winnie stand or sit in the mound, and if both, in what order? Back came the reply: 'Dear Mary Moore, In the first Act I stood, in the second I sat. Good luck.' As it happened, we'd arrived at the same conclusion. Very difficult, though, very uncomfortable, and producing odd reactions at times.

I remember, during one matinee performance, up to my waist, an enraged voice whipping up from the audience with the words, 'Say something funny!' Frustrated by seeing something the reverse of what he wanted, or was expecting, the interjector was frankly bamboozled. So was I for a minute. It was akin to a bucket of iced water in the face. Beckett would have been delighted.

Happy Days rehearsed in Sydney for a week or so and then transferred to Adelaide, where it was scheduled to open. As ever, I found the rehearsal period perilously short – four weeks for a massive and intricate role –, and was fond of remarking through gritted teeth that Beckett himself always insisted on six. In preparation, during the return Melbourne run of *The Importance of Being Earnest* earlier that year, Kirrily Nolan had come to stay with me, and we went over and over the play till madness threatened. I am not one who enjoys learning a role before rehearsals commence, and seldom do, but this was unique. Even with that belt of time with my very generous friend, it was still a nightmare. I often shout at the lines, 'Why are you putting up such a fight? Slot in there will you! You'll slide in ultimately, for God's sake do it sooner rather than later.' Ah, the passage of the years. Once, no study was made at all; the lines behaved themselves and were submissive. These days I sometimes *have* to learn. I hate it!

But I don't learn comedy before we begin. Ever!

We rehearsed and Simon was both inspirational and patient – and tender. We couldn't rehearse for eight hours every day, as *Happy Days* is virtually a one-woman piece. In the event, arriving at the production week, it was apparent I was in a little strife. Each note session, Simon would write notes on fresh scripts as, hopefully, helpful *aides-memoire*, but his final suggestion of a speaker in the mound for prompts – for the first preview at least – was sufficient to galvanise me into action. Rachel Landers, who as a Beckett enthusiast was assisting on the production, came back to my hotel, and by 2 or 3 a.m. the lines seemed safe. I don't recall much of the following day, but the first preview audience received a word perfect performance, and I am eternally grateful to Rachel for a night in a hotel which doesn't rank with my more pleasurable.

By opening night we were away. The opening and two-week run in Adelaide rounded everything, and by the time we got to Sydney we were fairly humming along, if that is the correct phrase to describe a Beckett journey.

Dot, dot, dot. Or dot, dot, or pause or long pause or maximum pause – a text peppered with these directions and signposts leaves no possibility of escape from their strictures. But who would want it? The text becomes a music score, and if the pauses and directions are faithfully adhered to will always have a base line that, *when* finally learned, becomes a watertight protection against memory lapse – in much the same way that Shakespeare cushions. But of course the iambic pentameter and the accessible images made *learning* Shakespeare simple by comparison with Beckett. The latter's iron prose at times seems devoid of meaning, even purpose. Until you stop analysing and just receive.

I should think Beckett's perfect audience member would have been the Aboriginal elder who travelled quite a distance to see the play when we took it to Alice Springs. Someone asked him at interval what he thought. Interval was the moment, particularly in Sydney, where roughly 10 per cent of the audience fled – except on the Wednesday matinees, and I like to think that that's not just because the mostly older women who make up these audiences lack the necessary nimbleness to extricate themselves. Perhaps they're more open. As was the elder, who said, 'I'm looking forward to the second act for I think it will explain the first.' At the end, he was very moved and his only comment was, 'It is very sad, it is very sad.' The play was simply *received*.

An ability to approach Beckett without intellectual baggage brings its own rewards. Billie Whitelaw, when doing the rounds of the universities and the societies of this and that in Sydney, firmly stated that she was not an intellectual and at times didn't know what they were all talking about. But she knew precisely what was what when Beckett said to her, 'Billie, there are only two dots there, you gave me three.' Interpretation is the first job of the actor. And occasionally it's an advantage not to think too much.

Being a committed traveller, touring with a production never bothers me, beyond missing those who have been left behind – this only ever assuaged by the odd visit. I'm never bothered, because touring, as with travel, brings its very special moments. One of the *most* special came during the *Happy Days* tour in Alice Springs. The man who acted as our dresser for most of the performances was responsible for much of what happened in performance in the town, and it was good to have someone added to the company who was so *au fait* with theatre. In addition to his theatrical attributes, he proffered a sister who owned a large property just outside the town. He arranged to take all connected with the production for a picnic. This was the largest property close to the town and it was a reasonably short drive to our destination. A walk with picnic baskets and rugs and lights and we found ourselves on the bank of a wide but, just then, completely dry river. We settled ourselves, looking onto smoothly white river stones below and, opposite, to the sheer cliff face that soared above us. Great river gums lined the banks, and as the evening descended shapes became etched; and the silence was another participant at the feast whenever we momentarily shut up to pay attention. Then, one of those moments you pray for. Opposite, high up, while there was still sufficient light, a great kangaroo, a euro, appeared, alone and massive. This statue gazed down at us for a long time and our talk was reduced to whispers between the sips of wine and the munching. He finally tired of watching and before night completely enveloped, turned slowly and majestically and hopped off. If I think of Alice Springs now it seems encapsulated in that night which journeyed on through its delectable food, its talk, its sudden hushes and, finally, to the moment when we started our trek back along the river bed. Then, out of an immense silence, every giant tree burst into a cacophony of noise and light as its colony of great white cockatoos took to the air as we passed beneath – a parade of epiphanies spreading high above and before us. It is at these moments that one's own size is revealed for what it is – small, in the scheme of things.

A season of a play in Perth in 1990 provided the opportunity for our introduction to the Kimberley. After a few relaxing days in Broome, we set out along the main road to Fitzroy Crossing, then Halls Creek and finally Kununurra.

Miles and miles of unchanging scenery on a tarred road that, at times, stretched straight from the horizon behind to the horizon ahead.

We were armed with an introduction from Marion von Adlerstein to Susan and David Bradley of Carlton Hill, near Kununurra. We hoped to meet over lunch, but in typical big country hospitality we were invited to stay. There in the midst of the arid dust was an oasis with green, green grass, trees, a house, a guest wing across the lawn, a peaceful billabong. Here we spent about four days, resting, talking, eating, drinking, joining the young jackeroos for smoko, meeting Susan's Aboriginal women friends who travelled in by ute. We were warned not to bank on their arrival, time being a completely different, much less binding concept for them. Thankfully, they did turn up and we had a great smoko. I spoke to Daisy Jandun, whose daughter had been taken away from her. She was about my age and she had finally met her daughter, for the first time since infancy, the year before. The daughter had been brought up in a Catholic mission, eventually became a nun, and ended up in New Guinea. At their meeting she told her mother she prayed every day of her life for her mother's well-being, and that one day she would find her; that one day they would meet. And they did. And, yes, that was wonderful, but scarcely recompense for a lifetime apart. You sit next to someone like that, drinking the scalding, strong tea, and wonder about things.

One thing you don't wonder about, you know with a certainty as steady as a candle flame in a vault, is that the Kimberley can change your life. Look at rock art going back into prehistory. Look at Wandjina figures, those heads white and staring, the ancestors, the creators, that carry all secrets. Look at the elegance of the even earlier Bradshaw paintings (known as Guyon Guyon), named for the first white man to bring them to the world's attention, with their headdresses and adornments, and above all just let the mysteries of the desert country seep through your skin. In the words of Albert Barunga:

> Wandjina, he said. You must believe Wandjina. If you won't believe Wandjina, you won't live. This is because Wandjina gave us that Law to follow. And then he says, I give you this Land, and you must keep your Tribal Land. You can't touch somebody's land because it is your body, and your body is right here, and the Aborigines believe his body is his own Tribal Land.

Soft voices, lots of laughs, many photos, myself called by them 'flour bag head'. Appropriate, if a little unkind. More talk and exchange of ideas and anecdotes and tall tales and true tales that in the telling defy credibility, but up there, in context, are completely believable. The story of the Aboriginal woman, a very important person, who died. Susan went to pay her respects and convey her own sadness, but they said, 'Don't be upset, Susan, she be *jabiru* now.' And Susan went back to Carlton Hill, did the washing up and looked out the kitchen window as a great jabiru flew down to the dam. Susan accepted that that was the departed one and felt comforted. And so does one also accept these things, sitting there under the boab tree.

Over one day and night we were taken on a fishing trip, camping on the banks of the great Ord. The young Bradley boys came with us. Our guide manoeuvred his aluminium craft to 'guaranteed' fishing spots and we fished and fished, occasionally catching sight of the great saltwater crocodiles. Whenever our group stepped onto a mud bank midstream for better access to the fish, I became slightly hysterical. There, to me, recklessness never bore fruit anyway, and, much to everyone's annoyance, the only fish caught was mine – a barramundi. We carried it back to the camp site and had the most delectable sashimi I've ever tasted. Sleep that night was a little broken as I remained unconvinced one or other of those great crocodiles could not quite easily climb up the high bank to our spot. I was comforted that the two boys were between me and the river.

From Kununurra we planned to return along the Gibb River Road, finishing up in Derby. This was before it became a popular adventure, and in one sense we pioneered. In Broome and in Kununurra, a few said, 'Don't risk it!', others inferred it would be a pushover – not least Susan. We trusted her. Well, it was something in between and still ranks as our most rewarding journey. As we set out I suggested a two-way radio might be helpful. Eric's flippant reply, 'Who'd be listening?', didn't fill me with confidence, but the knowledge that he can usually fix everything and knows much, did. We'd arranged accommodation along the way at big station properties, and the essentials did boil down to enough water, a bag of oranges, that day's lunch, and – provided the people we were heading for knew of our impending arrival – the decision to just stay put should there be a mechanical breakdown. This last essential fortunately never had to be put to the test!

We stayed at one place where cattle raising was being supplemented by about twenty adventurous guests. They were out being adventurous when we arrived, but we were informed that we would join everybody for dinner, which, surprisingly, would be formal. We were told it would be a 'silver service' dinner, drinks beforehand. I was a little anxious about the correct attire for this and added a drift of chiffon to the basic pants and shirt.

Everybody tumbled out of four-wheel-drives, noisy, dirty, full of bonhomie, and we gritted teeth a little at the prospect ahead, our great craving in the wilderness being for relative solitude. The noisy ones showered and turned into varying degrees of formality, drifted in for drinks, and we all sat down at a large U-shaped table complete with linen, candelabra – and, yes, the silver. One of the army of backpackers we met over the next two weeks had dropped anchor here for awhile, and, being French, was assigned the task of drink waiter, for which he was ill-equipped. Here we all were in the middle of a desert giving the impression of being at a suburban dinner party. Bizarre, but our host – cattleman, adventure leader, marketer – was determined to present something not to be repeated elsewhere. It wasn't. We ended up having fun despite our reclusive attitudes and trust he prospers, for since the big takeovers in the north and west, and the need to focus on the export of live beef to Asia – coupled with the disappearance of the abattoirs at Wyndham – , 'small' cattle people have little chance of survival through just practising their traditional roles. They have been forced to learn the hardest possible way about change. And the need for diversity.

We went on another Kimberley expedition some five years later, taking our friends Sue and John Rogers with us. This time we went the reverse way, which couldn't have been the reason for some slight hint of panic – despair? – within our beloved region, surely. It was still a wonderful journey, but now Carlton Hill was in other hands and the air was slick, efficient, hard edged, and no time for meandering smokos. The allotted time only for those young men we watched jumping in among flashing hooves and panicked beasts. Susan and David were still there, arriving a day after we did. The talk continued to be wonderful and outrageous and gossipy and John and Eric walked miles with David over land, every part of which he knew and loved. He and Susan are now in Darwin. Carlton Hill will become more profitable. We are all of us caught up in leaner, meaner times. Things get lost in the process.

Susan was responsible for a performance that celebrated the women of the Kimberley. This was filmed and was shown on the ABC. It was a wonderful night, a stage set up under the stars, a large audience, and entertainment and stories from all the women who have contributed their talent and energy to the advancement of this very special place. The stories were funny, moving and inspirational. We saw the Aboriginal women, some of whom we'd met, painting their bodies and performing their ancient ritual dances. The whole celebration was opened by the spectacular arrival, in full splendour, of one Dame Edna Everage, who appeared on the scene, the almost royal personage she is, waving gladioli from a jeep, and bursting onto the stage like cascading fireworks. As Susan said in her introduction, it was certainly the first time that Dame Edna had entered a stage down a cattle ramp. Dame Edna's Manager is a great friend of the Bradleys and had managed to persuade her to grace the occasion with her presence. One becomes aware at times like this of the generosity, the quite remarkable generosity, not only of Dame Edna, but also her Manager, Mr Humphries.

In October 1996 I was guest of honour at the welcome dinner for the ABC Rural Woman of the Year finalists. They flew in from all over Australia, exceptional women who have achieved great things through initiative and hard work and cleverness. Often, great things for the country at the same time. An utterly unselfconscious group of women, but very confident in their own abilities and contributions. We had a wonderful time together, and I was invited to the north, south, east and west of the land. Their connection with me through *Mother and Son* was real and important and very satisfying. One woman from the Kimberley recognised my Broome pearl, so we talked of Bill Reed from Linney's who sold it to me and who is another great Australian. Suddenly, I was hungry for Broome and that country filled with the larger than life.

At the end of the evening, a young woman from Western Australia said she would like to sing, unaccompanied, a song she had written. It was a ballad about a pioneer woman writing 'home' to her mother. A lonely woman. So often these moments are simply embarrassing. This time, this lawyer, actor, farmer, delivered herself of something that had the hairs rising on the back of the neck. It's a big country.

Seventeen

Shown a script all those years ago, is there just the faintest of possibilities I may have declined had the consequences of playing Maggie Beare been pointed out? Hesitated, at least? No such glimpse into the future being vouchsafed, the first response was a rush of gratitude that here, at last, was a situation comedy quite out of the ordinary and possessed of a bleak subtext that was neon lit. Rare, and utterly, painfully, believable. Gorgeous, it was. Delectable.

The man who proffered this gem was an architect, Geoffrey Atherden, who wrote a bit. The then producer was to be John Eastway. John duly hawked the treasure round all the commercial networks. Not a modicum of interest. Then it was shown to the ABC and without hesitation was snapped up. John O'Grady – son of 'Nino Culotta' – was the executive producer and script editor, and Geoffrey Portmann was director. A pilot was made, which didn't quite work, and then by some stroke of brilliance or fate one Garry McDonald was ushered into the role of Arthur, Maggie's son, and that was that; the special elusive quality that makes two disparate people metamorphose into a double act. No one can ever predict it and no one can analyse it, but in this most unlikely pairing something clicked. Garry and I developed an on-air relationship that could be continuing to this day if Geoffrey Atherden had not called it quits.

Garry and I understand one another and fitted into those two adversaries as if we'd been waiting for the opportunity forever. Two people, each with a well-developed killer instinct in comedy, happy to play ping pong and almost level the score for forty-two episodes. Simply, we trust one another. Without that, comedy won't work. At the same time we are incredibly different – as people and in the *way* we work. I am his greatest fan and, if honest, still a little desolate that the ball is over. Maggie's drab, sensible wardrobe is more prized by me than Cinderella's finery for *her* ball. Well, midnight always strikes.

How did we arrive at Maggie's look? A few lengthy trawls through the shabbier end of the ABC wardrobe yielded the odd cardigan and skirt – suitably plain, and one very nice cotton blouse with embroidery. A shopping expedition provided one or two more blouses and there were one or two plain and simple dresses. We needed a coat, and nothing the ABC wardrobe came up with seemed right. Then I remembered a houndstooth check A-line coat I'd bought in London in 1974. In 1982 it was correctly out of fashion – even timeless. The brown velvet hat, Maggie's signature, was director Geoff

Portmann's inspiration and became the most jealously guarded item of the wardrobe — re-blocked, squashed seemingly to extinction but forever capable of resurrection. The shoes were my inspiration — two sizes too big, which automatically ages by upwards of twenty years if necessary. And a long, maroon wool skirt for formal occasions (formal usually only in Maggie's eyes), topped with a splendid ruby coloured silk blouse from the Burlington Arcade in London. Had I billed the ABC it would have fractured their wardrobe budget.

With Henri Szeps as favoured son and Judy Morris as favoured son's obnoxious wife, our family from hell was complete. But because Arthur and Maggie, despite the manipulative manoeuvring on the one hand and the distracted coping on the other, are actually joined by a very golden thread of mutual love, need and protection — the last quality exclusively Arthur's — the series works at a compassionate level, which is why it makes such a strong connection with vast numbers here and abroad. Maggie's character is beautifully realised in the writing — from the playful to the senile. Also, of course, the scripts are extremely funny.

The responses to *Mother and Son* are varied, to say the least. The overwhelming majority simply love it in a very special way. This majority comprises all ages, genders, races. *Mother and Son*'s latest sighting is in Harare, Zimbabwe, where by a happy coincidence *Spider and Rose* has also been showing. I was big in Harare for a moment or two.

It's the extreme reactions that are the most fascinating. In a foyer, recently, making polite conversation to a theatre group who were eating sandwiches and quaffing champagne after a performance of *A Little Night Music* (Casts are always requested to mingle on these occasions; am I unreasonable in thinking the performance should be sufficient?), I am confronted by a grey suit with thin maroon stripe. Occupied by a man of late middle age. Respectable. He is nearly bursting out of his suit he is so agitated. His grey hair, disciplined within an inch of its life, is getting dangerously close to needing a shampoo. He tells me there is one role I have played he just hates. I smile and batten down the hatches. I am attacked for Maggie's conduct. Her vileness. Do I know what she is doing to Arthur? Am I aware of Arthur's pain? 'How would you feel if you were Arthur?' When he gets to 'I know it is meant to be a send-up', I swiftly and silkily interrupt the flow to assure him it is anything but. The briefest of pauses, then, somewhat grudgingly, 'I suppose it is in some ways a tribute to your abilities.' I gravely thank him.

'My mother,' he thunders – and I am now that person – , 'wanted me to live with her when she got older. She never let up, never! I know what it's like to be Arthur.' A brief pause while I throw down some wine. Then, 'I couldn't watch it. I couldn't watch it. Ever!'

I find that a little hard to believe. The sipping and nibbling goes on around us. I've tuned out, but snap to attention when we get to the moment, 'My mother is dead now, God rest her soul,' shooting a swift glance heavenwards. I begin to feel the diatribe may have been worth it. He stands there, empty of air, his gaze a little softer now – saddened as we share a moment in memory of Mother. Raise our glasses.

I am buoyed up remembering the fund-raiser luncheon at which a woman in charge of a nursing home specialising in patients with Alzheimer's came up to thank me for playing the role. Which nicely counterpoints the woman who stood up at a forum and demanded to know how I'd feel if I ever developed Alzheimer's. The only answer to that: 'It won't be my problem, will it?'

Letters have arrived from bureaucrats within the Health System who fear it is making too light or being too flippant about the terrible problem. Others purse lips and say it is demeaning to the elderly. This one I can never work out, with Maggie winning every battle. Primary school children adore her. They recognise the naughty child in her and anyway there's something of Maggie in their grandmothers, whom they love without any problems or emotional hangups, just very simply. And there are the genuine ones who cannot watch, seeing themselves in the firing line.

The favourite moment, though. A few years ago at yet another fund-raising occasion. Outdoors, somewhere in Sydney. There was a marquee. Just as I was leaving, a woman stepped up, smiling. 'My children have insisted that I thank you for saving a family.' She herself was caring for her mother. 'Every time we feel like murdering her we slap on a video of *Mother and Son*, and we laugh so much, I change my mind.'

At this point it is as well to note that the word Alzheimer's has never been mentioned in *Mother and Son*. The perception exists *outside* – though I would agree that Maggie is not 'normal', whatever that is. My own view? A degree of dementia in remission. But that's just my view.

So much a part of all our lives for ten years that withdrawal symptoms are inevitable. Henri's performance as the upwardly mobile, philandering, sentimental Robert – who can forget his distraught cries when he thought Maggie was dead and the swift recovery when he realised she wasn't? – could not have been bettered; and Judy's small role, managing to eat every scene she entered. We had a ball. Not quite in the way some anticipate, however. Well, lots of laughs at the first reading around the table, but from then on heads down. Geoff Atherden writes such intricate dialogue and such long scenes that there's precious little time for play, even if one were in the mood.

How did we get through an episode without laughing? I'll tell you how. The slightest error on taping night and back to the beginning of the scene. And again and again if necessary. Quite enough to stifle any incipient laugh. Notwithstanding, things did go marvellously wrong at times and all control evaporated. My favourite was the time Garry and I were going hammer and tongs – backwards and forwards – when he suddenly stopped and threw at me, in an aggrieved fashion, 'That was *my* line!' 'Well, why didn't you say it?' I snapped. We and the studio audience took a while to become serious again.

In the early days, we could still be in the studio at midnight, and as Garry and I mostly arrived at 11 a.m., this made for an exhausting session. Fortunately, some of Saturday's workload was later incorporated into Friday, and we had a more civilised life in the last series. We had a perfectionist in the person of director Geoff Portmann, and I won't ever complain about that, beyond pointing out that one's best work seldom occurred at midnight. Desperation lurks around the witching hour.

To tape one series – seven episodes – of *Mother and Son* took us about three months. The first two or three weeks were devoted to filming the exteriors. The Beare household exterior was at Five Dock. Exits and entrances and walks down the street and digging up Leo's ashes and apocalyptic storms all took place there. The rest of Sydney and sometimes much further afield would also be taken care of in those first weeks. Arthur's ancient Morris minor would arrive (there was a substitute when model number one finally gave up the ghost). The famous funeral scene was shot in the Northern Suburbs cemetery, and there were many visits to Centennial Park. There are two or three ducks I feel I know intimately. A week off before the serious business began and then we would make three episodes, have a week free, two more episodes, a further week off, and then the last two.

I have to confess that one moment stands out head and shoulders above all others from the filming sequences – this moment unscripted by Geoff Atherden. Arthur had fallen in the bay and was returning, dripping wet, to the house along the concrete path. It is never just one take, of course. Damp footpath had to be dried between takes. With little money to spare for extravagant equipment, the footpath was dried laboriously before each take with a hand-held hair dryer. In one of my more caustic moments between takes, waiting for the interminable process to finish, I made the withering observation to Henri – also in the scene – , 'Budget cuts!' Henry looked astounded. 'Bunch of *what* did you say?'

Mother and Son succeeded as much as anything because of the teamwork. The first reading of an episode would reveal what cuts needed to be made. These were dealt with in a huddle between John O'Grady and Geoff Atherden, and then work commenced. I trusted Geoff Portmann's judgment completely, and if he saw an approach to a moment differently from me I mostly went along with it. He is a comedy buff, and understanding and loving comedy are the main requirements for someone in that role. As well, wardrobe, make-up and crew remained virtually unchanged throughout the series, and our mutual aim for the best no matter what – even approaching midnight – played a tremendous part in the final result: the high and continuing popularity of the series both here and worldwide.

The best television demands a fine production team, a touch of magic between the leading players, and first-rate playing and meshing from everyone else. Lose just one of these components and the finest script in the world will be hard pressed to gain that highly elusive stamp of quality. I count myself lucky to have been part, even if only once, of just such a series.

But . . . one became 'known', a household name. There is no longer freedom to walk anonymously down a street, to go alone into an art gallery, a cinema or a department store.

Where I live, our family home, there is a supportive and cherishing community, and I feel relatively free. Nowhere else. The lifelong habit of observing people surreptitiously, a tool of trade, is no longer possible. Stop at traffic lights, stare straight ahead. Any deviation to right or left and a car load will be waving. And yes, it's delicious, and they're all simply lovely and there is enormous mutual warmth and the loveliest things are said. Real joy is a precious commodity. One is grateful for that. But what there isn't is privacy. Not now, not ever, and that is the one thing that may just have given me pause all those years ago before putting signature to contract. But I don't really think so. As the old Spanish proverb says: ' "Take what you want," said God. "Take what you want. And pay for it." ' And I wanted Maggie.

Eighteen

The Melbourne Theatre Company decided to schedule Oscar Wilde's *The Importance of Being Earnest*. Simon Phillips was to direct. I had never worked for the Melbourne Theatre Company so was surprised and delighted to be asked. Also, thanks to *Mother and Son*, I now might bring a different audience with me. Perish the thought that this is ever uppermost in management's minds – it isn't. Shall we say, it is never a drawback.

So I met Simon Phillips at a coffee shop in The Rocks in Sydney. Would I play Lady Bracknell? I said I thought the rhyme made it inescapable. The long involvement began – a season in Melbourne followed by a tour of country Victoria and over the next few years, with Sydney Theatre Company and State Theatre Company of South Australia involvement, a season in Sydney, a return season in Melbourne, and an interstate tour that took in Adelaide, Brisbane and Perth. And recently I was approached to do it all again!

Of all plays this is the sure fire success. I believe there will always be an audience for this most perfect of comedies. Having said that, it is not the play for schools and drama academies to attempt, which they will persist in doing. It may look like a romp but in reality it is a most controlled, elegant piece of writing, which needs precisely the same in playing. Control and elegance are not strong in the armour of school students and new graduates. Add to this brilliance of writing the fact that Wilde wrote the play in something like three weeks – albeit originally with four acts, one of which he was persuaded was one too many – and one permits him the accolade 'genius'. With Simon directing and with Tony Tripp's inspired design, we had a dazzling production.

Much has been written about Wilde and comedy. When you come to do it, especially with a fine director calling the shots, you quickly realise that not only is it as funny as anything you have ever read, but that also, while perfectly representing the period from which it emanates – with Wilde strongly setting the rules for his characters – its view of humankind with all its foibles, charms, and impossibilities, applies for any age. Hence its greatness. Gwendolen and Cecily can be updated and turned into post-modern proto-types, make them Generation X exemplars – scratch the surface a little, and out will pop Gwendolen and Cecily. The language will be different, the manners poles apart, the motivations will be identical. Women's liberation has failed to eradicate the Miss Prisms in our midst, heavily disguised though they may be. Jacks and Algernons still proliferate around Mayfair even if the accent has undergone a change. And there is still the occasional Canon Chasuble on the loose, avoiding the hot issues of modern Anglicanism and the ordination of women as he avoids the inroads of the rampant Prisms. Lady Bracknell is still hard at work, even in Melbourne. Merriman still occasionally totters in with the tea trolley in Point Piper and Toorak. But when we get to Lane, where is he? Where indeed is brilliant, perspicacious Lane. I suspect Lane died with Wilde.

Act I: LANE: . . . I have often observed that in married households the champagne is rarely of a first-rate brand.

ALGERNON: Good heavens? Is marriage so demoralising as that?

LANE: I believe it *is* a very pleasant state, sir. I have had very little experience of it myself up to the present. I have only been married once. That was in consequence of a misunderstanding between myself and a young person . . . (In that exchange, Lane has one joke, a clincher from Algernon, topped by two, possibly three more, effortlessly. Other writers of comedy usually make do with one 'feed' line, one pay-off. An embarrassment of riches from Wilde.)

And later in that first scene.

ALGERNON: I hope tomorrow will be a fine day, Lane.

LANE: It never is, sir.

ALGERNON: Lane, you're a perfect pessimist.

LANE: I do my best to give satisfaction, sir...

Lane, with that line, has taken on the persona of Wilde himself leaning against the chimney-piece at Oxford.

Simon had a grand cast – first time round it was Geoffrey Rush as Jack, Richard Piper as Algernon, Jane Menelaus as Gwendolen, Helen Buday as Cecily, Monica Maughan as Miss Prism, Bob Hornery as Chasuble and, in a brilliantly effective, not to say highly original double, Frank Thring played the two butlers Merriman and Lane. Tony Tripp's design was based on an Aubrey Beardsley book. The audience entered and saw a stage empty save for an elegant table with a Beardsley book on it, mirrored at the back by a huge closed Beardsley book, its covers held together by a white cord and tassel. The play began with Lane opening part of this huge book, which then became the set, and in the course of the next few minutes the rest of the stage furniture, precious little, was also placed by Lane, ending with the trolley set for tea. He then picked up the book from the table, opened it and slowly exited, immersed. Simple, elegant, and brilliantly effective. The play then began.

I loved these rehearsals, which is not always the case. Often that demon impatience sits on my shoulder. I struggle with the demon, but just can't wait for the audience. Here, it was always so delightful watching the performances evolve with such precise and funny detail. I loved watching Geoffrey and Jane manoeuvre their way through the proposal scene. I couldn't believe how far, but never *too* far, Helen and Frank would go in their second act moment of virtuosity in the tea scene that climaxes the icy exchange between Cecily and Gwendolen. There are just two stage directions for Cecily and one for Merriman. What happened with those directions in the hands of Frank and Helen is one of the funniest things I have ever seen on a stage, possibly adding a minute to the play, but totally within the bounds of reality for both characters. Inspired and blissful. In later emanations of this scene with Gordon Chater and Rachel Szalay it was equally delicious though quite different, with the addition on Gordon's part of a touch of Parkinson's disease.

Every part of this play was wonderful to watch in rehearsal, and Simon was as much in its grip as any of us. By that I mean quite often helpless with laughter. Miss Prism and Canon Chasuble were all hot passion, not to say lust, only just held in control. Gwendolen and Cecily, in their politely icy exchange, were devastingly effective, and the climax of Act II with a muffin fight between Jack and Algernon was outrageous and right. And, it goes without saying, complained about by some.

I had a fine time, too. Simon insisted that Lady Bracknell must, at all times, be the epitome of stern Victorianism — no relaxation permitted whatsoever. The young lovers needed to be in a fairly constant state of alarm — but never downtrodden — so that their extrication from her clutches and dictums happened by skill and charm and an ability to be fast on their feet. The dreaded 'handbag' moment, ruined for all time for other interpretations by the great English actress Dame Edith Evans's impossible and daring colouring of the moment – was a hurdle to be faced. There is a simply wonderful progression in the scene as Lady Bracknell quizzes Jack on his suitability as a candidate for her daughter's hand, eventually making the appalling discovery that Jack was found, as a baby, by a gentleman on his way to Worthing. This gentleman brought him up:

LADY BRACKNELL: Where did the charitable gentleman who had a first-class ticket for this seaside resort find you?

JACK (*gravely*): In a hand-bag.

LADY BRACKNELL: A hand-bag?

JACK (*very seriously*): Yes, Lady Bracknell. I was in a hand-bag – a somewhat large, black leather hand-bag, with handles to it – an ordinary hand-bag in fact.

LADY BRACKNELL: In what locality did this Mr. James, or Thomas, Cardew come across this ordinary hand-bag?

JACK: In the cloak-room at Victoria Station. It was given to him in mistake for his own.

LADY BRACKNELL: The cloak-room at Victoria Station?

JACK: Yes. The Brighton line.

LADY BRACKNELL: The line is immaterial . . .

Lady Bracknell's line 'A hand-bag?', while providing a moment for glorious shock and horror, is actually improved upon, in the comic sense, by Jack's reply, but Dame Edith's extraordinary delivery of the word has meant that every actress subsequently has probably thought, 'What do I do with it?' Having said that, there is a generation of actors now who know little of Evans so the problem solves itself. I was not blessed with ignorance, so simply avoided doing anything at all till the last week of rehearsal. It is ridiculous to have one moment ruined by a legendary delivery fifty years earlier, but it remained a hurdle. All I can say is I have now, too late, discovered the *perfect* approach to the dread word, and for that reason alone it may be worth having another crack at it. Or a recital series perhaps? 'Missed Moments in Literature Revisited.' Lady Bracknell, of course, is one of those roles one could, given possession of all one's marbles, still essay as an octogenarian – a wheelchair could be a most useful prop.

Which brings me to the only mild complaint about the set – minimalist. Looked wonderful, devoid of comfort. I got to sit down through the inquisition of Jack on one of the two drawing room chairs available, and that was that. In Act III, it was stand the whole time from the moment of sweeping into view. It probably looked grand, but it felt like purgatory, Lady Bracknell's beautiful costumes, one at any rate, being constructed out of furnishing fabric I suspect. Cheaper than the silk it so perfectly represented, but weighing a ton! The other costume was a mile of wool of the very heaviest weight. Simon, all compassion, wanted to give me an opportunity to sit – on the only thing available in Act III, which happened to be my shooting stick! For this to work it was necessary for Lady Bracknell to assume her pose while aiming the point of the shooting stick into a hole on the stage the size of a five-cent piece – all without sneaking a look. The reward of being able to sit down for a moment or two made me rehearse this spectacular moment many times, but the average for holing in one was not encouraging so Lady Bracknell stood and delivered . . . and stood some more.

At the end of the first Melbourne season came the Victorian country tour. We set off, Frank and I allotted a driver and a Holden, the drivers being part of the company, with a variety of transport modes for everyone else, argued about, I seem to recall, for much of the tour. One of the transports was driven by Dein Perry. 'We knew' he was a dancer. He moved on to Helen Montagu's production of *42nd Street* and is currently seeing his own show, *Tap Dogs*, tour the world. Life changes dramatically with a good idea.

We played for one or two nights only at most of the towns visited, a first for me. It was a matter of in and out at the different venues, do the play, and present ourselves for the supper – sandwiches, cakes, savouries in copious quantities, wines, beer, cups of tea, take your pick – all provided by the various ladies of the various organisations who were supporting us on our way. Most of these feasts from the 1950s took place in the foyers, but we were occasionally entertained in someone's house, and this was always a treat. You fleetingly meet charming people, some you would love to keep in touch with, but this never happens and fleeting means just that.

There were sometimes unexpected hazards along the way,

not usually met in the capitals. I seem to remember one night fighting, or trying to ignore, a swarm of crickets that bombarded us most of the evening. Monica Maughan had a moment of high alarm when she thought the audience was pelting her with boiled lollies. The crickets by then were ending it all in her straw hat. And vividly, another night when all the lights went out in the middle of one of my speeches. Calculating that not being able to see need not also cause temporary deafness in an audience, I just kept talking and, being a long speech, by the time it was over we were once more bathed in light. It might have been more sensible to suspend the action, maintain the gesture and pick up when lit as if the action of the play, by divine intervention, had simply frozen for a moment. Or maybe the audience would think they'd all gone mad and the lights hadn't failed at all. Mad audience disease. A lovely thought!

Touring was not a special joy for Frank, and the Thring groan was much in evidence. One town on our schedule was Nhill – a bit to the west in Victoria. Way out in Frank's view. He threatened to sell one of his pictures so he could buy the house and thus bypass Nhill – an offer not taken up by management. When he knew we would be staying at the Zero Inn his misery was total. 'Zero Inn in Nhill,' he groaned. 'And I suppose that's located in Fuck All Street.'

To redress the balance a little on the town's side, I have to say that after our performance we were entertained in the most delightful house by friends of Monica. The high spot of our journey, so it must be said that all was not ill in Nhill.

Perhaps it's unfortunate that Frank's last work was this tour, which, at the very least, taxed him. In all senses a giant, he was passionate about film and theatre. His own production of Wilde's *Salome*, in which he played Herod, had such an impact in Melbourne at the time that he was encouraged to take it on to London. Here his major talent was recognised and extraordinary role succeeded extraordinary role – mostly very evil indeed. Here was Frank epitomising the gross and evil in *Salome, King of Kings, Ben Hur, El Cid.* Frank always looming over one, with his strange, sonorous, sibilant voice. Black eminence. Did Frank garb himself in black to match that core of tragedy within him? I often thought so. Or was he just brilliantly theatrical? Always a lump of gold on his chest somewhere. Flamboyant. Somehow the cask of Ben Ean moselle that accompanied him everywhere didn't quite fit.

His career fell away a little towards the end, but was nicely rounded, starting and finishing as it did with Oscar.

Undoubtedly the most unforgettable night of the season in Melbourne occurred well into the run when Geoffrey Rush was ill and it was apparent he would not be able to appear. Simon has a facility for knowing every line of any play he directs, and this was put to the test when he stepped into the shoes of Jack with no warning. He moved through every word of that intricate role without a pause and, as far as I can remember, no substitution of dialogue. As he would, by then, have moved on to other work, this mental ability to pick up the one before quite effortlessly is something that doesn't happen too often. His grateful cast was, as they say, gob smacked at the control and elegance.

Control, elegance and a perfect sense of comic timing. Also admirable qualities in a cat. Philomena Freya arrived by chance. One dog, Bambi, plus one cat, Joseph, saw us through the childhood and adolescence of Anna, Jane and Jonathan, but the cats following Joseph, who died in advanced old age, hadn't lasted long due to their insatiable desires to beat the cars on the increasingly busy front road. I said 'Enough is enough', particularly as I seemed to be the one who did the bulk of the grieving. Or did I? They *do* all seem to have melded into one cat now in my memory of them.

Bambi was not the ideal name for our beloved dog. Named in puppyhood when she seemed all doe-eyed grace, she developed, in middle years, into comfortably ample pro-portions and resembled some of those stout and bejewelled European ladies with spindly, unreliable legs, who still totter about the eastern suburbs of Sydney. My eyes always mist over when I glimpse them these days, Bambi inevitably springing to mind.

When I came home from the theatre one night, Bambi went out for her midnight stroll and expired on the road, her heart finally giving out. She was well into her 90s in human terms, and I was too distraught for any replacement. The down-side of being the object of the affections of a one person dog.

So, if one excludes the possums, ours was an animal-free house for a number of years until I did a television promotion for pet care. I was offering wise words on the subject and introducing my own cat in the process of describing responsible cat care and ownership. My high-flown integrity insisted that if I said I had a cat I must have a cat, so Philomena Freya became part of the deal and was duly delivered, the idea being that, come the shoot, she and I would be sufficiently *au fait* with one another for the cameras to roll.

A fantasy. Animals in commercials are little – or big – stars who, by dint of much training and handling, more or less know what is required of them. And I emphasise 'more or less'. Philomena was rejected on all counts, and I confess to the deception that the big stripy animal filmed was not actually mine.

Philomena arrived in her carrying cage with all the necessary items for her survival and comfort. Toys, brush, scratching post (never used), kitty litter tray plus litter, a diet sheet and a most impressive pedigree. A Burmese Blue. To one who had been used to receiving the last to be placed of some neighbourly litter of kittens this all seemed grave responsibility. Hives erupted – on me, not her. She, on the other hand, was all cool containment, permitting a degree of handling and stroking before retiring to a corner, behind a table. It took about ten days and many phone calls to the breeder before I finally relaxed – Philomena Freya would keep disappearing. She had a heart-stopping ability to just vanish in the dining room. Seen to enter this average-sized space, but not emerge. There would be no sign of her. Search the sideboard, open drawers, look under the small table, look under the dining table – again and again — feel all the chairs, lift the lid of the wood box (always assuming she had herself first managed this not easy task for a cat), look up the chimney. Nowhere. Much later she would stroll out, smiling slightly. She was fussy with food until we, poor fools, grasped her requirements. She avoided all designated toys, and made her own, and swiftly created a lifestyle and regime for herself befitting her royal status.

Her saving grace is her comic ability. Impeccable timing, swift repartee, and a killer instinct second to none. And like all good comics never afraid of making a fool of herself.

She opens cupboard doors with ease, makes short work of the cast-iron doorstop placed in front of the linen cupboard doors — a vain attempt on my part to thwart her entry to a spot she regards as her inner sanctum. I am still bemused as to how she accomplishes it — and closes the door behind her.

Part of each day I find I'm wearing her. Velcroed to my right ear. The telephone, her great rival, becomes our daily battle ground until I throw her out of the study.

When I'm away she accepts Eric, her substitute attendant, with grace, but my return restores the status quo. The I now realise never-to-be-escaped status quo. I must have been mad. I shall resist any endorsement of horses, ferrets . . .

Philomena was named after my agent for the simple reason that neither gives me any peace. But a great deal of pleasure.

NINETEEN

In 1980 Rex Cramphorn gathered around him a number of Sydney actors for the purpose of studying two Shakespearean texts over six months. At the end of this period we were to present the results of our time together in one or two performances of the texts we had been studying, which would be viewed strictly as work in progress. This group consisted of John Gaden, Ron Haddrick, Arthur Dignam, Jennifer Hagan, Robert Menzies, Drew Forsythe, John Howard, Kerry Walker and me. Jim Waites, now drama critic at the *Sydney Morning Herald*, handled research for us. Rex had obtained a government grant for this work. We were a democracy and all decisions were to be arrived at after consultation among all. We were, in a very real sense, bound together and required, by no charter but a loose understanding, to devote all our time to this six months – no distractions. We were in retreat in the charming, if chilly, Darlington Public

School building, which has been preserved in the grounds of Sydney University. A small, stone, gabled building, with the glass houses of the Agricultural Science Department handy and the swimming pool, for the use of graduates, undergraduates and staff, nearby.

This was an unusual way to work at that time in Australia, though not overseas. It allowed Rex's extraordinary magic to work: something in his watching made the plants grow. We attended five days a week, from 10 until 5, and each was paid a salary of scrupulous equality.

So there we were in our own co-ed convent with Rex as our Mother Superior. We read the Sonnets and absorbed their fresh, youthful passion and idealism; we debated which plays we would concentrate on; we finally settled on *Measure for Measure*, that most elegantly complex play on good and evil, true morality and spurious morality. Our other choice was *The Two Gentlemen of Verona*, the springtime play, one that seems to rise up from the sonnets – or the earliest ones at any rate – like a fitting sequel. A delectable play, performed all too seldom. Our aim was to get as close as possible to the essence of Shakespeare. We would cross gender and sometimes share roles; for instance John Gaden and I shared Sylvia in Two Gentlemen. (In the event, come public performances, I never got near Sylvia, John becoming so possessive of her.) We were aiming for the essence in all characters, their male/female amalgams rather than their male/female particularity, exploring the point of connection between the sexes when all the barriers are removed. Our aim was not to play them *as* men or

Anton Chekhov's The Seagull, *with John Bell, 1974*

ABC drama series Ben Hall, *with Tom Farley, 1975*

Rex Cramphorn's A Shakespeare Company, with Shorty, 1980

Miss Ciss in John O'Donohue's A Happy and Holy Occasion, *with Sean Fonti, 1982*

The Crummles family, Nicholas Nickleby, *1983.*
Clockwise, from top left: Peter Phelps, Graham Harvey,
Ruth, Ron Haddrick and Amanda Muggleton

Maggie Beare

*Maggie with her sons, Robert (Henri Szeps) and
Arthur (Garry McDonald)*

Emma in Ray Lawler's The Doll Trilogy, *1985*

Irene in David Williamson's Emerald City, *1987*

Peter Schaffer's Lettice and Lovage, *1989*

Lady Bracknell in Oscar Wilde's The Importance
of Being Earnest, *1988*

Group shot celebrating the tenth anniversary of the
Sydney Theatre Company, 1988. Clockwise, from top centre:
Ruth, Ron Haddrick, Peter Carroll, Garry McDonald, Colin Friels,
Geraldine Turner, Robyn Nevin, Richard Wherrett, Jacki Weaver,
Judy Davis, Nancy Hayes, Drew Forsythe and John Bell

women, nor androgynous, simple 'straight' in the true meaning of the word. In the process, discoveries would be made.

First test of our brother/sisterhood, all for one, one for all ethos came quite early in our foregatherings. Sorrento in Italy was holding a film festival honouring Australia, and a number of Australians were invited to attend. Kerry Walker and I were on the list because of Patrick White's *The Night the Prowler*, in which we played mother and daughter. This film was directed by Jim Sharman and designed by Luciana Arrighi. Jim would be going to Sorrento as well. Our Shakespearean Order was summoned to an extraordinary meeting to debate the matter of attendance at the festival, Kerry and I abstaining but in attendance. The decision was reached that it was important for all of us, and the industry as a whole – not to mention the country and possibly God – that Kerry and I accept, which we did with alacrity. In a thrice we were on a plane headed for Rome. We were permitted ten days' absence from the Convent. Two pupils wagging school. Delicious.

We landed in Rome, where we spent the night at the charming Hotel d'Inghilterra, but not before seeing Rome first. It was Kerry's first visit, and she was not going to miss anything. Being jet-lagged, we opted for a bus tour, which was pretty pointless as we kept falling asleep on one shoulder or another, but at least Kerry could lie and say she had seen Rome. The next day we headed for Sorrento and prepared ourselves for:

Unpacked, balmy Sorrento evening, romance in the air, my travelling companion expressed desire for dalliance, disappeared, and left me with the distinct feeling of always the bridesmaid never the bride. Kerry returned later – the living embodiment, it seemed to me, of da Vinci's Mona Lisa. My lips are sealed as to what may or may not have happened over the ensuing days, but I do know that there was a waiter whose yearning glances always seemed close at hand, and that my travelling companion never found time hanging heavily thereafter. The Shakespearean Sonnets have a lot to answer for.

I, meanwhile, soberly attended press conferences, answering question after question, at one of these a little bewildered to be asked whether I was one of my country's leading feminists. This was assumed on the flimsy basis that Gillian Armstrong's short film *The Singer and the Dancer*, about the free spirit Mrs Bilson, was also appearing at the festival, and was showing within the category *Film di Ispirazione Femminista*. It was news to me. Momentarily stumped, but rallying, I stammered, 'No, no, I'm...ah...ah...' Desperate attempt to break through the language barrier. 'I'm ah...just a...(sudden inspiration) working actor!' Great applause from the floor, half the press that day being communist. 'Working' was music to their ears, and I found myself accepted on the spot as a member of yet another brother/sisterhood. *Molto bravo.*

We travelled en masse in a small bus to various functions, Judy Davis, Barry Humphries, Don Crosby and Wendy Hughes among us. Barry always looked elegant in white linen, panama, silk pocket handkerchief. He must have had several suits, or access to speedier laundry than the rest of us, because the odd dollop of pasta did land on the sparkling white. But was never there the next day. Life imitating art? Was Sir Les Patterson momentarily hovering? Perish the thought! Sir Les never has access to laundry. *I* couldn't talk, anyway, liberally covered with scampi as I was – tipped over me one day by Don Crosby, I seem to remember. The trouble was, we were always eating. And talking. And drinking. The typical Australian group abroad, one might say. Complete with tour bus.

And of course, never any tea! Don was distressed by this. He noted the absence of tea-making facilities in our splendid Italian hotel rooms. He felt they'd somehow failed us. It seemed to weigh on him, especially during those bus trips. He muttered a bit.

One afternoon, I wandered off alone and stumbled upon an exquisite lace and linen shop selling hand-made handkerchiefs. I bought a beautiful, minute square, and met the proprietor, an elegant 80 year old. She knew I was with the Australian film contingent, and, one thing leading to another, I was invited to call on her. Next day, I arrived at her villa – walled garden, citrus trees, absolute security, guard dogs, huge iron gates. Through we went into a place of quiet beauty. I remember the thick yellow tiles of the entrance hall. I remember the paintings, objects. We had coffee and talked of many things – film, art, opera; Sorrento today with all its drawbacks. There was a pressing invitation to return. In fifteen or so years I've not managed it. Well, maybe next year . . . She will be gone, but perhaps the tiny shop is still there. We made our farewells, the huge gates swung closed, and I was returned to the hotel.

There seemed at least two worlds in Sorrento – one locked away, fearful, part of a, perhaps, suspect older order, the other geared towards the tourist, or on the make, or unemployed. Under all the fun a faint whiff of violence – and not just a whiff in Sorrento/Naples in 1980. The Red Brigade was active in those days and, coinciding with out visit, the Queen was paying a state visit to Naples. Security was at a maximum, and there were some terrorists on the run, including Michele Viscardi and Maria Teresa Conti. These two were finally apprehended in Sorrento while we were there – it was rumoured that they were attending a performance of *The Singer and the Dancer* at the time. I hope they were. I'd love to think of them watching Gillian's film with me as Mrs Bilson running free over the grassy slopes near Picton. Press reports had the whole occasion of their arrest verging on the Keystone cops. The films were shown in the Cinema Tasso in the Piazza Tasso, and the local *carabinieri* or their agents received a tip-off that terrorists were somewhere close. So all the crowds attending the performances were studiously filmed by an agent, with what end in view one couldn't be sure. Suddenly, this day, he saw the terrorists and set off the alarm.

Confusion everywhere and the quarry escaped, but were eventually captured in a flat where four of them had been holed up. There were photos and detailed, if confusing, press reports. It all added a certain piquancy to that Sorrento film festival. One never knows where film buffs will turn up next. Nor, indeed, which one of us may be filed away in Italian police records.

The festival's grand finale was held in the Naples Opera House; a formal occasion. I had rustled up something or other in silk. Kerry had a Linda Jackson original – *we* wouldn't be letting the side down. My silk was handed to the maid for ironing and, as seemed inevitable at this film festival, disaster struck. She returned it to me with a piece missing, still attached to the iron, in fact. Any thought of dissolving in sadness was banished because the maid herself was utterly distraught and begged me not to mention it to the management. I have seldom been in the presence of such terror. One had the impression she would be sacked on the spot and as she was probably the sole breadwinner for her family, the consequences of the mildest complaint were not attractive. A tiny moment of ugly reality. It took a while to soothe her, and to convince her that no *coup de grâce* would be administered. Just a handful of pins. Or did we cleverly arrange the beautiful square of fine lawn from the handkerchief shop?

The Naples Opera House was packed. A number of us were to sit on the stage, and I seem to remember being between Judy Davis and Barry Humphries. Kerry was in a box, and very happy to be there, thank you. No strain at all for Kerry.

Simple, uncomplicated enjoyment. Then a little, tiny drama involving Wendy Hughes, who expressed the desire *not* to be there at all. Unfortunately, she was vital as she was meant to be accepting an award for *Newsfront*. Problems are meant to be solved and this one was by the charming David Roe, our Australian organiser, who thrust his head round the door of Kerry's box and announced that she would be accepting the award. No refusal possible and the reluctant and bewildered Kerry found herself up there with the rest of us.

Looking out into that beautiful auditorium was impressive, to say the least. I sat back to take it all in, careful to remember all the details for the brothers and sisters toiling away back in the Convent in Sydney — the glamour, the polite applause as various dignitaries and visiting unknown film stars were introduced — when Marcello Mastroianni strolled onto the stage. In denim. The entire audience leapt to its feet and the response was akin to a World Cup soccer final. As for me, Mastroianni had taken over. Ravished I was, in front of the thousands.

Kerry collected the *Newsfront* award; it had only shortly before been stuck to its base, and it leaked all over the Linda Jackson original. In the bus, later, she handed the sticky trophy to the ever placid David Roe, Wendy, by this time recovered, expressing a preference, understandably, for a bottle of scent. My thoughts were still with Mastroianni.

And that was Sorrento. Fun, but also rather special to be part of a festival in a film-making country. A country that has so often led the way, whose films, the best of them, have remained, and will continue to remain, classics. And a country which, for that short time, was honouring us. Taking notice. Being very serious about *us*. Kerry and I wouldn't have missed it for worlds.

We returned to the Convent — to sanctuary. There was momentary interest, but we weren't going to be allowed to swan it for long.

TWENTY

I have appeared in ten or so films over the years – the first being *Smiley Gets a Gun* in 1958. This film is something I would be quite happy to forget, apart from the delight of being with Gordon Chater again, but on the occasional rainy Sunday afternoon it will still surface. And that, of course, is the problem with film. I've enjoyed being with a variety of directors, all with their own particular style, and if I want to risk pulling names out I must say great enjoyment has come from being with Gillian Armstrong in one of her earliest forays, *The Singer and the Dancer*, Jim Sharman in *The Night the Prowler*, Fred Schepisi in *The Chant of Jimmy Blacksmith* and Bill Bennett in *Spider and Rose*. Gillian for quiet passion and humour, Jim for just letting the comedy happen, Fred for tenderness, Bill for subtle persuasiveness.

Film is always a joy after months of eight stage performances a week. Long, long days, but with the knowledge that the energy is required for such a comparatively short time. And so contained it is, so intimate at times. Thoughts are filmed. Of course by take 10, 15 or 20, however, the sheer effort of removing tension can become the priority.

The first day of rehearsal for *Lilian's Story* I drove to Rosebery. I crossed the Bridge, and as I drove towards Oxford Street, already they were appearing. Couples straggling along the footpath. Past Oxford Street it began to be a minor procession; some were distinctly bedraggled; some were wearing the remnants of costume. There were occasional small groups – four, six, the odd lone walker, aimlessly wandering, one could say an air of satiety pervading. A trail of tinsel here and there.

The day after Mardi Gras. If there is anything that demonstrates more clearly the highs and lows of existence than the morning after Mardi Gras, I don't know what it is. I keep promising myself I will watch the parade; one feels positively out of it. I am tempted, and then I remember: The crowds. Can't be part of a crowd. Any prospect of that was crushed forty years earlier at that other stupendous crowd puller – London, 1953, the Coronation. Or rather, the night of the Coronation. It was mandatory to go back to the heart of things that night, after a day of patriotic fervour when hearts seemed ready to burst with joy. To go back and just wander about, be a part of that last flowering of absurd optimism, though we didn't know it at the time, which confidently knew the future was golden and this momentous day meant the end of post-war drabness forever. The new Elizabethan

Age would be triumphant, happy and glorious, and altogether very nice. All such refreshing thoughts were banished in a flash as I became caught in the centre of a crowd that was moving inexorably along a small street near Whitehall. The street ended in a brick wall. I was swept along, further and further from my friends, who managed to toss a door key to me. If I ever escaped back to Earl's Court, I would at least find my bed again. A car came close to being overturned. Everyone was happy and stupid. I made a tiny space around me with bent arms, looked up at the sky, found some stars and tried to focus on them. I could feel the scream rising.

The street, as it happened, wasn't a dead end. I was swept around a corner, ultimately managing to escape into a side street, shaking, happy to be alive, and unable from that day to this to be part of any crowd – unless decently apart on a stage and preferably when there's an orchestra pit.

I drove on through the post-party Sydney streets. By now dozens and dozens of stragglers were walking on the pavements, some cutting through Moore Park, some just standing. They'd disappeared by the time I got to Rosebery and vanished from my thoughts, as we began our rehearsal in part of the production office. A reading with Toni Collette, Barry Otto and me. We concentrated on Toni's scenes as she was off to America to promote *Muriel's Wedding*. Our director, Jerzy Domeradsky, picked away at the text. We all chipped in. It had to be decided there and then whether Lilian was actually raped by Father. We made the decision. Even the tentative reading and shaping was chilling. Then, wardrobe inspections and decisions, and that first, tricky day dealt with.

The whole rehearsal period was two weeks, much of it reading and analysing – setting the fight with the police, going to the house in Middle Cove to plot moves and soak up the neo-Gothic atmosphere. Hours that screenwriter Steve Wright and I spent closeted, sorting through passage after passage of Shakespeare to arrive at the selection that would match Lilian's moods. Somewhere in that two weeks Jerzy and our director of photography, Slawomir Idziac, persuaded me to change my hair colour to dull brown. I did. And then we were shooting.

Lilian's Story ranges all over Sydney, much of it with a Harbour setting. Lilian's mother clocks the movements of the ferries across the Harbour; there is the attempted suicide by young Lil at a small beach. So many views of Sydney's most publicised natural glory, but – with the exception of a brief glimpse of a section of its arch – not one shot of the Bridge, nor one of the Opera House. We felt this may have been a record. It is an unfamiliar, but heart-breakingly beautiful look at the city.

The sleazy, lower end of Pitt Street stood in for Kings Cross, where much of the action takes place. During takes, make-up and stand-by wardrobe were secreted in a soon-to-be-opened Chinese emporium, which had a new facade for our purposes as Lil's bank. During long waits I made possibly the first purchase there – a glass dome containing an infant Buddha, encased in the inevitable snow storm that always fills these irresistible objects. The perfect birthday present for someone who has everything? A first purchase in a Chinese emporium has to be lucky. They are quietly, politely delighted to have a film crew camped among the brass and china.

Outside, in that wind tunnel, filming was torture. The body screamed for the blanket, wrapped around the instant 'cut' rang out. Isobel, who was managing this side of things, broke Olympic records in her dash from concealment. In the long days of filming, make-up, stand-by wardrobe and, in my case the third assistant director (prompt with tea in a cup and saucer, no mug, thank you, no polystyrene), make life possible and, even, enjoyable. I have decided these are the vital members of a unit. The director may direct, the director of photography may photograph, but creature comforts are what it is about.

And a clean loo. Tofer, our American second assistant director, took a few days to get this area fully operational, but daily inspection of the convenience in my tiny caravan soon ensured that the impossible standards of the two of us were upheld. In addition, when make-up is in the hands of my dear Peggy Carter, friend from way back, life will flow smoothly. My favourite moment, now that we speak of priorities, occurred when we were filming near First Fleet Park at the Quay. Unexpectedly, I had to stay back after an impossible day for a hair colour adjustment (the curse of rushes). Tofer's preppy manner quickly came to the fore as I intimated that the only thing that would make the process bearable was a dry martini. Half-way through the hair-colouring, Tofer arrived at the make-up van – where I sat at a back-breaking basin – bearing aloft a silver salver with a crystal tumbler and a jug containing a martini, which had been prized out of a reluctant barman at the nearby Regent. I hadn't had a martini in years and doubt I shall again, perfection having been achieved at that moment. Tofer was minus his watch. To be redeemed when silver and crystal were returned. These are the important moments in filming, which may come as a shock to the many splendid directors I have worked for. But lest there be any misunderstanding here, the martini was proffered and consumed at the completion of the day's filming. Alcohol is forbidden on a film set, and any time it is smuggled in by some dependent actor, a nightmare ensures.

So much of what I remember is external to the film, but will always, for me pervade it. Vignette in Pitt Street, Lil in a taxi. Outside, our prostitutes, our spruiker. Our street dressing. I glance up to the floor above the X-rated video shop — not ours. Above, the Wild Orchid, curtains fluttering. Beautiful, exquisite young Asian working girls peep at us play-acting, peep at our prostitutes. Those engaged in make-believe steal looks at the reality. Upstairs in the Wild Orchid, joss sticks are lit and a tiny, graceful hand appears, scattering rice for the birds. A young man looks out. Prostitute? Pimp? Client?

Aggression in the street, mostly from the old men drinking their pension cheques. Chinese wandering. Everyone gazing at us and we at them. Alcohol and drugs and deprivation, and the sounds and stench at this end of the city, repeated endlessly in every big city in the world. At least the weather's better here.

Making a film always provides moments of tension,

inevitable by the very nature of the activity. The pressures to get through the day, where the budget is limited, are often competing head-on with artistic requirements. It is amazing that any film ever gets made. Somehow they do. We had our Polish director and our Polish director of photography. And an Australian crew. The potential dangers here were beautifully encapsulated on our first day of shooting in a mental asylum – the old Gladesville Mental Hospital. Lilian is saying goodbye on her release. All the other inmates are partaking, noisily, of breakfast. Actors, extras, crew. There is a sour smell in the corridors. Flat, stale atmosphere of the once flourishing, bustling business of restraint and denial. Reminders, though. A hopscotch marked out on the flagging of the verandah; the remains of a mobile turning in desultory fashion. Our film concerns Lilian, who was locked away for forty years with comparative ease, and what happens after she is released. (These days people aren't locked away with such ease, but many who have an unexpected freedom thrust on them are not always a great deal better off.) There is a tunnel under the madly busy Victoria Road, leading to another less picturesque part of the mental hospital. It allowed for the decent arrival and departure of earlier occupants – no disturbing sights and sounds to alarm the populace. We would film Lil's departure by taxi in this tunnel, pursued there by Jewel, her most precious 'loony bin' connection: 'You said you would never leave me.' The most confronting line in the film, possibly.

Forty years earlier I, myself, had entered that other arm of Gladesville. Always the too willing volunteer, I had been pressed to join a grotesque concert party for the entertainment of the patients. One Freda Francks, performer of good works, had gathered together an unlikely group. Freda was a capable and energetic pianist and music teacher, and her greatest passion in life was an organisation called One World, to which I was willingly conscripted. World Government, we believed, with an unshakeable conviction, was the only hope for the human race, and I've no doubt that we sent off pamphlets and read many earnest and convincing arguments for the establishment of World Government, impressed as we were by the support of higher intellects. The fact that Russia was not in any way contributing to this to-ing and fro-ing of manifestos and articles of faith world wide did not just then deter us. I was well and truly caught up — until a degree of latent scepticism re-asserted itself.

Freda Francks's light relief, if it can be so described, was taking concert parties to where, in her view, they would be most appreciated. A mental asylum was, naturally, top of the list. Our group this day consisted of a pallid, not to say, anorexic, ballet dancer, myself to read poetry, Freda on piano for solos and accompaniments, and a baritone. We arrived at a door in the high green fence, were admitted to one of the buildings, and then, accompanied by two guards, entered a room the size of an average classroom, the door of which was promptly locked behind us. Our audience of about thirty men was seated on our level, and the first unwilling and rather disgruntled row was within touching distance. Not for the first time I remember thinking, What in God's name am I doing here? Terror began it's slow, but inexorable rise, only kept under control by an inner voice screaming, 'Don't let them see it! Don't let them see it!'

Proceedings began with a rousing and encouraging piano piece by Freda. I have no real memory of it. There is slight recollection of our baritone's contribution. Total recall of our ballerina! She was clad in an unsuitable, all things considered, slightly shop-worn, faded tutu, and she bravely attempted to execute pirouettes and the odd graceful lurch from one side of the smallish space to the other – on point. Our male audience was focused instantly. The applause that greeted her last provocative pose was not music to my ears. My turn. Shortly after I began, one man became extremely agitated, whether moved by the immortal stanzas I was reciting or enraged that I was saying anything at all, I don't know. I do know that he started to rise and move in my direction, and that a guard moved swiftly to his side and thrust him back into his seat. The guard stayed close – no comfort to me – and the rest of the audience, as one, sank back into a sullen acceptance of my offering. Little contest in the popularity stakes between the ballerina and me. I escaped from that room sure of only one thing. It was my last concert party.

Lilian's Story's other grim location was the Remand Centre at the Central Court in Sydney – this still being an active environment. A section of the prison was cleared for our use. There was a counter staffed by Corrective Services, the walls behind the counter covered with drugs and aids information, and a framed poem on heroin addiction written by a young woman who'd passed through: 'In cellophane bags I make my way/ To men in offices and children at play...'. There were passageways – unexplored – leading who knew where, and one passage used by us, flanked down one side by two large communal cells, one with stretchers attached to the wall, the other just a space with benches around, possibly for 'recreation'. Graffiti and names and messages. One scene required Lil, in a state of depression, not difficult to summon, to sit on a stretcher, knees drawn up – solitary; the other was Lil thrust by our warders into the 'recreation' area. The claustrophobic effect on cast and crew made escape to a quite pleasant courtyard, as often as possible, essential.

I met the director of the Centre, who spoke, among other things, of attempted suicide, self-mutilation – the latter mainly by women. 'They will do it,' he said, 'just to get attention.' He might have been speaking of recalcitrant children, but as some of those awaiting trial can be confined here for up to twelve months, I wasn't so sure. A nice man; great lover of *Mother and Son*. I may have had my photo taken with him. I certainly received a Corrective Services silver-plated teaspoon, boxed, and an asked-for copy of the heroin poem.

At one point, midway through a particularly difficult shot, our director and director of photography are engaged in the longest of discussions – or tirades, possibly – in Polish. They finish. Mark Turnbull, the first assistant director, pauses, and with a delicate edge enquires, 'Which means?' Jerzy has an ability to drag fine performances out of actors, but, at times it *was* difficult to comprehend exactly what he was after. Language barrier or no language barrier, though, he was determined to go for what was in his mind. Just occasionally bewilderment turned to frustration. At times, we lived, ate, slept tension. And if he didn't like what was on the page, out with it! A new look at Lilian's lover Frank's death scene on the day we shot it came as a great surprise, especially as I had to make it all up. Next time, a crash course in Polish first.

Tensions come with the job, however, and I shall always be profoundly grateful for the chance to appear in a film that went along the track of digging deeper into emotion than was the case in much of what was produced earlier. We have not always been comfortable, we Australians, when departing from the laconic view. Jerzy doesn't know the meaning of the word laconic.

Working with Swavek, the brilliant director of photography with films such as *Three Colours Blue* to his credit, was, quite simply, wonderful. He had an enormous effect on the result, so much of the film depending on his eye, his perceptions. Viewing it, one is constantly aware of brush strokes that can encompass the most delicate, the most tender, and then proceed to Gothic horror with seamless skill. Detail is all important, and I treasure the memory of his shout of delight when, off screen, my finger made an oval photo frame rock from side to side, thus securing his precious and perfect close-up of the frame. 'You are a witch, a genius!' Forget acting!

Actors are one's colleagues and should be one's closest

allies. Mostly they are, and those in *Lilian's Story* were no exception. Barry Otto I had worked with in Theatre years before – a performance of *Tom and Viv* in which he played T. S. Eliot and I Viv's mother to Robyn Nevin's Viv. And before that we had endured and survived a difficult set in a fine Australian play *A Happy and Holy Occasion*, by John O'Donoghue. In Lilian, his portrayal of the father/son double is quite breath-taking. Toni Collette I'd not worked with before, and really didn't this time around, as it is somewhat difficult to have scenes with someone who is playing a younger version of oneself. Our meetings were restricted to passing one another once in make-up and at the cast and crew viewing of the finished product. We embraced warmly at the end with that instinctive clutching for comfort that occurs on these occasions. The dark core of the film belongs to her and she is superb. Apart from Barry, my main scenes were with John Flaus as the older Frank, and a fine unlikely pairing we made. Two bears, perhaps.

The joy of *Lilian's Story* is the way myriad characters flow in and out and the clarity with which each is etched. Like a modern Dickensian canvas. Marian MacGowan first obtained the rights to Kate Grenville's novel, *Lilian's Story*, in 1986. *Lilian's Story* was inspired by the Sydney identity, Bee Miles, whom I'd tripped over all those years ago in Rushcutters' Bay. Inspired by, not the history of. Marian and Jerzy showed me the first draft of Steve Wright's screenplay some four years later. We thought the money was there in 1994, but expected funds vanished at the end of the financial year. The following year, the Australian Film Finance Corporation provided the major part of the finance, with private investors making up the balance. That's virtually a decade before the dream can be realised. Producers require an enormous amount of determination and passion to last the distance.

So we finished. One's last day on a set is always a little emotional, with the presentation of the signed poster and a silver brooch – a bird, of course –, but most touching and completely unexpected, a Limoges cup and saucer from the assistant director's department for the one who won't accept mugs or polystyrene.

Feathers were a good luck symbol on the film between Marian and me. A feather in front of either of us on the path had to be picked up and was assurance of a good day. We began to find them everywhere and duly reported to one another. I'm still doing it, and one has wrapped itself in some inexplicable fashion around a ring box in a drawer. It doesn't wish to remove itself and I don't encourage it to. Another is attached to the boot of my car and no amount of car washing has dislodged it. We take these matters to be a very good sign.

Some months after the completion of filming, Eric and I were travelling to Queenscliff in Victoria where I would be staying at Patricia O'Donnell's wonderful Queenscliff Hotel during the Geelong run of *Three Tall Women*. Three huge flocks of migratory birds, high in the sky, passed overhead. We stopped the car to watch and when we travelled on, a smaller flock accompanied us for a few miles. The fact that this happened just as I'd begun, for the first time, to listen to the sound track of *Lilian's Story* caused the hairs to rise slightly at the nape of the neck.

We mind all these tiny symbols of hope, clinging as to the lifebelt in water. We will be saved. All will be well.

September 1996. Eric and I are in Telluride, Colorado, in the United States for the annual film festival. *Lilian's Story* is showing here, and we have arrived by a circuitous route from Edinburgh, where it also appeared in that city's film festival. Such a warm response to the film there that I don't dare hope for its equal in Telluride. This festival is beloved of film buffs and film makers because it is possible to concentrate on the films, listen to seminars, talk with like-minded people, and never once have to face the media. There is no competition, and simple word of mouth decides which films are the ones to see. People possess passes of differing value, but even the holders of the $1500 passes have to stand in line, even if *their* line takes some precedence. Queues for the films can start forming hours before a screening, and there is a great scramble to gain admission to the popular films. Telluride pays tribute to certain people. This year's festival is dedicated to the late Louis Malle, the renowned director and a great supporter of Telluride, who when asked which were his favourite festivals remarked, 'For me, there is only Telluride.'

The absence of a competitive edge at Telluride is, I imagine, what makes it such a loved festival. This year there are to be special tributes to Shirley Maclaine, Mike Leigh and French film-maker, Alain Cavalier. Also, a silver medallion is to be presented to Roger Mayer for his work in preserving film, which has resulted in the Turner Film Library, the largest resource in the world, containing, as it does, more than 3000 movies, 2000 hours of television and over 2000 shorts and cartoons.

There was a smart reception on the first night of the festival at the house of American writer John Naisbett. It is a glamorous house set in trees, its various levels taking advantage of the mountain against which it nestles, its approach by way of the odd ramp and bridge over a gurgling stream, where engineering just may have assisted nature's natural fall. A crowd had already gathered, and we received a very warm welcome from our host. Eric and I knew no one but the festival director pointed out various luminaries, including Mike Leigh and Roger Mayer. Wonderful food. Flowing everything and pleasant servers, all of them volunteers and serious film buffs. Jerzy already ensconced. Wandering about I became aware of a woman in pink on the shadowed balcony in a fairly solid ring of men, talking, having food brought. No more than a casual glance from me, but enough to see that this was Shirley Maclaine, whose tribute the following night would launch the festival.

I had consecutive swift reactions. First, slightly weak at the knees, which sometimes still happens when I am in the presence of great talent. Second, genuine pleasure at the prospect of meeting her and passing on the Andrew Peacock story.

Earlier in the year, on the Friday night of the Grand Prix weekend, I had spoken to a group of two or three hundred celebrating International Women's Day in the Hyatt Ballroom in Collins Street, Melbourne. A wonderful confluence of opposites. There were awards at the end of the night presented to young, innovative Australian businesswomen, and their youth and success were especially encouraging on this night when elsewhere the macho weekend was getting off to a great start at the Grand Prix Ball. I confessed in my speech that ejaculating exhausts didn't turn me on any more than energetic spurts of champagne over winners. Better things to do with that incomparable elixir.

Next day at the airport there is Andrew Peacock. We'd never met, but he came up and introduced himself, and we had a pleasant ten minutes or so before boarding, during the course of which Shirley Maclaine's name entered the conversation. It appeared she was taking a long time to shake off a flu virus and was in need of a genuine break. I said he must get her to the Kimberley. It would fix her. I thought no more about it – but on the plane, Andrew sent messages across asking for phone numbers as he was determined that Shirley and I should meet. I think he was convinced we would be instant friends of the bosom.

We waved goodbye, and Andrew was even prepared to overlook my scathing comments on the Grand Prix, assuring me that I would have loved the Ball. I doubt it.

So, awaiting my moment on the balcony of the Naisbett residence – not so easy as the ring of bright men did not allow for easy access – I began my conversation with a genuine description of my regard for her brilliance, which as I proceeded was not yielding a deal of response from Miss Maclaine. To my horror, I seemed to be metamorphosing into one of my own gushing fans. Out of control in other words. Desperately striving to redeem the situation – the bright ring around her being polite and attentive, if glazed – I threw in Andrew's name prior to launching into airport anecdotes, but was stopped in my tracks by a snappy 'Andrew? Andrew who?' from the fair figure in pink. This was the moment for swift extrication. I melted into the gloom.

The evening moved on, snail's pace now. Our host invited Peter – or was it Paul? – of Peter, Paul and Mary to sing for us. I thought it would be breakfast before relief arrived. Paul – or was it Peter? – sang with soulful sincerity to a rapt group at his feet, but not Jerzy who, with brisk determination, took my elbow and propelled me through the disciples and to the front door. There I found my infinitely better half, and off we stumbled into a beautiful night.

Next evening was the Shirley Maclaine Tribute at the exquisite little opera house. We took our seats near the front, and on our right was the box for the guest of honour. My gaze was unflinchingly on the painted curtain, which I came to know intimately. Eric leaned over and said, 'I think that's Andrew Peacock trying to attract your attention.' My gaze stayed focused. The Tribute commenced: A collection of Maclaine film moments right back to the beginning – all showing that particular quality which, for me, is summed up by her ability to walk away with just about every scene in which she appears.

Then the final applause and the mandatory interview session, this time with a well-informed interviewer and the star performing with panache, wit and a killer instinct second to none. Well, it takes one to know one.

We leave and are chased by a breathless messenger: 'Andrew wants to see you. He's been trying to attract your attention.' 'Yes,' I say. No need for 'Andrew who?' So back to Miss Maclaine's dressing room. Fairly crowded. Andrew was excited and I made a more graceful speech, with more imprimatur than on the previous evening. Miss Maclaine smiled slightly and we decamped.

Finally, there was a lunch. Shirley and I had been at a forum, a long forum at which I seem to remember Mike Leigh described his method of working in some detail. As I was leaving, I was gathered up by one of the young men who'd just seen *Spider and Rose* at Disney: 'No you *have* to come to lunch.' So there were Shirley, some friends of hers, Andrew, Eric and me. Shirley seated us – she opposite me. A little constrained on my part till something said produced a swift, deadly response from me. Miss Maclaine's jaw dropped and she uttered a guffaw. Our eyes met briefly. It was a moment when Andrew's feeling that we were meant for one another evinced just a tiny grain of truth.

This Sunday at Telluride is Lilian's day. Eric photographs the queue running around the corner from the tiny opera house. I am nervous. Jerzy and I wait in the box that had been occupied two nights ago by Shirley Maclaine for her Tribute. *Lilian's*

Story is preceded by Dorthe Scheffman's short New Zealand film *The Beach* — skilfully and beautifully shot. Very subtly disturbing as the camera pans over the languid, sensuous beach landscape, past a father playing cricket with his son, other children, all fairly solitary, the odd swimmer entering or emerging from the water. We end on two reclining women, the scene unfolding through their sparse dialogue. Beautiful and slightly erotic, and then the dark theme is revealed: Abuse. Making it, of course, the perfect companion piece for *Lilian's Story*. After *The Beach* Jerzy and I deliver our speeches, and I make special mention of Marian's passion and commitment, which elicits whoops from her friends. It's a relief to know she is there because it was impossible to locate her. Jerzy, Eric and I disappear during Lilian's screening, returning just in time for co-director of the festival Tom Luddy to introduce us, and as I walk into the spotlight there is a spontaneous standing ovation. I stammer out thanks. Jerzy looks happy and we launch into a vigorous and stimulating question and answer session. Two more screenings that day, both of which we introduce, plus a screening on the final day in the big 650-seat auditorium. From being completely anonymous, suddenly we are recognised on all sides by film buffs and film makers. Their comments are manna from heaven. *Lilian's Story* seems to have universally touched and moved people.

Now, the film has been seen at two festivals overseas. It has swum bravely and happily for awhile. It remains a matter of luck as to how long the swim lasts. Whatever . . . we did love the festivals.

TWENTY ONE

As a performer, the joy of arriving at the Sydney Opera House, with its bustle and excitement and steady magnificence, is only surpassed by leaving at night and taking time to wander by the sea wall. On a moonlit night one could die of excess. Had the interior worked seamlessly the Opera House would be perfect and the angry gods might have had to smash it to the ground. We are grateful therefore, for the problems.

In the year the Opera House opened for business, actually gaining admission to the theatres was the hardest part of all. Many's the argument I had with Security to persuade them that not only was I legitimate and trustworthy and not concealing a bomb, but that I actually needed to be in my dressing room fairly speedily or there'd be no show. If one was driving it was more of a problem; actors on foot had an easier time. All that zealous commitment of the security guards did not stop my car from being driven out by someone else one night and taken all the way to Port Pirie in South Australia — a construction worker desperately wanting to get home? — but then none of us is perfect. And the original security guards bear no resemblance whatsoever to those who currently staff the complex, and whom I regard as my very dear friends.

I was one of the Old Tote actors who provided the first season of plays at the Opera House in 1973. Robin Lovejoy, whose task it was to mount the season, opted for a repertoire of three plays. It seemed, for a moment, as if I were going all the way back to 1952 and the adventurous days of that old pioneer Sydney John Kay. But these were tougher times, and the eyes of the whole country were now upon us. The Australian Opera was proceeding with its mighty *War and Peace*, and we embarked on a new play by David Williamson, *What If You Died Tomorrow?*, Shakespeare's *Richard II* and a production of Bertold Brecht's *The Threepenny Opera* with Jim Sharman as director. Robin Lovejoy had the task of ensuring that the first season worked, and in retrospect this could be seen as the most awesome task to befall an Australian director, certainly to that point. I played Irene in *What If You Died Tomorrow?* And the Duchess of Gloucester in *Richard II*. The Duchess of Gloucester has only one mighty scene of rage and grief with John of Gaunt about his part in the death of Gloucester, his brother: 'Finds brotherhood in thee no sharper spur?/Hath love in thy old blood no living fire?' Its added joy is that it is Act I Scene 2. The following scene takes place at Coventry and is the arranged joust between Bolingbroke and Norfolk with the

King and all the nobles in attendance. Into the season it was the greatest delight to make my escape along the tunnel where the lined-up nobles were waiting to make their entrances with the whispered advice of what awaited me in the dining room at home, particular emphasis resting on the wine chosen for the evening. I was lucky to run the gauntlet unscathed.

On the whole, *Richard II* was a bit unwieldy, and the staging was difficult. The decision to carpet the acting area in green wall-to-wall Axminster was not one of Robin's better choices. We had a revolving stage for the first time, so it had to be used, of course, but condemning John Gaden as Richard to rise up from the depths through the middle of the revolve, as if in an open department store lift, was not the easiest of entrances. We battle on, though, and John overcame the rides stoically, delivering a moving Richard.

I, myself, have no great fondness for the revolve, recalling the taking of the bow to the audience at the conclusion of William Congreve's *The Way of the World*. The revolve had brought us all round in spirited fashion, and in a moment of confusion, in a line-up of grace and style, I was to be seen bowing to the back wall, my well-camouflaged rear being all with which the audience was favoured. This is the curse of not having any sense of direction, and difficult to explain to those not similarly handicapped.

The Threepenny Opera was a great Jim Sharman production, and its cast included Robin Ramsay as Mac the Knife, Pamela Stephenson as Polly Peachum and Kate Fitzpatrick as Jenny Diver. Drew Forsythe also starred, and there was a memorable appearance by Gloria Dawn as Mrs Peachum. Drew Forsythe has the best Gloria story; one collects them. In the production week, the musical director was being forceful and over-heated at a note session. A bit of arm waving, with the whole cast seated in rows before him. During a pause, an audible sigh came from behind Drew, and the words, 'I *wish* I could win the lottery!' issued from the seat occupied by Miss Dawn. The moment succinctly sums up the Gloria I knew. She was in no way addicted to the business of performance. It's just that whatever she did was stunning – and it paid all the bills. For the rest she would have been happy collecting stray dogs and feeding the family. Gloria's married name was Cleary and it was as Mrs Cleary, and only as Mrs Cleary, that she was known by the butcher and baker and candlestick maker around Kingsford. As Mrs Cleary, Gloria always dressed down. When she performed in the clubs she was all glitter, glamour and upswept blonde hair. Her butcher, who had been used to slicing up the sausages and talking about the weather to Mrs Cleary, got the shock of his life at the local RSL Club when he turned up for a performance. The band struck up and on swept Gloria Dawn, who proceeded to belt it out in her incomparable fashion. The stunned butcher's shout of realisation, 'Jesus Christ, it's Mrs Cleary!', almost topped Gloria's opening bars.

Mention of Kate Fitzpatrick reminds me that I was the recipient of all her intimate confessions as we waited in bed prior to the commencement of a scene in Alan Ayckbourn's *Bedroom Farce*. This always put me into a frenzy of anxiety, because I was sure the lights would come up one night in the middle of one of Kate's better reminiscences, which, the professional she is, may have caused an instinctive increase in volume. And revelations no audience had paid for.

What If You Died Tomorrow? was the premiere of David Williamson's new play. This was my first experience in an Australian play. The Phillip Street revues had been my introduction to an Australian idiom, but this was the first actual play. In that cast, for what was a pretty memorable occasion, all things considered, were Shane Porteous, Kirrily Nolan, Ron Haddrick, Max Phipps, Dinah Shearing, Ron Falk, John Walton and myself. Robin Lovejoy directed the Williamson beautifully, and when we presented ourselves to our first audience we could not quite believe the response, nor our great good fortune at being part of this, for Sydney, historic moment – a play by an Australian playwright in the opening season of the Sydney Opera House. The comedy worked a treat, and the play finished up touring. We took What If You Died to Canberra, Newcastle and for a season in Melbourne. While playing in Melbourne we had the great news that, in association with H. M. Tennent and Company, the London theatrical entrepreneurs, the Old Tote would be presenting David's play in London.

So, there I was, almost twenty years to the day, returning to the city I'd not seen since. Going to London was a major family decision and only resolved by Eric's taking long-service leave, bringing the two younger children with us for a term in an English school and leaving Anna, who was coming up to the then School Certificate, with my sister, Gwenyth. The step was taken. I went with the Company ahead of Eric and he and Jane and Jonathan arrived a week or two later.

London, after all that time, was almost unbearably exciting for me. In the taxi from the airport I fell off the seat many times pointing out landmarks to Kirrily and only gained a degree of composure when, much to Kirrily's relief, we eventually arrived at Dover Street, where we would be sharing a flat pending the arrival of Eric plus the two children. Making our first forays revealed an unexpected bonus. Living in London in 1974 was going to be very different from that earlier stay in the 1950s. This time, the cost of living was working in our favour. A happy occurrence, and one not repeated subsequently. We had a feeling of modest wealth.

Our first experience of the then English theatrical scene occurred when Robin Lovejoy and the cast arrived on stage at the Comedy Theatre in Panton Street. There was a formal line waiting to greet us, which included Gloria Taylor, subsequently our landlady, and a woman who was to become a fairly major part of my life – Helen Montagu. Helen, an expatriate Australian, was then high in the echelon of Tennents, but had not yet begun her dizzy rise to her present position as possibly the most powerful woman producer in the UK.

The line-up was *faintly* intimidating, but not for long. My memory is of handshakes, brisk welcomes and two women who presented a display of fashion that made me, at least, not only envious, but extremely conscious of my own shortcomings. Helen looked impeccable. Gloria was dressed head to toe by Bill Gibb, and as an ex-Harpers house model, could never have looked anything other than a million dollars. Both of them were superb hostesses and sheep dogs for the whole company, and the bond struck up then between Ms Montagu and me has been, despite everything, one of the great joys of my life. She keeps me on my toes – a good place to be. This, of course, is only to be expected from one whose early days were spent under the wing of a notorious crime queen. Tilly Devine, some said, ruled Sydney's underworld pre and during the Second World War, wielding, by virtue of her position, not a little power in the seamier side of town, Among other interests Helen's father then owned a pub, with residence, in Darlinghurst, Tilly's domain. Obviously taking a liking to the spic and span schoolgirl attending the nearby Sydney Church of England Girls' Grammar School, Tilly sent out word that our Miss Montagu was never to come to harm. Under constant protection, in other words. I suppose having a devoted Bad Fairy hovering over one's early years is, in many respects, much better than having a Good Fairy, particularly if one intends to make theatrical production one's life work. Whatever, Helen's way is blessed, and, yes ... blessing. So linked have she and I been over the years, that she became, much later, the natural model for Elaine in David Williamson's *Emerald City*, searching, as I was, for something larger than life. The voice, for any who remember it, belonged, I have to say, elsewhere ...

Introductions over, that first day was spent familiarising ourselves with the Comedy. We were escorted backstage and to our dressing rooms by a delightful stage director whose chief claim to fame, as far as Kirrily and I were concerned, was his direct line to the Buckingham Palace downstairs fraternity. He was thus a rich source of Royal gossip, none of which, I am proud to say, sent us in the direction of the tabloids. (Of course, ever contemplating retirement, I could think again, though what we were privy to alongside today's revelations sounds positively suburban by comparison.)

Among the discoveries we made that first day was that we were expected to tip our dresser. Coming from egalitarian Australia, this was unexpected, but it soon became apparent that this was in no way largesse but, instead, an essential part of a remuneration that was all too small anyway. So, a little ceremony would take place every Saturday night as individual envelopes were handed over containing their designated amounts. To miss out on this would have been unthinkable.

What If You Died opened to a somewhat mixed response. Faint bewilderment, at times, perhaps. London was not then ready for the Australian idiom and the expletive-laden realism of the play – mild, by comparison with some of today's offerings – and the connection here was not going to be the joyous delight that it had been in Australia. No instant recognition in other words. Even today, audiences respond best to their own stories, if those stories are rooted in particular cultures. And why not? Despite this, we ran for six weeks, and still had fun playing it. David Williamson's pointed comic observation and realism are a delight for an actor.

The nights Australians were out front we zinged along.

The local acting fraternity, too, was very responsive. They were intrigued by the play, and the playing of it, and in that generous theatrical city it was not unusual to have the seriously famous line-up wanting to meet us at the dressing room doors. Yes, British actors had no trouble relating, bless them.

When Eric and the children arrived, Kirrily opted to stay with us, and we all moved into Gloria Taylor's flat in Bina Gardens, South Kensington. Gloria was happy to remove herself for awhile, as she was making up her mind about marriage to Lord Michael Birkett. They needed time. Her first marriage had been to the descendant of the Mahdi of Khartoum who'd been responsible for the death of General Gordon in 1885. I knew all about this. It had been drummed into me all those years ago at North Sydney Girls' High. There were small reproduced photos of the wicked black Mahdi and the noble, courageous General in the encyclopedia. So, we felt a certain glamour attaching to our abode because of it. Gloria's son, now an actor, was probably one of the most beautiful boys I have ever seen. He was away at school while we were there, but his presence remained. There was a bold stroke or two of nationalist graffiti in his bedroom. Gloria had lived for three years or so in Khartoum, royally, but without too much Western freedom I imagine. Ultimately, there was divorce. The kitchen shelves evidenced her exotic life, and we were the grateful beneficiaries. Cardamom, for instance, had been a mystery before then. We were advised to even add it to coffee. Fascinated with Gloria's whole story, and being an incurable romantic, I once asked what her marriage had been like. She smiled a green-eyed smile: 'It was like ... the meeting of the blue Nile and the white Nile.' I had no further questions.

Our play ended somewhat earlier than we had hoped. Most of the cast returned to Australia; only Drew Forsythe stayed on. Drew had taken over John Walton's original role, with John Allen and Melissa Jaffer providing the other changes. The big excitement for Drew, and news to us, was marriage. He and his bride-to-be, Trish, decided this was it and London the town, so Eric and I, in sort of double loco parentis, and Kirrily as witness/attendant, presented ourselves at the Chelsea Registry one fine, high autumn day and watched as two ecstatic people pledged troths. There was a snapshot or two outside, and we then escorted them to the Ritz and up to their room, where we sat on the bed with its satin sheets and slightly faded glory and consumed hors d'oeuvre and champagne before blessing them and stealing away into the fading afternoon. Quite the happiest thing we did in that whole London stay.

Meanwhile, we had major family decisions to make. Eric had arrived at a stage where he felt sure industry was about to take a dip in Australia and was, anyway, mid-life and ripe for change. We both loved London, and there had been a few expressions of interest in my direction from the odd casting director, including the National's. We began to seriously look for an alternative for him that would suit us both. We were very close to making this major change and only pulled back finally because of Eric's doubts about the future of the UK economy and our son's ill-concealed – What am I saying?, totally *revealed* – loathing of any such prospect. Jonathan was 11; he longed for the freer lifestyle back home; he railed against every visit to every stately home, historic house or Elizabethan palace, taking it to an extreme, we felt, the day he set off the alarm at Hampton Court by opening a forbidden door – an action that caused us to melt into the crowds very quickly.

Taking everything into consideration, we decided to return to Australia and deal with mid-life crises on home ground. The best decision we have ever made.

While still in London, I had been offered a role in the ABC television series *Ben Hall*. It was nice to have something in the work line to return to. I came home ahead of Eric and the three children – Anna having joined us before Christmas –, who continued exploring the British Isles.

Soon after landing in Sydney I headed for the Megalong Valley in the Blue Mountains. This was not what could be called a glamorous destination, nor was it by any means a new experience. I had spent many childhood holidays in the mountains, often with Auntie Ethel, who would wander rather vaguely down mountain tracks introducing me to strange things called mountain devils, sometimes murmuring, 'Ah, the ozone!' in much the same way as she used to murmur 'Ah, Wagner!' in different circumstances. As a small child I developed a respect for 'ozone', whatever it was. It certainly didn't have a hole in those days.

What did make this particular stint of filming unforgettable, however, was the fact that it occurred in the midst of a heat wave of such intensity that just getting through the day was a miracle. There were English actors in the cast – this was a joint production with the BBC – Evin Crowley, John Castle and Jon Finch. Theirs was a searing introduction to Australia. The valley itself had fire around it, the sky was pitiless, and the contrast with the ice of a London Christmas couldn't have been greater. The valley was stifling. I sat with my back against a tree, fanning off flies, gasping for the tiny airflow I was creating and wondering what my brood would be doing; envying their cold progress to the north of England, via Wales, where Eric would be pointing out places from which their forebears had emigrated. The thought of them bursting into an Inn and falling over themselves to get to the fire induced flickers of self pity. However, that dive into a real old-fashioned Aussie summer – the sort Auntie Bertha railed against to the Almighty – had a definite feeling of rightness to it. The decision to return was good. This – heat, flies, fires and all – was home.

On the *Ben Hall* set I met Jurgen Zielinski, a talented young make-up artist and wig-maker who had come to Australia at 24 in 1972, full of hope, anticipation and a burning desire to work in the new wonder of the world – the Sydney Opera House. His arrival was not auspicious. Sydney airport was 'a tin shed'. He clambered into the airport coach, exhausted, and by now nervous and bewildered, yearning for his first glimpse of the Opera House and the Bridge. No sign. Sydney must be quite a way from the airport! Finally plucking up his courage and in very broken English, Jurgen enquired of the driver when they would reach Sydney. Stopped at traffic lights near Hyde Park, the driver turned to look him up and down, and Jurgen's first communication with a Sydney-sider yielded the typically warm response, 'You're fuckin' here now, mate!'

This fortunately wasn't too discouraging for the new arrival. He now lives in Australia, and our paths have crossed many times over the years. The first occasion, in 1973, was in *Seven Little Australians*, which was the first colour television series produced by the ABC. Highly successful, it sold throughout the world, being dubbed into upwards of twenty-seven languages. Japan, I believe, being the first sale. This delighted QANTAS crews because invariably the first thing they would see when switching on television in hotel rooms in Tokyo was this Australian classic with its well-known characters communicating in impeccable Japanese.

Jurgen assures me that my first words to him on the *Ben Hall* set were, 'I'm exhausted, and I don't know why I'm doing this.' I repeated the identical words to him twenty years later when rehearsing Geoff Atherden's play *Hotspur*, written for Garry McDonald and me. I must watch myself. This must be why Garry's first greeting on the phone when I'm working is usually, 'Are you tired?' But then Geoff Atherden has stated publicly that I would have to be the most energetic tired person he's ever worked with. Score one to me.

TWENTY TWO

From those early days in Sydney when I worked with the stockbrokers A.W. Harvey & Lowe – now metamorphosed into the Ord Minnett Group – much of my leisure time was spent poking about in tiny galleries, around Rowe Street, Hosking Place, Angel Place, tiny streets that existed then in unwrecked charm. Sometimes, too, in nooks and crannies around the Quay. And, of course, I visited the Art Gallery and came to love the early Australian painters. In all this I was making the gradual discovery that visual art in all its forms – painting, sculpture, printmaking – was going to be both recreational and vital. I remember being taken with the strange and intricate shapes of Robert Klippel. I never hunted out galleries, I just took in whatever presented itself near my end of town. Lacking money, I made do with postcards and small reproduction masters – Corot and Cezanne were early favourites. And Tom Roberts and Arthur Streeton. Having no artistic ability whatsoever, the sheer joy of looking at something that, in execution, was completely beyond my comprehension was very special and very satisfying. But I had no knowledge. The visual had little place in my early life. What was on the walls was there purely to complement the rest of the furnishings. Pleasant but unmemorable. I remember when a friend gave me a framed small reproduction of a Van Gogh painting of a man going to work, I looked and looked again.

I loved watching scene and set painter and wondering how they made things happen on such a big scale. And I always loved colour.

Knowing absolutely nothing didn't stop me from hawking the commercial art of a friend of mine, Brownie Downing, around the various advertising agencies in Sydney. I had met Brownie through her sister, Desmonde, who was a scenic designer at the Independent Theatre when I was first there. An ability to fool people enabled quite a few sales to be made. I once remember ... visiting the office of the art director of one of the big department stores with a folio full and deciding that his life was very pleasant, really, sitting, working on designs in a quiet atmosphere, listening to classical music. And leaving his office with a lighter folio. Acting is selling, selling is acting.

Still, no knowledge. And not much experience of the greats, until I took off for London in the 1950s. *Then* I started to see many, many paintings, as everyone does, but the one quality I brought to viewing I suppose was a completely open mind, so that an ever growing appreciation covered all forms and all periods, and still does. And I think I have learned one very important thing – no period, no style, no movement, no fashion matters in the long run when you are looking at a great work of art. The great just sings and is beyond the moment. It cannot be explained. It just is.

Those early months in England took me into every gallery big and small that I could find. Paris provided the joy of impressionism along with the parade of great classical paintings and sculpture with which the Louvre overwhelms. And Italy threw up everything from sculpture to frescoes to mosaics. Once drunk on that, one is caught for life. But, still, interesting to find the changes in one's own taste over the years, so that now African and Persian and Chinese art and ceramics provide some of the deepest satisfactions. And Aboriginal art.

Millions and millions of words have been written about art. Experts and critics have explained or attempted to explain, and academics expound and sometimes enlighten, but in all that I have read I find the best description of an artistic 'process' is the one given by Aboriginal artist Queenie McKenzie, speaking about landscape and how she paints it: 'I like a do country. What you know country. And when you go to Sunday Road, somewhere walkabout, you look hill like that. You take notice. "Ah! I can draw this," you say. You go back to la camp. You camp might be that day. That morning you get up, just get your paint, and run that hill where he sit down. I got to run em that Bow River hill yet. I'm going for that I tell you.' In those few sentences, she speaks of atmosphere, inspiration, decision, focus and determination, A beautiful summing up of what making a picture is all about.

I suppose that when we returned from England in 1975 and Eric decided to look for some viable business, the fact that it turned out to be a framing business was not a major shock to the system. I knew he had been considering frozen fish and second-hand whitegoods. Framing seemed a godsend by comparison. His criterion was just 'a good business'. That framing shop is still there at Crows Nest – it is our headquarters, and it provides a wall display of framed reproduction old and modern masters, and in its second room shows antique prints. Over the years two galleries have been added to sell limited edition modern Australian prints by our leading artists, some paintings, together with Australian jewellery, glass and ceramics, all, we are thrilled to point out, showing just how fine Australian work is in these areas. One gallery is in Skygarden in Sydney, another is in North Sydney, and there is a snappy framing and poster outlet, also in North Sydney. Which is what happens when a marketer runs the show. Eric and I are partners in the business, but over recent years my sole contribution has had to be in some decision-making over the dining table. And phone. We also have a factory and through two recessions and continuing uncertainty have not retrenched; we still manage to employ twenty amusing and energetic people, full and part time.

There is no area of the business where I could perform today, other than selling, but in 1975 it was not unusual for me to breast the counter and work the bankcard machine; and make the tea and get the sandwiches; and when we acquired the shop next door, a sub-newsagency, to open the door through a bitter winter at 7 a.m., six days a week, and sell newspapers to a motley collection.

Eric revels in running the tiny empire, and daughter Jane comes in three days a week to punch accounts and invoices into computers and attend to like matters and keep my affairs in order. No one else is interested in joining the company, which means that neither Eric nor I will ever be able to retire. One just has to keep going the best way one can.

With, then, our love of art, journeys have always included some aspect of furthering that passionate regard. The visit to Telluride for *Lilian's Story* came by way of Santa Fe and Abiquiu in New Mexico – Abiquiu being the home of the great American artist, Georgia O'Keeffe. I have a shelf full of O'Keeffe and we couldn't wait to see the adobe house she had created, and soak up something of the atmosphere that had nourished and inspired her – the desert and the soaring, elemental mountains, the special New Mexico light.

Friday 27 August 1996: Georgia O'Keeffe day – which was via Ojo Caliente, an unprepossessing village in possibly the most arid country we have passed through, but the home of a health establishment that caters to every possible sensual activity this side of legality. Massages booked out, we settled for a private tub for two. Hot tub filled with the special spring water that makes the place so sought after, an arsenic component in the water being the very special ingredient. So there we were—Arsenic and Old Nudity...

They claim their combination of minerals, salts medicinal properties cannot be equalled. Supremely beneficial in other words. One is encouraged not only to bathe in it, but drink it. After the tub we wrapped ourselves in sheets and were led to beds and further wrapped, up to and including the head, this time in blankets. This for twenty minutes, and I found it wonderfully relaxing, if hot. E. can never relax in these circumstances and just felt hot. Then a shower in separate establishments. Every other conceivable massage and wrapping up and mud and lotion application and spa and pool dipping going on. Robed people wandering about. Social intercourse in healthful pools. I can't wait to return and must obviously find a companion! Lunch under a tree and one has seldom felt so relaxed. Then to Abiquiu and found O'Keeffe's house with great difficulty. Nothing to indicate she ever lived there. Enormously protected and private. We were early so drove on to view the terrain around Ghost Ranch, the other O'Keeffe dwelling, which is itself strictly private and not able to be glimpsed from the road. Majestic landscape, eternal...yet even at her most abstract she perfectly depicts its quality. Each bend in the road to Ghost Ranch revealed some further awesome stretch of desert or mountain, or massed rocks, the colours ranging from clotted cream, gold, through every shade of red to purple, to black. Great mountains etched into a sky that could be piercing blue one minute, the next send up boiling masses of storm clouds, blue, black, grey. Frightening when the lightning streaks through. Exciting, too. We pray the photographs do it justice. Then back to Abiquiu and our guide from the Georgia O'Keeffe Trust presenting at first a somewhat stern demeanour. '*No* photographs and *no* cameras please.' E. meekly returns his camera, which he'd not intended using, to the car. They jealously guard their treasure. About ten of us – all O'Keeffe aficionados – are escorted around the exterior of this beautiful and simple New Mexican dwelling. The dwelling itself covers three acres and, with the surrounding garden – still showing the patterns she created –, five acres in all. The talk by the young woman, herself a Georgia, was precise, succinct and informative. Gained a PhD in O'Keeffe, doubtless. The house would have been built in the 16th century. The pueblo country here belonged to Navajos and Anasazi people. Many of the local Indians were granted small plots of land as reward for assisting the Spaniards, or as gifts for working as virtual slave labour. Less friction at Abiquiu than, say, Acoma. But O'Keeffe's house by comparison vast. It was occupied by a retired army officer when she acquired it and in a very run-down state. She then set to work on it with the help of her Indian woman friend, Maria Chabot, who was a skilful designer/builder well able to realise O'Keeffe's vision. All this happened in the late 1940s, by which time O'Keeffe was into her 60s. Our group not permitted to enter the house, but one can easily see into all the rooms. You come away knowing that this was the perfect design for living for this very special woman. Sparse, spare, and simply furnished, and then you discover that that simple sofa or that chair at the table was designed by Saarinen! Naked electric light bulbs. Simple muslin curtains or bed covers. Still there, an occasional grouping of the stones and rocks she loved. House built around two courtyards, one containing the famous door. The light is trapped beautifully in the courtyards, geometrically cutting off corners of adobe walls. Subjects for a painter. One old sage bush remaining. Guest wing — two bedrooms with connecting bathroom; living, dining flowing down another wing; a roofless room; what would originally have been quarters for animals, her work space; on the corner of this wing *her* 'corner', her bedroom. The corner of her corner looks out onto desert and mountain and to the right shows the snaking road from Santa Fe which became at least one sublime winter painting, a breathtakingly original black on white. The views matchless, and here in her 60s she at last owned her own place. She alternated between nearby

Ghost Ranch in the summer and Abiquiu in winter when the snows obliterated and allowed other aspects to be caught. Her kitchen allowed her to prepare and store and freeze quantities of food. The garden provided vegetables. She followed her own regime for food preparation and ate healthily, which no doubt contributed to a life that lasted till 98. We were fascinated to discover that O'Keeffe had constructed a fallout shelter, which is still intact, a shelter that could have enclosed and protected if need be in a place that was perilously close to Los Alamos.

In all that time, and conscious always of the great experience, we were never, somehow, connected. We were always visitors. Welcomed everywhere, but visitors. We never felt a part, at one with the landscape, the way we do unconsciously here in the Kimberley, say, or the centre of *our* place. For all that white Australians have been in their country for such a short time, there is little doubt that roots have gone down. When away, I am always surprised at just how deep they tap.

I returned with an Ansel Adams photograph of Georgia O'Keeffe and Orville Cox, black garbed, black hatted against a background of gathering storm clouds split with light. I look at if often. I feel oddly close to O'Keeffe sometimes. Something familiar. Both of us birds in another life probably. She and I do have one thing in common. An early life surrounded by women – mother, aunts.

Winnie in Samuel Beckett's Happy Days, *1991*

Neil Simon's Lost in Yonkers, *1992. Standing, from left:*
Robert Grubb, Kirrily Nolan and Nicholas Hammond
Seated, centre: Pamela Rabe and Ruth
Front: Damon Herriman and Brian Rooney

William Congreve's The Way of the World,
with Suzanne Roylance, 1993

Geoffrey Atherden's Hotspur, *with Garry McDonald, 1994*

Edward Albee's Three Tall Women, *with Pippa Williamson and Pamela Rabe, 1995*

In my dressing room between matinee and evening performance.
Three Tall Women, *Sydney*

Lilian's Story, *with John Flaus, 1996*

Stephen Sondheim's A Little Night Music, *with Andrea McEwan,1997*

A Little Night Music, *with Helen Morse*

Forty years on

With Madeleine, my first grandchild

TWENTY THREE

In 1979 I was playing the vile Mrs Raffi in Edward Bond's *The Sea* at Nimrod. John Bell played the hapless Hatch, and my outrageous friend, Maggie Dence, was Mrs Raffi's browbeaten companion, Mrs Tilehouse. Richard Wherrett directed.

Richard, John and I had first come together in 1974 in the Nimrod production of *The Seagull*, an extremely controversial production that seemed to divide Sydney, some finding it definitely not reverent enough. John and I as Tregorin and Arkadina had a marvellous moment, I remember, rolling around the floor in rumbustious passion, and Jacki Weaver's Masha, to some, an unlikely casting, will live with me forever. A lovely cast included Anna Volska as Nina, intense and beautiful, Peter Carroll, Drew Forsythe as Konstantin, Tom Farley, Tony Llewellyn-Jones, Peter Collingwood and Maggie Blinco, who also, from memory, designed the costumes. *The Seagull*, of course, ends in a tragic moment – Konstantin shooting himself – but it needs to be remembered that it is described by Chekhov on the title page as 'A Comedy in Four Acts.'

The Sea was some years later, and Hatch's manic wielding of the scissors in his confrontation with Mrs Raffi over a bolt of velvet in his draper's shop was worth the price of admission alone. Particularly so at the 5 p.m. Sunday performance that followed Richard's 'farewell from Nimrod' luncheon. Richard was headed for the Sydney Theatre Company to take up his appointment as artistic director. At this occasion Richard was presented with the Obie that had been awarded for the New York production of Steve Spears' *The Elocution of Benjamin Franklin*, with its brilliant, overwhelming performance by Gordon Chater. It was a very special luncheon, and for the first time in his career, farewelling his friend and co-director and feeling a touch emotional, John Bell imbibed a little. I had removed Maggie Dence from the festivities early, insisting, in true prefect fashion, that we must rest.

The performance began. In the 'velvet' scene I have a vivid memory of flashing shears wielded by a hand not at times in direct touch with a mind – any mind, it seemed. John told me later *his* most vivid memory of an otherwise clouded evening was my ashen face dominated by two blue saucers of terror. The scene became focused on attempts on my part to anticipate which route the shears would take next. And John certainly had no intention of pulling his performance, which fact I knew full well and which naturally fuelled the terror. Maggie, as companion, was seated safely at the counter throughout the scene and was no help. On the contrary, she could give full vent to her enjoyment at the prospect of my imminent decapitation. Just one of the many nights through the run that she wet her pants. The audience found it one of the more electrifying scenes they'd witnessed. I don't know if Richard was watching. If he was, he would have to have been helped from the theatre, tears streaming down his face.

It was earlier during the run of *The Sea* that Richard led me aside one night as I was mingling in the foyer. We sat on the Nimrod steps. Richard took my hand and said, 'I'm not supposed to tell anybody, but I'm bursting. I've been asked to become the artistic director of the Sydney Theatre Company.' This Company was to rise out of the ashes of the Old Tote, which had been the main subsidised theatre in Sydney up to that time. Richard was appointed by three people – Gilles Kryger, Jim McClelland and Tony Llewellyn-Jones – who'd been given the task of finding someone to head the new Company. I'm sure I wasn't the only one privy to this fabulous piece of news (Richard is not known for his ability to keep things quiet), but just then I was the privileged recipient. I was thrilled. This was an appointment that surprised some. Certainly one reason among many that would have clinched it for Richard was his confidence of being able to live with and surmount the difficulties of the Drama Theatre stage. In 1979 that stage was regarded as virtually hopeless. These days it's become part of our lives. Richard at that moment on the stairs also asked me to be a board director. Thus began my long association with the Company, which continues to this day as I am its Patron.

For the first year the Sydney Theatre Company was administered by John Clark and Elizabeth Butcher, the director and administrator of the National Institute of Dramatic Art, acting as a bridge until Richard moved into top gear. He asked Donald McDonald to be the first general manager of the Company. They were exciting times, as Richard pushed forward his aim 'To provide first-class theatrical entertainment for the people of Sydney — theatre that is grand, vulgar, intelligent, challenging and fun. That entertainment should reflect the society in which we live, thus providing a point of focus, a frame of reference, by which we come to understand our place in the world as individuals, as a community and a nation.' Richard stayed faithful to that aim, but in the bitchy way of Sydney some latched onto only two words — 'vulgar' and 'fun' — and accused him whenever they felt there was the slightest pretext of creating a Sydney theatre that had glitter, style, but no substance. When the attacks start, you can be sure of only one thing — the object of the barbs is *seriously successful.*

In 1983 the Sydney Theatre Company and the Australian Opera put into production *Nicholas Nickleby* — a mammoth undertaking. Richard Wherrett and John Gaden were both to direct — with Richard having overall responsibility.

I took a while to make up my mind about this one. Not sure why. I'd been reared on Dickens by the Watts aunts. Beat was even a member of the Dickensian society. All Dickens's characters seemed intimates of my Auntie Beat. Was it a hangover from the times when, as a 12 year old I'd argued with Uncle Arch Parkhill about the merits or otherwise of Dickens? He, too, loved Dickens, but I told him I couldn't stand the heroines; they were all so namby pamby. Who could stomach Little Nell? With a great deal of amused patience he insisted that there was more to Dickens than that. Which, of course, I subsequently discovered.

I knew about the Royal Shakespeare Company production of *Nicholas Nickleby*. That shouldn't have deterred, though — I'm a glutton for punishment. It was on Lord Howe Island, probably bicycling under the palms after visiting some Dignam or other, that I decided, 'Oh, alright. Give it a go.' Actually, I'd had a dream about my father the night before and *he* said, 'Give it a go.' So, basically it was his decision.

Richard and John were to split up some of the rehearsals so that we might have a better than even chance of getting through everything by opening night. As usual, much less time than the Royal Shakespeare Company would have had at their disposal. John Howard was to play Nicholas; I still think this was his great role. Whoever plays the role of Nicholas has to have enormous strength, apart from everything else, and John just powered through it, never once losing energy or commitment, and being the central focus for hour upon hour. The whole of the massive *Nicholas Nickleby* novel is presented, with little left out, in great halves totalling nine hours in all — each half playing on different nights in what seemed at times chaotic programming but wasn't, just occasionally hard to remember which half one was doing. On certain afternoons/nights, we would tackle the whole play. It was a large cast, but there still needed to be a deal of doubling. John Howard and Tony Taylor, who played the set-upon Smike, were not, of course, involved in doubling. From memory most of the rest of us coped with a multiplicity of characters and even provided stage dressing at times. We were required to be many things. On one occasion I was a wall – part of a wall – which has to rate as my least favourite moment, or eternity as it seemed, on any stage at any time anywhere. What provided a much happier memory in the crowd scene/extra department was the role – part of a swirling London street scene – of a young consumptive street seller, complete with tray. I insisted she be youthful because it added to the pathos, and was thrilled to shed the years in performance after performance. It became a test of ingenuity to dress this tray so that others could never be quite sure what would be on offer. It kept one sane. Sue Lyons, once she discovered I was selling weeds, was most helpful in keeping that portion of the tray topped up.

There were brilliant performances, brilliant cameos, the top cast never flagging for a moment and always highly inventive in everything they tackled. Sitting here remembering, looking out the window occasionally for inspiration, a parade of actors flashes by (Heavens, am I dying?): Peter Cousens, Julie Hamilton, David Downer, Suzanne Roylance, Kirrily Nolan, Ralph Cotterill, Ron Falk, Jon Ewing, and Brian James, Bea Aston, Linda Cropper, Julieanne Newbould . . . it was like a telephone directory of, in the main, Sydney actors. John Stanton, the Melbourne importation, made a chilling Ralph Nickleby, and Joan Bruce and Sue Lyons completed the

Nickleby family as if stepping straight off the page. Amanda Muggleton, Jennifer Hagan and Kerry McGuire joined later when we toured. My contributions were as the beastly Mrs Squeers, brutalising the boys at Dotheboys Hall, administering brimstone and treacle the while, and the much more lovable Mrs Crummles, wife of the well-known actor/manager, Mr Crummles, with Ron Haddrick slipping into that task as into a glove. The Crummles toured the country with their theatrical troupe and provided the great light moments of the story. As Mrs Crummles I have a memory of pinks and reds – certainly the wig with its huge topknot was vastly red. This is firmly lodged in the mind because of the night, during the big banqueting scene, that I missed the chair and sat on the floor. The audience was left with a view of desperate eyes, triumphant wig. Bustled and corseted, it took quite a while to hoist me back into position, particularly as everyone else on stage was by then in a state of sore collapse. Ron and I had great fun with the Crummles, and if only we'd been married in real life might have been tempted to take on the roles of the tourers ourselves. The Crummles had an exemplary life and were never less than buoyant.

Completely and thoroughly rehearsed, the music under our belts through the skills of our musical director, Julia de Plater, all the costumes and props mastered, we moved into the Theatre Royal for our production week. Backstage was a world of its own, all wing space being taken up with individual mini-stalls, each containing our props and some minor costume changes. Stage management, at times, seemed a more vital component in this adventure than anyone *on* stage, particularly in the second play when there were so many swift changes of character. One would rush off and be guided, when faced with a momentary blackout, to exactly the right prop. The assistant stage managers' knowledge of the play was second to none, and they became one's lifeline to sanity.

Opening day/night arrived – 10 December 1983. We were ready. An army going into battle. We moved to our positions like Henry V's battalions on St Crispin's Day. The great, adventurous, ever moving story began.

First play completed, we dined (unlike Henry's battalions), and set off on the long, long second half, moving though all Nicholas's noble journey, ever closer to our triumphant climax, when, all ills over, we mounted the stairs and scaffolding and gave vent to 'God Rest Ye Merry Gentlemen,' throwing our handfuls of snow into the sky as the closing moments unfolded beneath us. We sang lustily and operatically, and that moment, that first night, saw not only the audience awash with emotion, but cast as well. All restraint was cast to the winds, by virtue of which it remains one of the precious few *great* theatrical memories of my past fifty years. So finally, thanks to father, a unique experience it would actually have been criminal to miss.

The season proceeded, and Sydney received this production rapturously. You were out of it if you hadn't seen it. The evening commenced for audiences with cast mingling in the foyers and within the stalls and dress circles, so that people were able to talk to Dickens's characters before the play commenced. They formed a connection with us, which seemed beneficial to the night's enjoyment. There was a high buzz of excitement before curtain up. People compared their preferred method of seeing the play – consecutive nights, one week apart, or all in one hit, dinner in between. The cast felt that those who had seen the epic in one day were the winners. On those day/nights, audiences themselves became conscious of setting out on a long, exhilarating journey and were always the ones who were most affected by the finale. The finale that I ruined one night by throwing my handful of snow into the air a beat ahead of everyone else in not so glorious solo.

We told our tale in Sydney, finishing in March 1984, and moved on to Melbourne for more of the same at the newish Arts Centre on 29 December 1984. We were there over the festive season, which added to the emotions when 'God Rest Ye ...' swelled out. The response in Melbourne was every bit as joyous as Sydney's and almost succeeded in making one forget the exhaustion of the long second half, which at times equated with a stopover at one's least favourite airport.

I stayed with the production through the Melbourne season, but had to leave prior to Adelaide to take up a commitment with the Sydney Theatre Company to play Emma in Ray Lawler's *The Doll Trilogy*. Kirrily was to take over my roles.

One great thing about leaving. I was able to fly to Adelaide and sit in the audience and actually see what all the fuss was about. Richard Wherrett and I saw that whole long story, and, sitting there, it was with a sense of pride that I'd once been part of it, and gratitude that I was able to be out front now, part of a common joy that was palpable on every side. I, too, found it thrilling watching that triumphant journey.

All great theatre has a sense of ceremony, communion. There is an uplifting quality to it. In a sense it performs a religious function. One is encouraged to soar. It doesn't happen very often. *Nicholas Nickleby* was blessed with that quality, had a shine to it.

1984 was an exciting year for the Company. The Wharf complex was opened by the then Premier, Neville Wran. The flags broke out along the Hickson Street bridge, and the STC at last had its own home. The Wharf has been its home ever since.

Richard left in 1990. I thought we'd never survive. Put that down to my, till now, almost pathological inability to accept change. Of course, there is no other way for life to continue, and the Sydney Theatre Company *has* continued splendidly, under Wayne. And will, I have no doubt, when *he* decides to call it a day. Or is it just a case of *La plus ça change?*

The Company today has a subscription list of around 20,000 and with its turnover of over $17 million it stands as the largest theatre company in the country. Over the years, people come and go from the various departments. Change as a fact of life is accommodated. But I tend to believe that if the head of the Wardrobe department, Graham Wills, ever calls it a day, we *will* all pack it in. I can't think who could ever replace *him*. One change not to be contemplated!

When I started in theatre in Sydney, there was, of course, a parallel theatre developing in Melbourne. In many ways, this parallel activity could have been occurring on the moon. We were two principalities, and seldom did twain meet. Actors in the two cities stayed on their home ground and there was virtually no opportunity, nor interest, in exchange. Directors would have been hard put to know what was going on outside their immediate sphere of interest. Melbourne was Melbourne, Sydney was Sydney, and the occasional tours didn't make much of a dent in this attitude. Today, there is a very healthy cross fertilisation between not just Melbourne and Sydney, but Brisbane as well, and the three state companies regularly swap productions and co-produce, a most sensible and mutually beneficial arrangement. Where once actors from each city barely knew one another, today an actor will work in any city, and when touring, of course, can go from one side of the continent to the other. Companies cut costs in the process. Vital in these days of shrinking subsidies.

The Sydney Theatre Company is, of course, still subsidised, as are many companies large and small, to varying degrees. However, theatre companies, all arts organisations, won't survive on subsidies alone these days – vital though they are. There has to be competition for the 'Arts dollar' outside that umbrella, and all companies must aggressively pursue the task of obtaining corporate support and sponsorship at the highest level, and all the way down to that precious individual donation. A time-consuming business, and nothing to do with artistic endeavour, of course, but absolutely necessary to guarantee that vital top-up of funds. Thankfully, big organisations are now very happy to lend their names and support. It lends a certain cachet.

One thing is certain. No one wants to lose what has been gained over the years. Audiences have been built and are, thank goodness, a fact of life. They expect to be able to go into the theatre of their choice and know that it will be there for them. It has become a right. In responding to that right, all the companies big and small will ultimately realise that there is nothing to be gained without mutual respect and co-operation and everything to be lost by denying these and re-awakening tribal attitudes. Competition, and mutual support and respect can co-exist.

The great changes that have occurred since I started out have resulted, as a side effect, in an ever increasing supply of theatre practitioners – actors, directors, designers, administrators. The performing arts have become a highly desirable area for many young Australians. Everywhere I go, universities and drama academies throughout the country, shopping malls, even suburban streets, and certainly through the mail, I am made aware of just how passionate many young people are about making 'the Arts' their life's work. The tragedy is that only the smallest of percentages can hope to succeed. The talent is, at times, heart-breakingly high, but as more and more keep bubbling out of drama academies the sad reality is that they won't all be accommodated.

The result of all this is that audiences are the winners. The actors who do make it – even if only for a time – are of such a high order that the level of performance presented, the energy, and, most of the time, the focus, make for a splendid night in the theatre. In performance, anyway. If I may be permitted – a quibble here. The people in the back row are often the most perceptive theatre goers. It pays to let them hear what's being said. The curse of the theatre, I'm afraid. We actors have the luxury of being 'natural' only in films and on radio. In the crucible it's high energy or don't bother. And it is useful to remember that the voice is a musical instrument and must be used like one. After all, it is the great asset – 80 per cent of performance. 'So likewise ye, except, ye utter by the tongue words easy to be understood, how shall it be known what is spoken? For ye shall speak into the air.' (I Corinthians XIV, 9) The fate an actor should dread!

There is only one piece of wisdom I can pass on. 'The Arts', whether visual or performing, mean work. Hard, grafting work. And making mistakes – again and again. The only virtue in this continuing process of error is that I know no other way to learn. That's the comfort.

There are no words of comfort to pass on for occasions that by their very nature call for extra disciplines. Grit the teeth and pray to get through. Such an occasion was the memorial service for Andrew Olle in December 1995. I was asked. There is no way of saying no.

The day of Andrew's thanksgiving dawns – 22 December 1995. I feel numb and a bit weak. All goes to plan, the hire car (hired by me) arrives and we set out, unsure of what the traffic will be. I try to focus, anchoring the breathing, and we turn into Druitt Street alongside the Town Hall. A technician escorts. The remembrance service for Andrew Olle at Sydney's Town Hall is being televised nationally. Technicians, crew, go about their precise tasks, efficiently, quietly. There is an air of purpose, but shot through with a palpable sadness. Everything quiet, except for the rehearsal, which proceeds relentlessly.

I am taken to make-up. Dorothy Baker, a rock for us all, points out procedures, running order. I meet the first assistant.

Into make-up. No gossip, no jokes. I wait in the wings. Am shown the cue from London, move to the lectern and wait for the first assistant's cue. I say hullo to Mike Carlton and Margaret Throsby. We all look like death. Then back to make-up and hair. That attended to, Margaret and I are taken to a quiet place, except the a cappella is rehearsing. We look out into St Andrew's Square – and suddenly the chimes begin. Chimes for Andrew. And the cicadas add their din. I speak of ABC perfidy and there is much to discuss, but all is forgiven as this extraordinary hour unfolds. For, finally, when the chips are down, no one does it like the ABC. Not with that sense of unaffected occasion. The moment approaches.

We are now all on stand-by. Pat O'Shane says, 'I feel awful, but I'm thinking only of what I'm going to say. That helps. I have to say it.' I don't hear it, but they say her speech is full of fire and passion directed straight at the media – their crassness, their idiocy, their lack of integrity, their lack of intelligence. Typical Pat O'Shane firing. But there is, was, she affirms, one shining exception – Andrew Olle. As the thanks-giving proceeds, the same sentiments emerge, again and again, but not so seriously always, sometimes lightness mixed with the warmth. I think Chris Masters is the most affected. He is quiet, backstage and his words, as much as I can hear, are serious and thoughtful. Paul Lyneham has taped his contribution – one suspects he may have broken down, live. His is perhaps the most heartfelt. Ten years of conversing with someone publicly every morning and touching amusingly and with discernment on all the political issues of the day, and then, suddenly, without warning, one of you is no longer there.

There was Nathan Waks playing a cello piece by Peter Sculthorpe. He knew there was no time to organise others so Peter was approached to come up with something suitable for cello and piano. ('Just re-working this, oddly enough. Will it do?') The piece is called 'Parting'. It transpires it was composed in 1947, which is the year Andrew was born. There is a Schubert solo, Peter Luck speaks amusingly – it's a week after Andrew's funeral so there's less shock. Mike Carlton pairs with Margaret Throsby to compere.

I'm now waiting near the entrance at the bottom of a small flight of stairs. I can see the audience – they are rapt and focused, all 2000 of them and more in George Street watching, listening. My hands are like ice – Dorothy Baker rubs them. She is to precede me on stage, place a Louis MacNeice poem on the lectern. She is monumentally calm. The video from London with Mark Colvin begins. I enter, eyes glued to the first assistant director to my right and at floor level. The cue comes and I pray for vocal control. Just a little earlier someone had spoken of Andrew's kindness – a group of colleagues was gathered once and it came out, quite by accident, that each had been the recipient of a special kindness from Andrew in a time of difficulty. It had surprised and united them in an odd way. When Peter Luck spoke of this, I had my great present – the poem I am to read contains three perfect lines descriptive of 'one man's kindliness . . .'. Those lines were invested with more than I'd given them in all rehearsed readings at home.

After me, the a cappella, and it was all over. The thousands filed out, the crowds outside took their eyes from the giant screen, the building workers opposite went back to work, their sign to Andrew still there. And those of us who could stay drank a glass, lost some of the numbness and mingled with others who had been in the audience. Andrew's wife was there smiling, smiling, thanking, thanking. His surgeon was there. Managing directors past and present were there. ABC 'heavies' – all of them startled into the realisation, too late perhaps, that this man was the most precious asset they had ever had and one that all their viewers considered, quite simply, irreplaceable.

TWENTY FOUR

In line with the coincidences that have sprung out on all sides since commencing this book, and not having seen Rodney Fisher, other than across a crowded foyer, for a considerable time, I, of course, bumped into him at The Wharf the day before writing this little piece of history. He wanted me to launch a CD he was bringing out shortly; how odd, I thought, as you are very much to the forefront of my mind at the moment. A string of coincidences it has been with people resurfacing and letters turning up relevant to what I'm doing, the writers of the letters unaware of the preciseness of their timing. Just coincidences, of course.

My first introduction to Rodney was in Simon Gray's *Close of Play*, which he directed for the new Sydney Theatre Company's first season in 1980. This play opened at the Drama Theatre of the Opera House, and due to its success transferred to the Theatre Royal for a season. Frank Thring and I headed the cast. Which was a beauty – John Gaden, Julie Hamilton, Andrew Tighe, Jennifer Hagan, Ron Falk and Janice Finn. A bleak play, beneath the wit and the acute observation of the English middle class – in this case an English family. Simon Gray requires a consummate director to develop all the facets and with Rodney he was thus blessed. When the play transferred to the Royal, Robyn Nevin took over Jennifer's role.

The play called upon Frank Thring to be seated, comatose from stroke, throughout the entire evening. His ability to maintain the tension and concentration never wavered – even on those occasions when a not altogether *sotto voce* groan emerged from him in telling comment on the action going on around him. This happened not infrequently; I suppose it was Frank's only way of coping with nearly three hours of being stuck in a chair, speechless, except for one line at the end: 'The door is open.' A long wait for a line! Extraordinary to think of the great Thring voice, distinctive if ever a voice was, heard just once all night. Those members of the audience who had come especially to hear it could well have wanted their money back.

Each of us was the recipient of one of Frank's groans at some stage – he didn't play favourites. What was certain was that he was possessed of an acute ear that never failed. He would pick up the slightest deviation in performance, the slightest blurred moment, and it was never allowed to pass unnoticed. Rather like having a critic permanently there on stage. Unnerving, but kept us on our toes.

If the play did nothing else it made me familiar with Mozart's clarinet concerto, the melody of which I had to hum. It did a lot more, but every time I hear that concerto now, the years peel back.

I wrote once, after dining with him in Brisbane, that Rodney's mind is second to none. Certainly it is encyclopaedic. His wealth of knowledge over the broadest of areas never ceases to amaze. Ask him a question on any subject — artistic, scientific, academic — and he comes up with the answer, and if not at that moment, certainly within twenty-four hours. Research probably gives him as much pleasure as directing, and he owns the books to satisfy that pleasure.

After *Close of Play* came *The Man from Mukinupin*, a fine interpretation of Dorothy Hewett's play also at the Drama Theatre. This was followed by Ronald Harwood's *The Dresser*, with Gordon Chater and Warren Mitchell sharing the honours. *The Dresser* had a major involvement by Helen Montagu, which was fun for me, and travelled to Melbourne and elsewhere. It was the occasion for one of my rare flashes of rage. My contract was for Sydney and Melbourne only and when, during rehearsals in Sydney, Warren became aware, for the first time (I can't think why no one had told him earlier), that I would not be proceeding beyond Melbourne he delivered himself of a piece of invective on the professionalism of Australians in general and me in particular that caused me to kick my shoe high into the air in a perfect arc, much to the surprise of all. It was certainly not aimed at Warren but I imparted the feeling that it should have been. We made up, of course, and

he presented me a farewell present in Melbourne when I left –
a book on the brand of yoga he practised, with the message
that if I thought him difficult now I should have known him
before yoga was part of his life! Glad not to have, if I'm
honest. He is such a fine actor, detailed and precise, and I
thought he and Gordon made a grand team. Gordon played a
Shakespearean actor of the old school in the play, Warren was
his dresser, and I played his actress wife. I had very little to do
really, and when we got to Melbourne I had the energy to have
a lovely time there, which is one of the bonuses of not being
on stage all night. Rodney directed with his usual flair, and I
then waited till 1985 before our next collaboration.

The Doll Trilogy was to be presented in Sydney and Melbourne to coincide with the thirtieth anniversary of Ray
Lawler's great play, *Summer of the Seventeenth Doll*.

I believe we had an eleven-week rehearsal period. This
was for three plays, and the arithmetic will show that there was
actually less time for this complicated exercise than there
would have been for each play singly. Rodney has a deep interest in text and is always determined to make a text work to its
best potential, which incidentally is an actor's aim as well.
With the first two plays in the trilogy, written much later than
The Doll, some moments seemed to need clarification, and
occasionally, in the light of what is revealed later in The Doll,
others seemed to need simplifying. Working closely with him
in this complicated process the cast's task was to get on with
it and realise the characters.

In the trilogy I was playing Emma, which meant I had

the opportunity for a marvellous range of age throughout the plays, starting with Emma in early middle age and finishing with the more familiar Emma of old age. Those two earlier Emmas gave me as much pleasure as any roles I have played. They were created by Ray Lawler, interpreted by me.

We finally got there. All the work was done, and we awaited our first audience for the three plays — a matinee and an evening performance. A long journey. The adrenalin was running and we felt on top. It was, therefore, an unbelievable disappointment to hear that Ray Lawler was, to say the least, not happy with the result of the work on those two earlier plays of his story. Quite obviously, there had been *insufficient* communication. Once again one realises that communication and information on what is occurring in a rehearsal room — with complete agreement on what is happening — is essential if goodwill is to be maintained, particularly in the relationship between director and writer. It is understandable that with the time pressures of those eleven weeks, some things didn't get checked, and double checked. Understandable, but not excusable.

In the event, some of the changes were removed, and by the time we had reworked and re-accommodated I hope Ray finished with a happier memory of his tribute. Audiences, knowing nothing of any problems, took to the plays with gusto and relish, as they should, and I finished with a Victorian Green Room Best Actress award for Emma. As usual in these situations it is the actors who have the most difficult role. They have to continue as if nothing untoward has happened — performance after performance. It would be nice to know sometimes that these efforts are appreciated all round because there is only one thing certain — the actors are the *only* ones who have to stand up there night after night, unwavering. It is, I can attest, never easy. The fine actors who soldiered on on this occasion were Celia de Burgh, Olivia Brown, Heather Mitchell, Harold Hopkins, Steve Bisley, Russell Kiefel, Kaarin Fairfax, Shane Connor and James Higgins.

We had a lovely set. Brian Thomson's was a cut-away of a Victorian terrace — small, tight, but still permitting a minuscule garden, fence and gate leading to the street. In creating the upstairs section of the house, Brian only needed to show a foot or so of Emma's bedroom. This was a marvellous idea, but meant that every time I departed the action on stage to go to the bedroom, for once that didn't mean retreating to the dressing room and putting feet up awhile with a cup of tea. No, I had to climb up to the bedroom and remained trapped there until the action had me returning again. Very effective from the audience's viewpoint to see Emma actually enter that bedroom, half her legs only on view, moving about. It didn't take too long into the season to decide that Emma needed many rests upon that bed. But Brian created all the necessary dressing there, and I had much to look at!

The worst 'dry' I can recall — every actor's nightmare; the moment when you lose all contact with reality, become deaf to all prompts, and fear, as the sweat breaks out all over you, that you will never be able to speak again — happened on the first Trilogy night in Sydney to one of my favourite people, Harold Hopkins, in the role of Barney. From my dressing room I heard the awful silence that paradoxically can sound louder than a battle scene. I crossed the corridor at the Drama Theatre and stood at the top of the steps leading to the stage, which gave a view of Harold seated on the sofa. He might as well have been stripped naked. What I thought I was doing just standing there, I don't know. Willing him to pick up the prompt, perhaps. There was nothing *anyone* could do, of course. Not in that sort of a situation. Harold kept clearing his throat, which prompted Celia de Burgh to think he may have needed a glass of water. So she went into Emma's kitchen, which became wing space on entering the door. Illusory in other words, as was any tap or connected water. She ultimately came back with water from the prompt corner, but in any case it wasn't going to fix Harold's deadly problem. It seemed much worse to be watching him than being in the same position. I think I was praying for a space craft to drop out of the sky, but as that wasn't a likely occurrence in Sydney — prior to November 1996, that is — it wasn't much help. Eventually, the black cloud lifted and Harold was able to hear his prompt, make sense of it and move on. There is nothing worse in the world for an actor. It is not so bad for an audience, other than an audience full of other actors, which of course that opening day/night was. It should have been anyone but Harold, which is probably why it *was* Harold. We all told him to forget it, that it was of little importance in the scheme of things, but even as we were uttering the soothing words, we were well aware that for Harold it was probably the worst thing that had ever happened in his acting life.

Looking back all those years now, it *was* the worst thing that night. In my mind it diminishes all other troubles.

Rodney and I have not worked together for awhile. Too long. We've both been caught up elsewhere, but have promised each other this will be rectified. I hope so. I feel in need of a period of research and delving and finding and agreeing and not agreeing and both of us writing a bit. No interruptions, no other agendas – just the two of us. And the text there for both of us to create – the responsibility of just two people together. Heaven.

TWENTY FIVE

Christmas rushing towards us. The best of days – this year, 1996, celebrated on the back verandah surrounded by the ferns and palms. Looking cool, but it's not a scorcher, anyway. Only fifteen of us this year – Jonathan and Lisa absent. I breathe it in. In three days' time Eric and I will fly to Melbourne where I begin rehearsals for *A Little Night Music*. It has arrived too quickly. The last six months of writing, sandwiched between two film festivals and other commitments, have evaporated, and scant time to think of *A Little Night Music* other than listen to a song or two in the car. With rehearsal, I'll be away about nine weeks.

In the event *A Little Night Music* was such a success that a return season became inevitable. So, it was arranged. We had a two-week break and then transferred to the Princess Theatre, which meant that the original nine weeks became four months. One can be certain of nothing in this business.

I resided in Melbourne through the hottest summer since *King Oedipus* in 1971, also at the Princess. Records for drought and heat fell all around us as we launched into our adventure. I'd never been in a musical — an honest-to-God musical, that is. Revues, of course, but they're quite different, with the melody line never too far away. *The Duenna* is more a play with music, and the singing in *Nicholas Nickleby* is mostly rousing choruses. But at least Revue had provided many point numbers, so the prospect of singing solo was not unduly daunting.

Except this was Stephen Sondheim. The intricacies of the music were comparable to learning Japanese for one who doesn't read music. I was comforted on this score by the knowledge that neither does John O'May, who carried much of the singing thrust.

What makes a genuine hit? Oh, if producers could confidently pick this each time they begin how ecstatic they'd be. I think this one may have caught people by surprise. A Melbourne Theatre Company production, it would be done with high seriousness of purpose, would sit happily in the Playhouse at the Victorian Arts Centre, subscribers and others would be more than satisfied. It would have a particular stamp to it — well crafted, faithful to Sondheim's intention, and would be a highly delightful start to the year. I'm not sure anyone thought outside these parameters. Actually, one doesn't think along these lines at all. One is too busy trying to create the piece day by day. We all presented at the outset with that commitment to do the very best by the work.

We didn't realise we had that mysterious X factor flicking

around the rehearsal room. That little something that takes one on a rollercoaster ride. It all started quite soberly, really. There was a reading, there was in-depth analysis around the table, we got up and moved it. We had our individual music calls, we came, we went. The nature of *A Little Night Music* means that schedules allow for quite a bit of down time, waiting around, passing people in corridors, meeting in the green room. By lunch time one could be off – or not called till afternoon. I suppose it was when the runs of the musical started, with all in attendance, that I began to get a prickle at the back of the neck. I'm seldom one to get excited during 'the process'. Too conscious of all the work to be got through, like most actors. But this time, watching others, hearing the songs, hearing every word of those incomparable lyrics, watching the choreography evolve, knowing the sound would be in expert hands, yes, this time I did start to get a little excited. Partly, of course, because Madame Armfeldt spends most of the performance in a wheelchair and does a lot of watching when not actively involved. The excitement, a tiny bubble to begin with, grew nicely. By the time the orchestra joined, I'd have put money on a smash. A shame there was never time to organise it.

We opened. The first night response was all one could hope for. Audience over the moon, and the first night party an excited, noisy babble – the very best of tests. An enjoyable occasion for once. Mostly, I'm not over fond of these times. On a much smaller scale, the crush in the tiny foyer outside Wharf 2 in Sydney after Gale Edwards's work-in-progress presentation of *Miracle City*, the musical by Max Lambert and

Nick Enright, had that same electric charge. It's like manna from heaven.

So why? How? Simply, Roger Hodgman had supervised, drawn together, quietly directed a near perfect mix. The musical director, Jean McQuarrie, silkily, persuasively and, where necessary, with steel, gathered this group of fifteen disparate people and turned them – with orchestra – into a whole that, musically was absolutely *right*. Kim Walker evolved a seductive, elegant and tender choreography. Jamieson Lewis's lighting softened, pointed, flattered and never for one moment distracted an audience's attention from where it should be. And Tony Tripp's design was elegant, romantic, non-intrusive, his costumes all the above, with wit and style added. Finally, the sound delivered as we had been assured it would.

A Little Night Music itself is a bittersweet piece with an edge of cynicism, but also a tenderness lurking, which, under Roger, we plumbed, and which audiences just now seem hungry for. It is a fine time for this production. Is that the secret? The timing? It must be added that, of course Roger managed to get his first choice in performers. An important ingredient that can't be over emphasised.

So, we were into our season. Roger's dream a reality. For me, waiting in the wings each night in my wheelchair, Frid, my manservant, in attendance, watching the rest of the cast line up at the back of the stage while the opening was performed in front of the gauze by the five who were our chorus/ observers, was like watching a line of thoroughbreds at the barrier. Every time they moved downstage to take up their positions, I found it both exciting and moving. When we transferred to the Princess for the return season I spent a deal more time in the wings – there being no on-stage dressing rooms. I never tired of watching. Sondheim permits everyone his/her moment. Each moment was taken without fail. And with relish.

One afternoon I just managed to catch the moment in the Academy Awards ceremony where Geoffrey Rush accepts his Oscar for *Shine*. Thrilling for us all – especially those of us who have worked with him. Geoffrey's speech surely the most graceful and articulate ever made by an Australian collecting any honour in any field. For once, the words flowed. On a high, I walked to the Princess that evening and gave the best performance I've ever given of Madame Armfeldt. Just as well, as the previous night's had been my worst. I remember it vividly. Sitting next to Pamela Rabe in the fast change dressing room I remarked just that. And paused. Then, 'Of course, my worst performance is better than most people's best.' Pamela smiled. 'I knew I just had to let that hang in the air a minute or two.'

Independent of each other, Pamela and Lisa McCune swear to seeing Federici, the ghost of the Princess Theatre, in the upper circle on the night of the Academy Awards. An appropriate, ghostly tribute to Geoffrey.

We moved to our last night, and this wasn't, as can be the case, an anti-climax. Half the audience at the Princess that night had seen *A Little Night Music* twice, thrice or even five times already. At the end, they simply stood and expressed their joy. A most emotional night and for me, among a handful of truly great occasions in the theatre. We made the most of it.

A Little Night Music will tour nationally. I hope we all return to it. Salutary for me to remember that I very nearly declined the offer, thinking I was pushing things. I am forever grateful I was quietly persuaded by the Puppet Master, though Roger may have had a little help from my guardian angel.

TWENTY SIX

July 1996: Eric and I attend the opening of Treasures From the Kremlin, mainly Fabergé, at the Powerhouse in Sydney. Outside, we pass through a flurry of fake snow, which, inside, leaves the gentlemen looking as if they have a bad case of dandruff. The entrance is guarded by Russian soldiers in winter greatcoats and Astrakhan direct from Central Casting. We can hardly move inside, it's all intriguingly bizarre as the lighting and strobe induce a feeling of imminent epilepsy, or is it just that ecstasy is being passed with the vodka? Energetic dancing on a minute stage. Cossack style. Later, as I'm snatched for a photo with one of the dancers, female, all floating ribbons and authenticity of costume, I say, breaking the silence, 'Where are you from?' A moment or two of obvious agony as she tries to remember the name of a Russian city or town — *any* Russian town. I feel instant rapport, remembering my own past agonies and quickly add, 'Which *studio*?' 'Leichhardt,' she breathes with enormous relief. We smile happily as the camera flashes. The speeches end and we queue to view the treasures.

Premier Bob Carr and I are lined up for yet another photo opportunity. He expresses a desire for a copy and the photographer says, all innocent of face, 'Sure. And the name?' 'Bastard!' says the Premier. I suspect that Sydney is the only place in the world where such an exchange could occur. The Premier asks politely what I'm doing at the moment. A small hesitation, then I grit my teeth and confess. 'Writing an autobiography.' Assuming his most Lincoln-like pose, he commands, 'Denounce yourself! All the great autobiographers – Rousseau, for instance – denounce themselves.' I make a mental note.

Writing a book is a strange thing to do – when it's about yourself, I mean. A panicky feeling that one must rush back and remove all first person pronouns. An affecting modesty, but useless. Without them whose story would it be? Someone else's. And that's no good. That's not the contract. 'Tell *your* story!' they said. But who wants it? And whose business is it anyway? They convince me someone wants it. 'Name him,' I say. They gently tell me my attitude is not right. So I am endeavouring to fix my attitude, well aware that a woman without attitude today might as well crawl into a burrow.

Well, a nicely set up burrow . . .

One thing I do know is that it is not an easy thing to do. Looking back almost seventy years – I claim total recall to infancy – is not simply challenging, not simply bewildering, not amazing, not amusing, not sad, not bad, not right, not wrong, but all of them. And over and above all these, at times it is deeply disturbing. On the basis of that discovery alone, one would say it is not an undertaking to be recommended. At times, recollection can plunge one into dangerous territory. For me, there were sleepless nights; there were times when revisiting some stages of the incredible journey – incredible by virtue of its length, which is still hard to comprehend – caused a depression in one not ever before, and I hope not ever again, accustomed to such a state, and which made me regret the decision in the first place. But now, the final feeling – and this has been about feeling if it's been about anything – is one of gratitude that the journey *was* undertaken. Looking at the past has meant, for the first time, being able to let it go.

When Rebecca Gibney lent me the book *The Tibetan Book of Living and Dying* when we were making the children's film *Joey* recently in Brisbane, a dip into it at the right moment crystalised thinking, just at that coincident time in my life that I was being forced to re-live it. The book has shown me a number of things, perhaps the most important that I am not really a Buddhist, but, irrespective, forever grateful for being reminded that there are two, only two, certainties. One, that life is about change. Two, that we die. Knowing that one dies in the abstract is one thing, really understanding it for the first time is quite something else again. One's *own* death only, of course. Others? Those close? That's something else. But notwithstanding the limitations, that personal acceptance has brought with it a peace that before was elusive to say the least.

The other kernel I've taken away from The Tibetan Book is that it is useless, if at times pleasurable, to fantasise about the future. It is not here and it is not known. In the same way, the past is just that. Past. Gone. To be relinquished. 'What's done cannot be undone.' *Now* is what it's about. Not easy to arrive at this point, but once there, and held onto firmly, all else seems to slot into place – the correct place, neither given too much importance, nor too little. This does not mean instant relocation to some carefree Elysian field. Life is still to be lived, suffered, enjoyed, battled over. But trying to live in the Now provided a key that opened a vital door. As Frank Thring said, all those years ago in *Close of Play*, 'The door is open . . . ' A long time to wait to understand a line – or nearly understand, should I say. Complete comprehension obviously still awaits.

And paradoxically, while reading this book, I experienced some sort of re-affirmation of – one hesitates to use the word these days, it has been so damaged – the Christian ethic, one that had probably never completely deserted me, anyway. The ethic and belief that has forgiveness and love as its central tenets – the particularly difficult to achieve and maintain love of one's neighbour. Difficult, but inescapable, if there is to be some way through the mess that seems increasingly to press in on us these days. Compassion, acceptance and a sinewy determination not to reject what's different is absolutely vital. Surely. Even when that acceptance seems painful. What is 'different' anyway? Am I different, or are you different? Tricky times. We have to work it out, though. Or go back to the cave.

For me then, even in my muddled state, a sureness that

life without some spiritual centre is unthinkable. Bleak. Devoid of energy. And how strange that the Catholic Teilhard de Chardin's idea of 'becoming' is so close to some of those things I read in The Tibetan Book. And how easily it sits alongside so much scientific thought. Evolution. A spiralling to chaos. And beyond?

But I can't live exclusively – in Buddhism, in Shinto, in the Aboriginal connection to the land, lie other truths. A trembling stumble towards grace it is. One hopes to arrive...

Mind you, I was always rather open to evangelism in my early days. Gullible, my mother called it. On the beach at Collaroy on family outings with friends, where would I be? In the front row at the roped-off area of whichever hot gospeller was holding forth on the day. I suppose it became an easy form of baby-sitting for my mother. Come lunch time with Ida Coulson's matchless cold meat pie, the salads of shredded lettuce, tomato and hard-boiled egg, cucumber and beetroot, mayonnaise (condensed milk, vinegar and a pinch of Keen's mustard), the cakes, the thermoses, someone would be despatched to gather me up, and whoever it was would always know in which direction to head. How glad those evangelists must have been to have me there in the front row gazing seriously up at them, 8 years old, meekly receiving the texts and tracts. My mother wisely ignored this hothouse religious fervour – though, in fairness, I was never one to proselytise – and simply hoped that the less zealous attitudes at the Anglican Sunday School would hose me down a bit. I can still remember those texts with their primary colours. Tiny stamps of fundamentalism.

I was kidnapped once by a very strict and pious sect, gathered up and taken into a Gospel Hall at Chatswood for an afternoon's brainwashing. This, certainly, caused my mother a degree of alarm, until I was returned by my kidnappers in the fullness of time, quite unharmed. They were the parents of my current schoolfriend and only wished to do their best for me. I'm sure they all thought they were onto a very good thing, but I was just sampling the various wares. And finally turned my back on all of them – but something remained, and I do thank God.

These spiritual discoveries and insights penned, I'm in contemplative mood, thoughts meandering, when, unexpectedly, I find myself face to face with my most complex demon – pride. I am not sure why this should happen. At this precise moment. Denunciation perhaps?

I had dallied for a time with an aborted ABC television series to be based on the Seven Deadlies. This was long before the ABC showed a very different version. Tom Manefield, of the highly successful Checkerboard documentary series, had gathered together a number of people. I remember Gwen Friend, John Laws, Michael Boddy – here memory fails. Gwen was to tackle Envy, John opted for Lust oddly enough (this was a long time ago), and Michael Boddy, the splendid writer/cook of ample proportions, was Gluttony. I was Pride cursed with Sloth for a daughter. We represented a family warring over our deceased father's will. We were to meet over dinner, cooked by Michael, in the Gothic dining room of my grandiose house, where, with cameras roaming free and wine flowing we would presumably let our hair down.

Beforehand, we had written essays on our characters, their backgrounds, their journeys to this moment. I wrote carefully and with enjoyment and was quite proud of my insight into Pride.

We had a Fellini-type day and night shooting the first episode, and when ABC management reviewed it later they ran for cover. Where is that episode now? Probably destroyed, along with many other black and white treasures. This one, all things considered, could probably help the ABC out of its current parlous financial straits if marketed skilfully. I seem to remember we got quite ugly, stopping just this side of complete mayhem and the occasioning of actual bodily harm. Not to mention character assassination. Decades ahead of its day! Ah well . . .

I had barely written of pride and judgemental falls when I hurled myself down our side steps, concrete, cracking my head with great force on the path, also concrete. The immediate and intense agony that ripped through my head convinced me that death was imminent.

What I experienced at that moment was no calm acceptance, more an overwhelming panic, if I'm honest. Naked fear. As I crawled up the steps and stumbled towards ice, a degree of composure returned, but I didn't relax completely for a couple of weeks, by which time I reckoned the worst of the danger had passed.

As in anything else the readiness is all. It would seem I

still have some little way to go. Now why this stumble at this particular moment? Perhaps Auntie Beat had given me a push. She certainly wanted to sixty or so years ago when I stamped up the hill from 5 Inglethorpe Avenue, tossing a smart remark over a shoulder.

'Watch out, Madam,' she'd said. 'You'll fall.'

Going back, seeing the coincidences unroll along the whole way, has finally made this task of writing, recalling, an exhilarating experience. The coincidences have poured in all around. Write a page or two on the happenings of 1948 and the next day a letter from a stranger with a vital connection. Finish one subject, the phone will ring, causing an extra paragraph to be written.

One other reason for writing the book was an attempt to analyse why on earth it all happened. I know the how, the where and the when, but the why is much more elusive, and a rigorous honesty needs to function here. Was it that lovely sound of clapping when a spotlight was played on me at age 2? Was it that I wanted always to be the centre of attention, to hang onto that immature need long past the childhood where it certainly existed and where it should have remained? Did I inherit something from my mother that couldn't be stamped out? Was it Miss Farrell at North Sydney Girls' High, with her passion for the poets? Was it the simple act of walking through that other door at the St James's Hall? If Marjorie Webb hadn't had a spare ticket for the performance, would I not have set forth? Is it a true vocation? No false modesty permitted at this moment, so I say it *is* a gift. As it is a gift, it is polite to say thank you. I know it is addictive and do not seek a cure. And fame? Neither sought, nor expected. That by-product sneaked up as I looked the other way, and still confounds and amazes — and disturbs.

Whatever the reason, or amalgam thereof, what I am in no doubt of is that I am so very, very delighted that it *did* happen — one stumbling step after another. I would not have missed it for the world, and all those actors who have thronged through the pages with me, and through a long life, have been some of the most vital ingredients of that life.

The last word always belongs to the audience. I remember their involvement, that blessed connection, that silken thread that links two hundred, five hundred, a thousand people to a small circle of concentrated energy. Yes, that is a most powerful feeling. One that is worth savouring on dark nights when the wind blows. On the other hand, there is no way of ever knowing, when one steps out into that circle, if the connection will be made. The promise is there, the hope is there, but no certainty whatsoever. Which is, I suppose, the attraction. That connection, when it happens, is magic. When it doesn't . . . Turn out the lights.

THE AUTHOR AND PUBLISHER WOULD LIKE TO THANK THE
FOLLOWING FOR PERMISSION TO INCLUDE MATERIAL

Many of the photographs in this book are from the author's private collection.

PHOTOGRAPH SECTION 1: *Gracious Living*, the Australian Broadcasting Corporation
(ABC).

PHOTOGRAPH SECTION 2: *A Cup of Tea, a Bex and a Good Lie Down*, the Fairfax Photo
Library. *But I Wouldn't Want to Live There*, John Hearder. *I'm Alright Now*, John Pearson. Studio pose, John Hearder.

PHOTOGRAPH SECTION 3: *Ben Hall*, the ABC. Rex Cramphorn's *A Shakespeare
Company*, Robert Simms. *Nicholas Nickleby*, Brett Hilder. Maggie Beare, the ABC.
Maggie with her sons, the ABC. *The Doll Trilogy*, Andrew Southam and the Sydney Theatre Company. *Emerald City*, Branco Gaica. *Lettice and Lovage*, Branco Gaica.
Lady Bracknell, Stuart Campbell and the Sydney Theatre Company. The Sydney
Theatre Company's tenth anniversary, Andrew Rankin and the *Australian
Magazine*.

PHOTOGRAPH SECTION 4: *Happy Days*, David Wilson and the State Theatre Company of South Australia. *Lost in Yonkers*, Gary Heaney and the Sydney Theatre Company. *The Way of the World*, Sandy Edwards and the Sydney Theatre Company.
Hotspur, Branco Gaica and the Sydney Theatre Company. *Three Tall Women*, Branco
Gaica and the Sydney Theatre Company. Ruth in her dressing room, Jennifer Soo
and the Fairfax Photo Library. *Lilian's Story*, CML Production Pty Ltd. *A Little
Night Music*, Jeff Busby and the Melbourne Theatre Company. With Madeleine,
Henry Talbot.

Poem entitled 'A Tribute to Ruth', David Williamson.
Quotation from 'The White Cliffs' by Alice Duer Miller, Buccaneer Books.
Quotation from *Batsford Century*, edited by Hector Bolitho, Batsford Publishing Co.
Quotation from *Australia's Living Heritage — Arts of the Dreaming* by Jennifer Isaacs,
Lansdowne Publishing. Thank you also to the Mowanjum Community and the
wife of Albert Barunga.
Marchéta by Victor L. Schertzinger, 1913, The John Franklin Music Co.

Every effort has been made to contact the copyright holders of the photographic
and text quotation material for permissions. The author and publisher welcome
any further information regarding copyright ownership.

INDEX